THE BEST BUSINESS BOOKS EVER

THE

Best
Business
Books
Ever

REVISED AND
EXPANDED EDITION

*The Most Influential
Management Books You'll
Never Have Time to Read*

BASIC BOOKS

A MEMBER OF THE PERSEUS BOOKS GROUP
New York

Books published by Basic Books are available at special discounts for bulk
purchases in the United States by corporations, institutions, and other
organizations. For more information, please contact the Special Markets
Department at the Perseus Books Group, 2300 Chestnut Street, Suite 200,
Philadelphia, PA 19103, or call (800) 810-4145, ext. 5000, or e-mail
special.markets@perseusbooks.com.

Designed by Timm Bryson

The Library of Congress has cataloged the printed edition as follows:
 The best business books ever : the most influential management books you'll
never have time to read. -- Rev. and expanded ed.
   p. cm.
 Includes bibliographical references and index.
 ISBN 978-0-465-02236-6 (pbk. : alk. paper) -- ISBN 978-0-465-02634-0 (e-
book : alk. paper) 1. Management--Bibliography. 2. Business--Bibliography.
 Z7164.O7B323 2011
 [HD31]
 016.658--dc22
                                    2010054564

10 9 8 7 6 5 4 3 2 1

CONTENTS

USER'S GUIDE

There is a vast literature of business and the world of work, and thousands of new publications emerge each year. *The Best Business Books Ever* aims to distill in an accessible format the main lessons from the best and most influential titles ever published.

Taking in the perspectives of authors, practitioners, and theorists around the world and across the centuries, the contents range from timeless texts on strategy such as *The Art of War* and *The Prince*, to the management classics *The Principles of Scientific Management* and *The Human Problems of an Industrial Civilization*, to contemporary titles such as *The Practice of Management*, *The Age of Unreason*, and *Blur*.

A two-page digest of each work contains the following features:

- **Why Read It?**—a capsule introduction describing the book's key contribution to management
- **Getting Started**—an introduction to the main themes that each author sets out to address
- **Contribution**—a detailed summary of the book's most important points
- **Context**—an overview of both the immediate reaction to the book and its long-term significance
- **For More Information**—essential bibliographic information on each title

THE BEST BUSINESS BOOKS EVER

Action Learning
REG REVANS

WHY READ IT?
What is the difference between a puzzle and a problem? According to Revans, there is an existing solution to a puzzle; it simply needs to be found. There is no existing solution to a problem. The solution has to be worked out by a process of inquiry that begins at the point where one does not know what to do next and expertise is no help. *Action Learning* explains that process and offers an alternative method of learning to the traditional one, which is based on programmed knowledge instead of encouraging students to ask questions and roam widely around a subject.

GETTING STARTED
As a young man Reg Revans competed in the 1928 Olympics and worked in the famous Cavendish laboratories at Cambridge in the United Kingdom, alongside such fathers of nuclear physics as Ernest Rutherford and J. J. Thompson. Action learning is his systematization of the methods used by the Cambridge team to deal with problems. He developed them further when working for the National Coal Board after World War II. He also went on to become Britain's first professor of industrial administration at the University of Manchester.

Action Learning is all about an alternative to traditional education and training. The method it sets out is a form of "learning by doing," but its proponents are careful to distinguish it from "learning on the job" or "learning by experience." It involves a collaborative effort, humility, a "trading of one's confusion with that of others," and deep reflection on one's experience and the nature of the problem. Its outcome is personal growth as much as a way out of a current difficulty.

CONTRIBUTION
1. Action Learning
The concept of action learning is based on a simple equation: $L = P + Q$. Learning (L) occurs through a combination of programmed knowledge (P) and the ability to ask insightful questions (Q). It does not deny all usefulness to existing knowledge, but its focus is on asking questions. Learning must be opened up, argues Revans. Programmed knowledge is one-dimensional and rigid; the ability to ask questions opens up other dimensions and is free flowing.

The first step toward asking constructive questions is to acknowledge one's own ignorance. In the author's view, too many people conceal their ignorance under a veneer of knowledge. Instead of hiding our ignorance, we should be bartering it.

The essence of action learning is to become better acquainted with the self through observing what one actually tries to do, endeavoring to ascertain the reasons for the attempt, and tracing the consequences that result from it. Revans said he sought "to focus [his] own doubt by keeping away from experts with prefabricated answers."

2. The Importance of Small Team Learning
The structure linking the two elements in the equation is the small team or set. The central idea of this approach is collaboration within the set; its members strive to learn with and from each other as they confess failures and expand on victories.

3. A Better Way to Develop Managers

Action learning is also the antithesis of the traditional approach to developing managers. We keep solving the same problems because we do not learn from them. We bring in consultants to provide solutions or send managers to courses where they are taught a lot but learn little. Action learning is about teaching a little and learning a lot.

Unless your ideas are ridiculed by experts they are worth nothing.

4. Collaboration Counts

In industry, managers and workers need to acknowledge the problems they face and then attempt to solve them. When doctors listen to nurses, patients recover more quickly. If mining engineers pay more attention to their workers than to their machinery, the pits are more efficient. Managers learn most not from books or seminars, but from here-and-now exchanges about the operational job at hand.

According to Revans, "The ultimate power of a successful general staff lies not in the brilliance of its individual members, but in the cross-fertilization of its collective abilities."

CONTEXT

For a long time Revans's ideas were comparatively little known and undervalued, at least in the English-speaking world. They were received much better in mainland Europe (in Belgium in particular), and he spent the final period of his working life abroad. Many management ideas that are currently fashionable, such as teamworking, reengineering, and the learning organization, contain elements of "action learning."

One of the critical points about action learning is its relation to action. In a way it appears misnamed. At first sight the name suggests learning in practical situations or performing tasks rather than studying theory. It tends to conceal the centrality to the process of reflection; questioning, especially questioning one's own actions in a deliberate and precise way; ignorance bartering; and collaborative effort. The solutions that are eventually arrived at must be tested in action, but that is very much the final stage.

Interest in Revans's ideas nevertheless continues to grow. The Pentagon is said to be enthusiastic, and General Electric uses action teams to tackle particular problems. There is also the Revans Foundation at the University of Manchester in the United Kingdom, where the theory and practice of action learning are particularly studied.

FOR MORE INFORMATION

Revans, Reg. *Action Learning*. London: Blond & Briggs, 1974.

Administrative Behavior
HERBERT SIMON

WHY READ IT?
Decision making, according to Simon, is synonymous with management. But what is decision making, and how are decisions made? Simon realized that most people's assumptions were hopelessly unrealistic. He set out to inject some realism into the subject, but not in a merely reductive way; he also elaborated a very modern concept of the organization as an interrelated and intercommunicating body. He said that the ability to make decisions effectively was the difference between effectiveness and ineffectiveness in organizations. On that basis alone, his book is worth reading.

> Organization is not an organizational chart, but a complex pattern of communications and other relationships in a group of human beings.

GETTING STARTED
Herbert Simon, the son of German immigrants to Milwaukee and a graduate of the University of Chicago, won the Nobel prize for economics in 1978 for his work on administrative behavior, the subject of his doctoral thesis and this book. He is said to have been inspired to write it by observations made while working part time for Milwaukee's recreation department as a student. He is also said to have told the Nobel committee, when collecting his award, that his real interest was in artificial intelligence—the field into which his interest in how decisions and choices are made ultimately led him.

In *Administrative Behavior: A Study of Decision-making Processes in Administrative Organization*, he developed a theory of human choice or decision making that aimed to be sufficiently broad and realistic to accommodate both the rational views of economists and the human concerns of psychologists and practical decision makers.

CONTRIBUTION
1. The Problems of Organizational Theory
According to *Administrative Behavior*, the way in which administration is usually described suffers from superficiality, gross oversimplification, and a lack of realism. Theorists have refused to undertake the tiresome task of studying the actual allocation of decision-making functions. Instead, they have been satisfied with talking loosely about authority, centralization, span of control, function, and the like, without seeking operational definitions of these terms.

Classic economic theory also suggests that decisions are made by obtaining all the available information, assessing it, and coming to an objective and rational conclusion about how the best result can be achieved. In reality, nobody has the time and the mental resources to do this. Instead of aiming for "the best," management is content with what is "good enough," a solution that is "satisficing" (satisfies and suffices).

2. Organization Is Important
Organization is important, first because in our society, people spend most of their waking adult lives in organizations, and this environment provides much of the force that molds

and develops personal qualities and habits. Second, it provides those in responsible positions with the means for exercising authority and influence over others.

3. The Complexity of Organizational Interaction
It is not sufficient to regard organizational behavior as a matter of understanding people or measuring their performance more effectively. Each act in an organization exists in a complex interaction with the organizational system as a whole.

4. Understanding Decision Making
A complex decision is like a great river, drawing from its many tributaries the innumerable component premises of which it is constituted. Many individuals and organizational units contribute to every large decision, and the problem of centralization and decentralization is one of arranging the complex system into an effective plan.

5. The Importance of Relationships
An organization is not an organizational chart, but rather a complex pattern of communications and other relationships in a group of human beings. This pattern provides the members of the group with much of the information, assumptions, goals, and attitudes that enter into the decisions made by each and every one of them. It also provides them with a set of stable and comprehensible expectations about what the other members of the group are doing and how they will react to what any individual says and does.

CONTEXT
Simon later observed that he must have had a prophetic gift when he included the words "behavior," "decision-making," and "organization" in the book's full title, because they quickly became the fashionable phrases of social science.

Organizational theory had been deeply embedded in vagueness before the publication of *Administrative Behavior*. Its clearest proponent up to that time had been Chester Barnard, who contributed the foreword to Simon's book.

In response, Simon developed a theory of human choice or decision making that aimed to accommodate
- the rational aspects of choice that have always been the principal concern of the economist and
- the properties and limitations of the human decision-making mechanisms that have attracted the attention of psychologists and practical decision makers.

He thus formed a bridge between the humanists and engineers in management thinking.

Simon's views were ahead of their time. For the next 40 years organization, in the West at least, continued to be seen as an act of ordering, simplifying, and categorizing rather than as a powerful, dynamic, and ever-changing force. Only in the early 1990s, partly through the success of Peter Senge's *The Fifth Discipline*, did systems thinking make the leap from academic obscurity to the executive agenda.

FOR MORE INFORMATION
Simon, Herbert. *Administrative Behavior: A Study of Decision-Making Processes in Administrative Organization*. 4th ed. New York: Free Press, 1997.

The Age of Discontinuity
PETER F. DRUCKER

WHY READ IT?
Peter Drucker predicted the rise of the "knowledge worker" long before the term came into common usage. His definition is much broader than the IT-led version in current usage. He provides valuable insight into the changing nature of management roles and responsibilities in the knowledge economy.

GETTING STARTED
According to Drucker, the manager as knowledge worker is a new breed of thoughtful, intelligent executive. The manager is reincarnated as a responsible individual, paid for applying knowledge, exercising judgment, and taking responsible leadership within the organization.

The knowledge worker sees himself or herself as another professional. While dependent on the organization for access to income and opportunity, the organization equally depends on him or her.

Drucker maintains that knowledge, rather than labor, is the new measure of economic society—and the knowledge worker is the true capitalist in the knowledge society. Knowledge is not only power but also ownership of the means of production.

CONTRIBUTION
1. The Manager as Knowledge Worker
Drucker coined the term *knowledge worker*. This was a new breed of executive: a highly trained, intelligent managerial professional who realized his or her own worth and contribution to the organization. Drucker bade farewell to the concept of the manager as mere supervisor or paper shuffler.

Though the knowledge worker is not a laborer, and certainly not proletarian, neither is he or she a subordinate (in the sense of being told what to do). On the contrary, the knowledge worker is paid for applying his or her knowledge, exercising judgment, and taking responsible leadership.

2. The Nature of the Knowledge Worker
According to Drucker, the knowledge worker sees himself or herself as another professional, no different from the lawyer, the teacher, the preacher, the doctor, or the government servant of yesterday. He or she has the same education, but more income—and probably greater opportunities as well.

The knowledge worker may well realize that he or she depends on the organization for access to income and opportunity, and that without the organization, there would be no job. But there is also the realization that the organization depends equally on him or her.

Drucker effectively wrote the obituary for the obedient, gray-suited, loyal, corporate man and woman. The only trouble was, it took this corporate creature another 20 years to die.

3. The Impact of Knowledge Workers
The social ramifications of this new breed of corporate executive were significant. If knowledge, rather than labor, was the new measure of economic society, then the fabric of capitalist

society had to change. The knowledge worker is both the true capitalist in the knowledge society and dependent on his or her job.

Collectively the knowledge workers—the employed, educated middle class of today's society—own the means of production through pension funds, investment trusts, and so on. Knowledge is not only power, it is also ownership.

CONTEXT

The book effectively mapped out the demise of the age of mass, labor-based production and the advent of the knowledge-based information age. Drucker's realization that the role of the manager had fundamentally changed was not a sudden one. The foundations of the idea of the knowledge worker can be seen in his description of management by objectives in *The Practice of Management* (1954). Knowledge management, intellectual capital, and the like are now the height of corporate fashion. The modern idea of the knowledge worker is a creature of the technological age, the mobile executive, the hot-desker. Drucker provided a characteristically broader perspective, placing the rise of the knowledge worker in the evolution of management into a respectable and influential discipline.

> If knowledge, rather than labor, is the new measure of economic society then the fabric of capitalist society must change.

Drucker continued to develop his thinking on the role of knowledge, most notably in his 1992 book *Managing for the Future*, in which he observed, "From now on the key is knowledge. The world is becoming not labor intensive, not materials intensive, not energy intensive, but knowledge intensive."

The Age of Discontinuity was startlingly correct in its predictions. Much of it would fit easily into business books of today.

Prior to Drucker's death, management guru Gary Hamel said,

> Peter Drucker's reputation is as a management theorist. He has also been a management prophet. Writing in 1969, he clearly anticipated the emergence of the knowledge economy. I'd like to set a challenge for would-be management gurus: Try to find something to say that Peter Drucker has not said first, and has not said well. This high hurdle should substantially reduce the number of business books clogging the bookshelves of booksellers, and offer managers the hope of gaining some truly fresh insights.

FOR MORE INFORMATION

Drucker, Peter F. *The Age of Discontinuity*. rev. ed. Woburn, MA: Butterworth-Heinemann, 1992.

The Age of E-tail
ALEX BIRCH, PHILIPP GERBERT, AND DIRK SCHNEIDER

> Many view the Internet merely as a sales channel and treat it as an add-on without fundamentally questioning their current business system.

WHY READ IT?

This book, written by three specialists in e-tailing, is a practical guide to building a successful retailing business on the Internet. It describes the current state of the market and identifies success factors as well as risks.

GETTING STARTED

The future of shopping is online. It has already reached a mass-market audience in the United States. The Net has diminished the strength of traditional brands, as Internet success doesn't come for operations that are simply cloned from the physical world. Customer loyalty is important but increasingly difficult to create, meaning that soon all successful e-tailers will offer almost everything tailored individually to the customer. Because the Internet is the central medium of the future, companies should consider offering complementing online and off-line services.

CONTRIBUTION

1. The Future of Shopping Is Online

E-shopping has already reached a mass-market audience in the United States, and it is set to take off in the rest of the world. For established retailers and entrepreneurs, the question is not which sector is ripe for Internet trading, but whether the opportunity is still open.

2. Traditional Physical Assets No Longer Have Value

Established companies must question the fundamentals of their business. E-shopping is not about exploiting an additional sales channel, but rather about establishing a whole new business. Traditional physical retail formats must be fundamentally restructured or disappear.

3. New Players Are Seizing Power

New players are building up a lead in e-shopping; competitors are springing up everywhere, and competition is becoming increasingly intense.

4. Successful E-tailing Is the Survival of the Fastest

In the Internet economy, survival and winning are equivalent. Market leadership and the creation of successful new retail formats are critical. However, most e-shopping sites lose money on a large scale because of high start-up and investment costs.

5. Internet Shops Need New Brands

The Internet has diminished the strength of traditional brands. Prudential's online bank made little of the company's traditional virtues: solid, dependable, long established. The emphasis was on a brand that was modern, technology friendly, convenient, and different.

6. Context Makes the Difference

Internet success won't come for operations that are simply cloned from the physical world. The key to success is to design a retail site around three factors: convenience; content that adds value; and a sense of community and belonging for the customer. The successful site must also have traditional commercial *nous*.

7. Customer Loyalty Is Important but Increasingly Difficult to Create
E-tailers need repeat business to achieve profitability. However, the e-customer is a fickle entity. Winning loyalty depends on
- knowing more about customers and offering more;
- addressing customers individually;
- giving customers control of the business relationship by enabling them to design personalized products or manage transactions themselves; and
- creating a sense of community.

8. Built-to-order Offerings Will Upset Traditional Value Chains
There are hardly any limits to personalization. Most cars and PCs are now made to individual specifications, and soon all successful e-tailers will offer almost everything tailored individually to the customer. Even if the product is uniform, the surrounding experience can be tailored.

9. Innovation Will Be Driven by the Duality of Product and Service
Duality is the idea that "each product is a service and each service is a product." A product that is personalized contains a strong element of service in the transaction.

10. E-shopping Is Currently a U.S. Phenomenon
The United States enjoys a tremendous structural advantage for e-tailers: it is the largest homogeneous market; it has the largest online consumer base; the Web has penetrated everyday life; and Internet sales in most states receive a subsidy from the absence of sales tax.

11. Traditional Companies Can Offer Online/Offline Services
The U.S. sales tax regime forces companies into an online strategy, preventing most of the "bricks-and-mortar" players there from developing combined online/offline concepts. In the rest of the world the current absence of dominant online players gives traditional companies a better chance of successfully entering the Internet space.

12. The Internet Is the Central Medium of the Future
Many companies view the Internet merely as a sales channel without fundamentally questioning their current business system. However, companies should concentrate on developing truly complementary offline value (context and convenience, entertainment, customer acquisition and loyalty).

CONTEXT
E-commerce has attracted its fair share of hype, and it is difficult to predict its long-term acceptance. The failure of a large number of companies and a drift away from investor confidence in the sector saw critics predicting a short life. This book steers away from the hype and provides a practical guide to success and risk factors in setting up an e-tail operation.

FOR MORE INFORMATION
Birch, Alex, Philipp Gerbert, and Dirk Schneider. *The Age of E-tail: Conquering the New World of Electronic Shopping.* Milford, CT : Capstone Pub., 2001.

The Age of Unreason
CHARLES HANDY

WHY READ IT?
Written in 1989, this book includes a number of predictions about the way work would develop. The author provides insights into changing organizational structures and developments, such as knowledge working, outsourcing, and strategic alliances—the hallmarks of today's economy.

GETTING STARTED
In the author's view, in the age of unreason, a number of organizational forms will emerge, as will new working patterns, such as outsourcing, telecommuting, the intellectual capital movement, and the rise of knowledge workers.

The portfolio worker will become more important, contributing to a greater work-life balance. A portfolio describes how the different bits of work in our lives fit together to form a balanced whole. Portfolio work includes wage work and fee work, homework, gift work, and study work.

Handy states that the social changes resulting from these developments will be reflected in changing patterns of business, with a mix of small enterprises and large conglomerates. There will also be temporary alliances of large and small organizations to deliver a particular project.

CONTRIBUTION
1. The Concept of an Age of Unreason
The age of unreason is a time when the future, in so many areas, is to be shaped by us and for us. The only prediction that will hold true is that no predictions will hold true. It will be a time for thinking the unlikely and doing the unreasonable.

2. New Organizational Forms
The author suggests that a number of organizational forms will emerge in an age of unreason:
- the shamrock organization
- the federal organization
- the Triple I organization

The shamrock organization is a form of organization based on a core of essential executives and workers supported by outside contractors and part-time help.

The federal organization is a form of decentralized setup, in which the center's powers are given to it by the outlying groups; the center therefore coordinates, advises, influences, and suggests rather than directs or controls. Federalism is the way to combine the autonomy of individual parts with the economics of coordination.

The Triple I organization is based on Information, Intelligence, and Ideas. This type of organization resembles a university and seeks to make added value out of knowledge. To achieve this, the Triple I organization increasingly uses smart machines, with smart people to work with them.

3. New Working Patterns
Handy anticipated the growth of outsourcing, telecommuting, the intellectual capital movement, and the rise of knowledge workers. He also foresaw how these developments might

affect the individual. His concept of the portfolio worker helped redefine the nature of work, as well as questions of work-life balance.

4. Portfolio Working
A portfolio describes how the different bits of work in our lives fit together to form a balanced whole. The five main categories of portfolio work are

- wage work,
- homework,
- study work.
- fee work,
- gift work, and

Wage (or salary) work represents money paid for time given. Fee work is money paid for results delivered. Employees do wage work; professionals, craftspeople, and freelancers do fee work. Fee work is increasing as jobs move outside the organization. Some employees get fees (bonuses) as well as wages.

Homework includes tasks that go on in the home, from cooking and cleaning to child care and carpentry. Gift work is done for free outside the home, for charities and local groups, neighbors, or the community. Study work done seriously is a form of work, not recreation.

> The age of unreason is a time for bold imaginings, for thinking the unlikely and doing the unreasonable.

5. A Broader Portfolio
In the past, for most people the work portfolio had only one item in it—their career. This was a risky strategy. Few people would put all their money into one asset, yet that is what most people were doing with their lives. The career had to provide many things at once: interest or satisfaction in the work, interesting people and good company, security, money, and the opportunity for development.

6. Funding the Portfolio
Portfolio people think in terms of portfolio money, not salary money. Money comes in fits and starts from various sources, for example a pension, some part-time work, some fees to charge, or some things to sell. They lead cash-flow lives, not salary lives, planning always to have enough inflows to cover outflows.

Portfolio people think in terms of barter and know that most skills are saleable if one wants to sell them.

7. Changing Patterns of Business
The age of unreason will be a world of "fleas and elephants": large conglomerates and small individual entities, or large political and economic blocs and small countries. There will also be ad hoc organizations, temporary alliances of large and small organizations to deliver a particular project.

CONTEXT
The book predicts many of the important changes in working patterns that are now commonplace, including outsourcing, telecommuting, and virtual project teams from different organizations. It also recognizes the growing importance of knowledge workers and intellectual capital.

FOR MORE INFORMATION
Handy, Charles. *The Age of Unreason*. Boston: Harvard Business School Press, 1998.

The Art of Japanese Management
RICHARD T. PASCALE AND ANTHONY ATHOS

WHY READ IT?

First published in 1981, this book was one of the first genuine business best sellers, playing a crucial role in the discovery of Japanese management techniques. In its comparisons of Japanese and U.S. companies, it provides rare insights into the truth behind the mythology of Japanese management and the inadequacy of much Western practice.

GETTING STARTED

By the late 1990s, growing Japanese superiority threatened the dominant position of the United States in world markets. In the authors' view, a major factor in Japan's favor was its managerial ethos. Japanese managers had vision, something thought to be notably lacking in the West. In Japan, visions are dynamic, rather than generic statements of corporate intent. Managers in the United States are constrained by their beliefs and assumptions. The seven S framework (strategy, structure, skills, staff, shared values, systems, and style) represents the key categories requiring managers' attention. The Japanese succeeded through attention to the "soft" Ss—style, shared values, skills, and staff—while the West remained squarely focused on the "hard" Ss of strategy, structure, and systems.

> The Western vision of management circumscribes our effectiveness.

CONTRIBUTION

1. Growing Japanese Superiority

In 1980 Japan's GNP was third highest in the world, and extrapolating trends at the time, it appeared likely that it would become the highest by the year 2000.

For the U.S. readership, *The Art of Japanese Management* contains some hard-hitting truths. If anything, the extent of Japanese superiority over the United States in industrial competitiveness had been underestimated.

2. Managerial Skills

The visionary managerial style adopted in Japan is a major reason for its success, according to the authors. In contrast, despite having a variety of tools at hand, in the West vision has been limited. Beliefs, assumptions, and perceptions about management frequently constrain U.S. managers. The Western vision of management circumscribes our effectiveness.

In Japan managers enhance their way of doing business with dynamic visions rather than pallid or generic statements of corporate intent. The working practice of the Matsushita Electric Company (now Panasonic) was a particular focus of interest for the authors.

3. The Seven S Framework

The book is best known for its central concept, the seven S framework. As a general statement of the issues facing organizations, the framework is unremarkable, but it did gain a great deal of attention. The framework is a simple list of the seven important categories that managers should take into account: strategy, structure, skills, staff, shared values, systems, and style.

According to Pascale and Athos, the value of a framework such as the seven Ss is that it imposes an interesting discipline on the researcher.

4. Comparing Management Styles

The seven S is a framework for comparing Japanese and U.S. management approaches. The Matsushita approach was compared with that of the ITT Corporation.

The Japanese succeeded largely because of the attention they gave to the "soft" Ss—style, shared values, skills, and staff—whereas the West remained preoccupied with the "hard" Ss of strategy, structure, and systems. Since the book's publication, however, the general trend of Western managerial thinking has been directed toward the "soft" Ss, which are particularly helpful when managers and leaders have to deal with ambiguous situations and uncertain times—as many have to.

CONTEXT

The book's roots lie in Pascale's work with the U.S. National Commission on Productivity. Having initially thought that lessons from Japan were limited for cultural reasons, Pascale and Athos decided it would be more productive to look at Japanese companies in the United States. The research for the book eventually covered 34 companies over six years.

The authors' championing of vision proved highly influential. It was Athos who really started the entire "visioning" industry in the United States. Soon after *The Art of Japanese Management* was published, a flurry of books appeared highlighting so-called visionaries. Today, corporate visions are a fact of life.

Speaking about the book, business author Gary Hamel commented:

> Japan-phobia has subsided a bit, helped by a strong yen, inept Japanese macro-economic policy, and the substantial efforts of many Western companies to re-build their competitiveness. While Pascale and Athos undoubtedly overstated the unique capabilities of Japanese management (is Matsushita really that much better managed than Hewlett-Packard?), they successfully challenged the unstated assumption that the United States was the font of all managerial wisdom. Since *The Art of Japanese Management* hit the bookstores, U.S. companies have learned much from Japan. Pascale and Athos deserve credit for setting the learning agenda.

FOR MORE INFORMATION

Pascale, Richard T., and Anthony Athos. *The Art of Japanese Management*. New York: Simon & Schuster, 1981.

The Art of the Long View
PETER SCHWARTZ

WHY READ IT?
It may be impossible to predict the future, but it *is* possible to prepare for it and lessen the effects of any shocks it may bring. The "scenario method," presented in this book by Peter Schwartz, enables managers to cover the possible outcomes of their actions and take account of external events outside their control. It has been widely used in major corporations to prevent problems caused by unexpected developments.

GETTING STARTED
The book describes the use of scenarios to investigate and test decisions about the future. A scenario is a way of looking ahead, a description of how the world might turn out if certain events take place. Schwartz believes that scenarios enable an organization to plot routes through necessarily uncertain terrain. They are not predictions; accurate predictions are impossible. Nor are they extrapolations of trends. According to the author, scenarios are an approach to making better decisions about the future.

CONTRIBUTION
1. What Type of Scenario?
The author highlights three possible scenarios for the future:
- more of the same, but better;
- worse, leading to decay and depression; and
- different but better, with profound social changes.

It is possible to identify what types of business would succeed in each of those scenarios.

2. The Problem of Denial
Schwartz explains that some scenarios predict situations that people are not prepared to contemplate. He refers to this as a state of denial. Scenarios, he suggests, should be treated as stories to overcome the problem of denial. Putting figures in the scenario makes them believable. With stories, readers can suspend disbelief.

3. Responses to Scenarios
People have different mind sets and so respond to scenarios differently. Schwartz categorizes people as optimists, pessimists, and those who prefer the status quo. Some commentators dismiss scenarios as impossible dreams, but the author believes it is important to ask awkward questions and be prepared for the unexpected.

4. The Right Perspective
Schwartz recommends changing focus between the broad picture and the specific area of concern. For someone looking at the future prospects of an industry, it is important to take account of global developments as well as industry trends.

5. Wide-ranging Research
Research into areas such as science, technology, politics, and economics underpins the development of scenarios, but conventional research sources may simply point to the contin-

uation of the status quo. The author believes that "fringe research" may be equally important.

6. Certainty and Uncertainty

> To act with confidence, one must be able to look ahead and consider uncertainties.

The author explains that the building blocks of scenarios are society, technology, economics, politics, and the environment. Looking at developments in each area gives the scenario builder a series of useful perspectives. The author describes how Shell established the Global Business Network to bring together people with different perspectives. Scenario builders use multiple perspectives to create a series of challenges and possible responses and to identify potential winners and losers.

CONTEXT

The book draws on the author's wide-ranging experience in scenario development within Shell. He uses real-life examples to demonstrate the importance of scenarios in an industry like energy, which is influenced by technology, politics, and economic and environmental factors. He explains how unexpected events such as war or major political change could have had a significant impact on the industry if it had not prepared for change through the use of scenarios.

Schwartz is careful to highlight the difference between scenarios and predictions about the future. His book is not a prediction about the way the world might look, but a method for assessing what might change if unforeseen circumstances occur. In that sense, the book is a valuable complement to books on strategy development based on "business as usual."

FOR MORE INFORMATION

Schwartz, Peter. *The Art of the Long View.* Hoboken, NJ: Wiley, 1997.

The Art of War
SUN TZU

WHY READ IT?
When the postwar achievements of Japanese industry began to make a significant impression in the West, and Western businesspeople began to inquire into the thinking that underlay the success of their Eastern counterparts, Sun Tzu's *The Art of War* was often mentioned. This may seem surprising, because it was probably written more than 2,000 years ago. But military language and imagery have played an important role in the development of management thinking, and if one wishes to gain an insight into strategy, leadership, and survival in a hostile, competitive environment, who better to turn to than a general whose name is a byword for sagacity?

GETTING STARTED
Sun Tzu is thought to have lived more than 2,400 years ago, at roughly the same time as Confucius. Historians are generally agreed that he was a general who led a number of successful military campaigns in present-day Anhui Province; the state of Wu, under whose sovereign he served, became a dominant power at that time. Since then it has become standard practice for Chinese military chiefs to familiarize themselves with his writings.

The Art of War (the book's actual title is *Sun Tzu Ping Fa*, literally "The Military Method of Mr. Sun") is a compilation of the legendary general's thinking on the strategies that underlie military success. His anecdotes and thoughts, which fill no more than about 25 pages of text in all, are divided into 13 sections. Not all are relevant to modern-day concerns, but some strike a significant chord. Rather like a proponent of judo, Sun Tzu particularly recommends using the momentum of one's enemy's own moves to defeat him.

CONTRIBUTION
1. Get the Strategy Right
Sun Tzu, like most good and seasoned generals, is anything but an adventurer and anything but gung-ho. "Why destroy," he asks, "when you can win by stealth and cunning? To subdue the enemy's forces without fighting is the summit of skill."

His advice shows subtlety and restraint: "A sovereign should not start a war out of anger, nor should a general give battle out of rage. While anger can revert to happiness and rage to delight, a nation that has been destroyed cannot be restored, nor can the dead be brought back to life."

He continues: "The best approach is to attack the other side's strategy; next best is to attack his alliances; next best is to attack his soldiers; the worst is to attack cities."

2. Get Information from the Right Sources
Sun Tzu also gives sound advice on knowing one's markets: "Advance knowledge cannot be gained from ghosts and spirits, but must be obtained from people who know the enemy situation."

3. Stay Focused
His view on strategy leaves no room for sentiment or distraction: "Deploy forces to defend the strategic points; exercise vigilance in preparation, do not be indolent. Deeply investigate

the true situation, secretly await their laxity. Wait until they leave their strongholds, then seize what they love."

CONTEXT

So what does *The Art of War* have to offer the manager of, for example, a small components factory in Peoria or Nottingham? Sun Tzu's admirers argue that his pithy sayings encapsulate basic and eternal truths. According to Gary Hamel, "Strategy didn't start with Igor Ansoff; neither did it start with Machiavelli. It probably didn't even start with Sun Tzu. Strategy is as old as human conflict." Anyone who has to devise a plan or give a lead can do with all the help he or she can get.

> Water flows in accordance with the ground; an army achieves victory in accordance with the enemy.

Hamel adds, "[A]nd, if the stakes are high in business, they're rather higher in the military sphere." One of the attractions of the military analogy and the military role model in business is that they elevate proceedings to a loftier plane. Not only are the issues larger, and the scale more heroic, but it is clear who the enemy is, and when the enemy is clear, the world appears clearer, whether one is a military general or a managing director.

Embattled managers in particular may benefit from the stimulus that military authors like Sun Tzu, Clausewitz, or Liddell-Hart, and the writings of modern military leaders like Colin Powell or General Sir Mike Jackson, can give to their civilian imaginations.

Finally, as has often been pointed out, Sun Tzu has long been revered in the East. He is said to be required reading not only for Eastern military tacticians but also for Eastern businesspeople. To know one's enemies—or indeed to know one's friends, partners, and colleagues—it is useful to read what they have read.

FOR MORE INFORMATION

Tzu, Sun. *The Art of War* (trans. Griffith). Rev. ed. New York: Dover Publications, 2002.

Barbarians at the Gate
BRYAN BURROUGH AND JOHN HELYAR

WHY READ IT?

Barbarians at the Gate explores the takeover battle for RJR Nabisco in 1988, one of the largest ever leveraged buyouts (LBOs). It is both a biography of CEO Ross Johnson and an analysis of why the planned LBO went awry. Unknown to Johnson and his supporters, other bidders emerged, including Kohlberg Kravis Roberts (KKR), who were highly experienced at LBOs. For several weeks these two main groups, among others, fought to control the company. Eventually KKR's $25 billion was decisive. Johnson initiated the LBO as a cheap way to consolidate his standing—and lost everything. *Barbarians at the Gate* addresses both the financial and human aspects of investment banking. Financial issues are explored alongside "softer" aspects of business, such as negotiating. Like Lewis's *Liar's Poker*, *Barbarians at the Gate* teaches the lessons of an entire age. It shows how financial matters are dominated by human characters and captures the culture of competition at that time, a valuable lesson for current and future generations.

> We've got our fee, let's go on with the next deal.

GETTING STARTED

Leveraged buyouts are debt-financed transactions (using bank loans and bond sales) to take a public corporation private. They enable a single party to gain control of a publicly traded company, using vast sums of capital to buy out shareholders. Such deals became possible for two reasons. First, in the early 1980s the Internal Revenue Code made interest, but not dividends, deductible from taxable income, making it possible to obtain large bank loans. Second, the demand for junk bonds exploded in the 1980s, enabling the sale of bonds to raise finance for such transactions. Consequently, the LBO of RJR Nabisco was part of a wider economic trend. What Johnson and his supporters ignored was that if they could use this mechanism to take over a public company, then others would be able to as well. They overlooked economic trends at their peril.

Barbarians at the Gate highlights a milestone in financial history: the LBO of the Gibson Greeting Card Company, when the company was first taken private in 1982. Only 18 months later, it was made public again with a significantly higher share price, despite few managerial changes. LBOs were one of the most lucrative investments throughout the 1980s. Consequently, corporations faced numerous takeover battles, and the competition surrounding this could be disastrous.

CONTRIBUTION

The authors draw the following key conclusions from this roller coaster business ride.

1. Never Pay in Cash

Johnson's team underestimated the importance of the initial offer. Their offer was excessively low, proposing to the board of directors an LBO at $75/share, after concerns that the price was undervalued at $55. Consequently, rival bidders emerged, who could otherwise have been deterred. The authors maintain that Johnson, by showing his financial position before gaining control over RJR, allowed his weaknesses to be exploited. His concern that falling tobacco sales were dragging down the share price was insignificant compared to the threat of losing his stake in RJR Nabisco. The authors speculate about whether Johnson was unwilling to incur the large debt a higher bid would require because of the cost cutting it would necessitate. No valuation put RJR's value beneath $80 a share, and the authors suggest that Johnson's low bid invited better-financed parties to tender bids.

2. Never Tell the Truth

The book details how, ignoring Johnson's offer of directorship seats and soaring share holdings, the independent board evaluating the offer issued a press release, rather than keep the deal quiet. The board members knew their strengths: any potential buyer would reward them handsomely for their support. In the authors' view, Johnson had shown his cards too early. This allowed other bidders to enter the fray with a good understanding of how to undermine Johnson and win control of RJR Nabisco. The plan was that nobody would know about the deal until the last moment, by which time Johnson would already have gained control. By revealing his plan too early, Johnson undermined his strategy. Nowadays, investors are far more adept at handling the media.

3. Never Play by the Rules

Johnson's key mistake, the authors suggest, was to rely on Shearson Lehman Hutton and Salomon Bros. to support the bid. Both firms were hurt by the 1987 stock market crash and had little LBO experience. Johnson's competitors were KKR and Drexel, the biggest players in LBOs and junk bonds, respectively. Now firms are more diligent about choosing partners. According to Burrough and Halyar, Johnson's decisions were based more on loyalty and personality than on due diligence. A better strategy would have been to gain more finance, in case it was needed, while acting more unpredictably. Because KKR could anticipate Johnson's actions, they were able to attack his character in the media, undermining his popularity base. *Barbarians at the Gate* maintains that in a game of mavericks, one cannot win through playing by the rules.

CONTEXT

In many ways, the dot-com bubble of the late 1990s was a repeat of the stock market crash of the late 1980s. *Barbarians at the Gate* shows how irrational personalities precipitate such economic recessions. While Johnson's failure was on a relatively small scale, it demonstrates the kind of irrationality that leads to fluctuating asset prices. Eagerness to lend unjustifiable amounts of venture capital to high-tech start-ups in the late 1990s was mirrored in the LBO boom, which consumed similarly large sums of capital.

Much of investment banking has changed since the 1980s. Nowadays shareholders are unlikely to accept such turbulent management, because of the disruption to organizational culture it produces. The LBO wave of the 1980s was defined by an eagerness to make quick gains. Today the focus is on building sustainable increases in value. Most LBO firms in the 1980s leveraged capital with bank loans or junk bond borrowings. Now most capital comes in larger quantities from global pension or hedge funds. Now the philosophy is "buy and build," with bidders often keeping their holdings for three to ten years. They sell for the highest price possible through adding as much value to the organization as possible, and takeovers are usually management-led. However, the lessons from Johnson's failed takeover bid still apply.

FOR MORE INFORMATION

Burrough, Bryan, and John Helyar. *Barbarians at the Gate: The Fall of RJR Nabisco*. Rev ed. New York: HarperPerennial, 2003.

A Behavioral Theory of the Firm
RICHARD M. CYERT AND JAMES G. MARCH

WHY READ IT?
The book is a powerful introduction to the complex world of decision making. James G. March is one of the foremost decision-making theorists of the 20th century. The book evaluates traditional approaches to decision making and puts forward real-world alternatives.

GETTING STARTED
An entire academic discipline, decision science, is devoted to understanding management decision making. Early theorists in the field believed that the decision process could be rationalized and systematized, and that decision making can therefore be distilled into a formula. However, reality is often more confused and messy, and managers make decisions based on a combination of intuition, experience, and analysis.

CONTRIBUTION
1. The Evolution of Decision-making Theory
Early theories were based on the premise that, under a given set of circumstances, human behavior is logical and therefore predictable. A profusion of models and analytical tools followed, seeking to distill decision making into a formula. The danger is in concluding that the solution provided by a software package is the right one.

2. The Rational Theory of Decision Making
The authors suggest that the rational, or synoptic, model of decision making involves a series of steps:

- identifying and clarifying the problem,
- prioritizing goals,
- generating and evaluating options,
- comparing predicted outcomes of each option with the goals, and
- choosing the option that matches best.

These models rely on a number of assumptions about the way in which people will behave when confronted with a set of circumstances. The assumptions allow mathematicians to derive formulae based on probability theory. The decision-making tools include such things as cost/benefit analysis, which aims to help managers evaluate various options.

3. Problems in the Rational Theory
Reality is often more confused and messy than a neat model can allow for. Underpinning the mathematical approach are a number of flawed assumptions. The model assumes that decision making is

- consistent,
- based on accurate information,
- free from emotion or prejudice, and
- rational.

4. Real-world Decision Making
According to the authors, the reality is that managers make decisions based on a combination of intuition, experience, and analysis. Because intuition and experience are impossible to quantify, the temptation is to focus on the analytical side of decision making.

5. The Relevance of Decision-making Models

This does not mean that decision theory is redundant or that decision-making models should be cast aside. Decision making is becoming ever more demanding, for a number of reasons. The growth in complexity means that companies no longer encounter simple problems. Managers are having to deal with a flood of information; a 1996 Reuters survey of 1,200 managers worldwide found that 43 percent thought their ability to make decisions was affected as a result of having too much information.

Decision theory and the use of models is reassuring, as the models lend legitimacy to decisions that may be based on hunches. However, no models are foolproof; none is universally applicable or can yet cope with the idiosyncrasies of human behavior.

6. The Challenge for Organizational Decision Making

Business decision-making theory faces a crucial and immediate problem: Individuals have goals; collective groups do not. There is a need, therefore, to create useful organizational goals, while not believing there is such a thing as an organizational mind.

Organizations should be regarded as coalitions that negotiate goals. Creating goals requires three processes:
- bargaining, which establishes the composition and general terms of the coalition;
- internal organizational control, which clarifies and develops the objectives; and
- adjustment to experience, which alters agreements in accord with changing circumstances.

Goals are inconsistent for three reasons:
- Decision making is decentralized.
- Short-term goals are given the most attention.
- The resources available to the organization are insufficient to maintain the coalition.

> Managers make decisions based on a combination of intuition, experience, and analysis.

7. A New Decision-making Model

The authors assert that the five principal goals of the modern organization are production, inventory, sales, market share, and profit. There are nine steps in the decision process: forecast competitors' behavior, forecast demand, estimate costs, specify objectives, evaluate plans, reexamine costs, reexamine demand, reexamine objectives, and select alternatives. To work successfully, this decision-making model demands that there be standard operating procedures. The procedures may be divided into general ones based on avoiding uncertainty, maintaining the rules, and using simple rules. There are also specifics, such as task performance rules, continuing records and reports, information-handling rules, and plans.

CONTEXT

Much of decision science rests on foundations set by early business thinkers, such as computer pioneer Charles Babbage and scientific management founder Frederick W. Taylor, who believed that, under given circumstances, human behavior was logical and therefore predictable. Based on this premise, models emerged to explain the workings of commerce, which, it was thought, could be extended to the way in which decisions were made.

FOR MORE INFORMATION

Cyert, Richard M., and James G. March. *A Behavioral Theory of the Firm*. 2nd ed. Malden, MA: Blackwell Publishing, 1992.

Being Digital
NICHOLAS NEGROPONTE

WHY READ IT?
This book explains why knowledge is more important than physical commodities. Although it argues that organizations of any size can break into the new economy, this is not a book that offers practical guidelines.

GETTING STARTED
Negroponte was a regular contributor to *Wired* magazine and provided many insights into the digital world. He introduced the terms "bits" and "atoms," which are used to describe the elements of the digital world. He explains that most information, despite being digital, is delivered to us in the form of atoms, that is to say, as newspapers, magazines, and books.

Economists still measure trade and write balance sheets with atoms in mind, he points out. But looking ahead, he explains why bits are easy to make and keep. They can travel easily around the world, he argues, and they are the basis of a global economy that allows the smallest company to participate.

CONTRIBUTION
1. The Concept of "Bits" and "Atoms"
According to Negroponte, the best way to appreciate the merits and consequences of being digital is to reflect on the difference between "atoms" and "bits." Atoms, he explains, are the elements of the old economy. Bits are digital. However, he points out that while we are undoubtedly in a new digital age, most information is still delivered to us in the form of atoms: newspapers, magazines, and books.

The author argues that although the economy may be moving toward an information economy, we measure trade and write our balance sheets in the traditional way, using atoms as the measure.

2. Describing the Digital World
According to Negroponte, the bits and atoms distinction has increased, not weakened, over time. He claims that people quickly grasp the idea of bits that have no weight, no size, no shape, and no color, and can travel at the speed of light.

3. The Value of Bits
Bits, claims Negroponte, are the key elements of the new information economy. He explains how the marginal cost of making more bits is zero, and no inventory is needed. It is possible to sell bits and keep them at the same time because the originals and the copies are indistinguishable.

4. Toward a Global Marketplace
The author believes that bits will form the basis of a global marketplace that is accessible to even the smallest company. That is because bits don't stop at customs. Governments cannot tell where they are, and regulators cannot determine their appropriate jurisdiction.

CONTEXT

The book consists of a "repurposing" of many of the themes first visited in the author's monthly *Wired* column in the early to mid-1990s. The book offers practical insights into the future of communications, but allows little opportunity for considered reflection on big-picture issues.

According to critics, Negroponte seems content to describe rather than to analyze, and the book lacks an incisive conclusion bringing together the key themes that he touches on but never really makes explicit.

Our economy may be moving toward an information economy, but we measure trade and we write our balance sheets with atoms in mind.

FOR MORE INFORMATION

Negroponte, Nicholas. *Being Digital.* New York: Knopf, 1995.

Blown to Bits
PHILIP EVANS AND THOMAS WURSTER

WHY READ IT?

This is a valuable book for someone putting together a business strategy. It shows that the key to success will be control of information, rather than size. Technology enables organizations of any size to acquire, control, and distribute information. This is a consultative-level book that sets out a framework for developing strategy.

GETTING STARTED

Information is changing the structure and behavior of businesses. In the past, organizations could provide rich, customized information about a product or service only to a small number of customers. Alternatively, they could reach a wider audience, but with less customization. Advanced digital technology eliminates the compromise, but also makes many traditional business structures and strategies obsolete.

Information holds traditional value chains, supply chains, consumer franchises, and organizations together. However, connectivity and common information standards are radically transforming economic relationships. New players are emerging to pick off the most profitable sectors, unencumbered by traditional physical assets.

Leaders must assess the vulnerability of their own businesses and respond. New electronic retailers and "navigators" will become an important element in the new business model. Companies must use the "ungluing" of industries to establish a competitive advantage or simply fall apart at the seams.

> Advanced digital technologies are allowing information to separate from its physical carrier.

CONTRIBUTION
1. Changing Patterns in the Information Business

Those in the business of communicating information to others have until now faced a strategic choice—go for richness or reach.

Providing rich, customized information about a product or service limited the number of potential customers who could be reached with that information. On the other hand, going for reach meant the degree of customization of the information was reduced in direct correlation to the widening universe of customers.

Information providers reflect a trade-off between richness and reach. They provide a physical infrastructure and established behavioral patterns that enable and govern the sharing of information vital to the work of business.

2. Technology Eliminates Compromise

Advanced digital technologies are allowing information to separate from its physical carrier. This removes the richness/reach trade-off and renders obsolete many traditional business structures and the strategies that drive them.

An example is Microsoft's Encarta, which destroyed *Encyclopaedia Britannica*. Since 1990, sales of printed encyclopedias have plummeted by 80 percent, destroyed by the CD-ROM. In the music industry, the struggle is between MP3 and related technologies.

3. Transforming Economic Relationships

This does not just apply to explicit "information" businesses. Information is the "glue" that holds together value chains, supply chains, consumer franchises, and organizations across the entire economy. The melting of this glue has major implications.

The explosion in connectivity and the adoption of common information standards are radically transforming economic relationships. Assets such as a sales force, a system of branches, a printing press, a chain of stores, or a delivery fleet once served as formidable barriers to entry because they took years and heavy investment to build. Now they are perceived as expensive liabilities.

4. Changes in Business Structure

New players will emerge to pick off the most profitable sectors. They will have the ability to provide both richness and reach to customers and will not be burdened by cumbersome physical assets. This will engender a process of deconstruction, involving the breaking apart and recombining of traditional business structures. Deconstruction is most likely to strike in exactly the area of the business an incumbent can least afford to lose.

5. Toward a New Business Model

A new form of disintermediation, driven by the new economics of information, threatens not just to resegment markets, but to destroy the intermediary business model entirely.

6. The Rise of Navigators

One of the most dramatic aspects of deconstruction will be the rise of navigators as independent businesses. New electronic retailers and navigators will prove as powerful and aggressive as today's category-killing retailers.

The competitive battles will be fought across three dimensions: reach, affiliation, and richness. In the new world of navigation, the importance of achieving critical mass is essential. The critical shift in affiliation from the seller to the customer will occur. The only options available in the new economics of information are to use the "ungluing" of industries to establish a competitive advantage or simply to fall apart at the seams.

CONTEXT

Like Davis and Meyer's *Blur*, this book is a valuable guide to the way markets and organizations are changing. It provides information on the new infrastructure that companies must understand and embrace.

FOR MORE INFORMATION

Evans, Philip, and Thomas Wurster. *Blown to Bits: How the New Economics of Information Transforms Strategy.* Boston: Harvard Business School Press, 2000.

Blur
STAN DAVIS AND CHRISTOPHER MEYER

WHY READ IT?

Blur is a book about the future, but the authors do not offer prescriptions. Instead, they offer a starting point: provocative ideas, observations, and predictions to get readers to think creatively about their business and future.

GETTING STARTED

At the heart of *Blur* are three forces that are redefining businesses and destroying solutions that worked for the industrial world. These forces are known as the blur of desires, the blur of fulfillment, and the blur of resources.

A product offer and exchange were once clear-cut, but buyers and sellers are now in a constantly evolving relationship. The entire theory and practice of competitive strategy is changing, and intellectual capital has emerged as the key resource.

Change no longer carries the huge weight it did only a few years ago, and connectivity is speeding up the economy and changing the way it works.

CONTRIBUTION
1. The Nature of Blur

At the heart of the authors' blur theory are three forces: connectivity, speed, and intangibles. These forces are blurring the rules and redefining our businesses and lives. They are destroying solutions, such as mass production, segmented pricing, and standardized jobs, that worked for the relatively slow, unconnected industrial world.

The three forces are shaping the behavior of the new economy and are affecting what Davis and Meyer label the blur of desires, the blur of fulfillment, and the blur of resources.

The Blur of Desires   The blur of desires has two central elements: the offer and the exchange, which were once clear-cut.

In the product-dominated age, a company offered a product for sale. Money was exchanged, and the customer disappeared into the distance. Now, however, products and services are often indistinguishable from each other. Buyers and sellers are in a constantly evolving relationship—a mutual exchange—which is driven by information and emotion as well as by money.

The Blur of Fulfillment   As organizations change to meet changing demands, so, too, must the entire theory and practice of competitive strategy.

Connectivity produces different forms of organization operating on different first principles.

The blur of businesses has created a new economic model in which returns increase rather than diminish; supermarkets mimic stock markets, and we want the market, not our strategy, to price, market, and manage our offers.

The Blur of Resources   Intellectual capital has emerged as the key resource. Hard assets have become intangibles; intangibles have become our only assets.

2. Change Is Less Critical

The authors assert that "built to last" now means "built to change." However, change and the ambiguity it brings no longer carry the huge weight they did only a few years ago.

3. The Impact of Connectivity

In the information economy, small things are connected in a variety of ways to create a complex adaptive system. Instantaneous, myriad connections are speeding up the economy and changing the way it works. The problem is that the connections are so many and so complex, they can bring things to a grinding, inexplicable halt.

CONTEXT

From Dale Carnegie to Stephen Covey, Frederick Taylor to Michael Porter, business book readers have been weaned on a diet of prescriptions for success. Books are distilled down to a handful of key points or simple models. The trouble is that lists of the essential ingredients for success are becoming increasingly more questionable.

> Built to last
> now means
> built to change.

Uncertainty is uncharted territory, and *Blur* is a book of the new breed. *Blur* would not even have been considered just a few years ago, when blind faith and certainty ruled. It would have been too weak, too suggestive of managerial confusion and impotence, and too realistic.

FOR MORE INFORMATION

Davis, Stan, and Christopher Meyer. *Blur: The Speed of Change in the Connected Economy.* Cambridge, MA: Perseus, 1998.

The Borderless World
KENICHI OHMAE

WHY READ IT?
Like Ohmae's *The Mind of the Strategist*, this book provides valuable insights into the strategic thinking behind Japanese corporate success. The author adds new elements to the structure of business strategy, showing how it operates on a global scale.

GETTING STARTED

It's time for big companies to relearn the art of invention.

According to Ohmae, in the global marketplace the concepts of country and currency are important to business strategy. Fluctuations in trade policy or exchange rates can affect an otherwise brilliant strategy. Strategy is about more than being better than the competition. Big companies must relearn the art of invention in global industries. Customers are not driven to purchase things through nationalistic sentiments; therefore, strategy should be formulated around a determination to create value for customers. Global business balances world-scale economies with products tailored to key markets. The role of central governments must change to allow individuals access to the best and cheapest goods and services from anywhere in the world.

CONTRIBUTION
1. The Key Elements of Business Strategy
To the three Cs of his previous works (commitment, creativity, and competitiveness), Ohmae adds

- country—the government-created environments in which global organizations must operate; and
- currency—the exposure of such organizations to fluctuations in foreign exchange rates.

These two additional elements are now key to the formulation of any strategy.

An otherwise brilliant strategy can be ruined by a sudden fluctuation in trade policy or exchange rates, leading to a seemingly irreparable hemorrhage of cash. Making arrangements to deal with fluctuations must lie at the very heart of strategy. Strategy is creating sustained values for the customer more effectively than competitors do.

2. Invention Is Critical
In the author's view, invention and the commercialization of invention are essential. Most people in big companies have forgotten how to invent, so they must relearn the art. This time they must learn to manage invention in industries or businesses that are global, where it is necessary to achieve world-scale economies and yet tailor products to key markets.

3. Going Beyond the Competition
Strategy is about more than simply being better than the competition, which only encourages companies to become fixated on the competition. This fixation drives them to formulate their strategy according to those of their competitors.

Possible strategies should be tested against competitive realities.

Tactical responses to what competitors are doing may be appropriate, but they should come second to the real strategy. Before testing oneself against the competition, the strategy should encompass the determination to create value for customers.

4. The Interlinked Economy

In the author's view, countries are merely government creations. In the interlinked economy (made up of the triad of the United States, Europe, and Japan), consumers are not driven to purchase things through nationalistic sentiments, no matter what politicians may say. At the cash register, people don't care about country of origin or country of residence. They don't think about employment figures or trade deficits. This also applies to industrial consumers.

5. Declaration of Interdependence

The role of central governments must change to
- allow individuals access to the best and cheapest goods and services from anywhere in the world;
- help corporations provide stable and rewarding jobs anywhere in the world, regardless of the corporation's national identity;
- coordinate activities with other governments to minimize conflicts arising from narrow interests; and
- avoid abrupt changes in economic and social fundamentals.

In addition, governments must deal collectively with traditionally parochial affairs, including taxation.

CONTEXT

The Borderless World explores the new logic of the global marketplace as well as what Ohmae calls power and strategy in the interlinked economy. This manifesto for the future is as broad ranging as it is, in political reality, unlikely.

However, the book has fueled debates about the role of governments, as well as the relationship between governments and the business world, which have yet to be resolved.

Ohmae has since gone on to further explore the role of nations and now suggests that we have reached a time when the end of the nation-state is imminent (see *The End of the Nation State* [Free Press, 1996], and *The Invisible Continent* [HarperBusiness, 2001]).

Leading business author Gary Hamel commented about *The Borderless World*:

> So the world is becoming interdependent. Hardly news to companies like Dow Chemical, IBM, Ford, or Nestlé. But in 1990 this was still news to Japanese companies (and politicians) who typically defined globalization as big open export markets, and maybe a factory in Tennessee. Kenichi challenged Japanese companies, and myopic executives elsewhere, to develop a more sophisticated view of what it means to be global. Just what balance will ultimately be struck between the forces of globalization and the forces of nationalism and tribalism remains to be seen.

FOR MORE INFORMATION

Ohmae, Kenichi. *The Borderless World: Power and Strategy in the Interlinked Economy.* Rev. ed. New York: Collins, 1999.

The Brand You 50
TOM PETERS

WHY READ IT?
Tom Peters's books have a habit of being provocative, and this one is no exception. Depending on one's point of view, one can either be motivated or irritated by Tom Peters. This book looks at the changing career opportunities in the new economy and challenges individuals to promote themselves like brands. For someone looking for a career change, this book could give him or her a boost.

> It's this simple: You are a brand. You are in charge of your brand. There is no single path to success. And there is no one right way to create the brand called You. Except this: Start today. Or else.

GETTING STARTED
Changes at the corporate, national, and global levels have an impact on the nature of work for individuals. Knowledge workers are now an important part of the economy, and new work patterns such as hot-desking and telecommuting are emerging.

The individual has become the fundamental unit in the new economy, and people should consider themselves as brands that must stand out. There is no single path to success and no one right way to create a brand.

CONTRIBUTION
1. Changing Work Roles
Changes at all levels affect the nature of work for us as individuals. Knowledge workers are making a living out of "thin air," and the biggest challenge for companies is "the war for talent."

Commentators offer advice on why it pays to quit: how workers should be hot-desking with colleagues, telecommuting from home, and generally reconsidering their entire futures.

2. The Individual as a Brand
Individuals are brands. They can't move up if they don't stand out. People are in charge of their own brands. There is no single path to success, and there is no one right way to create the brand called You. It is essential for individuals to transform themselves from employees into brands that shout distinction, commitment, and passion.

CONTEXT
The book focuses on how changes at corporate, national, and global levels impact the nature of work for us as individuals. The theme appears in a number of other books: knowledge workers making a living out of Charles Leadbetter's "thin air"; McKinsey warning its clients that the biggest challenge for companies is "the war for talent"; Charles Handy's "portfolio workers"; Harriet Rubin's "soloists"; business magazines like *Fast Company* being devoted to Me Inc. or me.com and full of advice on "why it pays to quit."

In *Future Perfect*, Stan Davis argues, "Most people on the political left—particularly in Europe—share Peters' fundamental analysis while drawing the opposite conclusions. They believe that the very forces that Peters celebrates—technology, globalization, the shift toward services—are breaking down the old social contract, leaving workers at the mercy of a new and ruthless variety of capitalism."

FOR MORE INFORMATION
Peters, Tom. *The Brand You 50*. New York: Knopf, 1999.

Built to Last
JAMES COLLINS AND JERRY PORRAS

WHY READ IT?

According to the authors, companies that enjoy enduring success have core values and a core purpose that remain fixed, while their business strategies and practices endlessly adapt to a changing world. The book shows the importance of developing and sticking to a set of guiding principles and identifies the qualities essential to building a great and enduring organization.

GETTING STARTED

Values are important in the context of business and corporations, and many companies have long recognized the importance of possessing a set of guiding principles. In the authors' view, enduring organizations with strong guiding principles have outperformed the general stock market by a factor of 12 since 1925.

Core values drive the way the company operates at a level that transcends strategic objectives. Such values don't change, although strategies and practices adapt endlessly to change.

Core ideology complements the envisioned future—what the company aspires to become. Any effective vision must embody the core ideology of the organization.

CONTRIBUTION
1. The Importance of Corporate Values

Honesty, integrity, wealth, and fairness are all values that we may be able to relate to on an individual basis. But what about values in the context of business and corporations?

While the term *corporate values* is a relative newcomer to the business lexicon, the concept of values as an important aspect of corporate life is not. Many companies have long recognized the importance of possessing a set of guiding principles, and the evolution of the concept can be traced through some of the most influential business books over the last 50 years.

Thomas Watson Jr., CEO of IBM, observed that any great organization that has lasted over the years owes its resiliency to the power of its beliefs and the appeal these beliefs have for its people.

2. The Qualities of an Enduring Organization

The book sets out to identify the qualities essential to building a great and enduring organization—the successful habits of truly visionary companies. The 18 companies chosen as subjects had outperformed the general stock market by a factor of 12 since 1925.

Core values are the organization's essential and enduring tenets. These are a small set of guiding principles (not to be confused with specific cultural or operating practices), which are never to be compromised for financial gain or short-term expediency.

Values are timeless guiding principles that drive the way the company operates at a level that transcends strategic objectives. For Hewlett-Packard, for example, values include a strong sense of responsibility to the community. For Disney, they include creativity, dreams, imagination, and the promulgation of wholesome American values.

3. Core Values Don't Change

Companies that enjoy enduring success have core values and a core purpose that remain fixed while their business strategies and practices endlessly adapt to a changing world. This constancy is a key factor in the success of companies such as Hewlett-Packard, Johnson & Johnson, Procter & Gamble, and Sony.

> Companies that enjoy enduring success have core values and a core purpose that remain fixed while their business strategies and practices endlessly adapt to a changing world.

4. A Model for Core Values

The authors recommend a conceptual framework to cut through some of the confusion surrounding the issues. In their model, vision has two components: core ideology and envisioned future. *Core ideology*, the Yin in their plan, defines what the company stands for and why it exists. Yin is unchanging and complements Yang, the envisioned future.

The *envisioned future* is what the company aspires to become, to achieve, to create—something that will require considerable change and progress to attain. Core ideology provides the glue that holds an organization together over time.

5. An Effective Vision

Any effective vision must embody the core ideology of the organization. This has two components: core values (a system of guiding principles and tenets) and core purpose (the organization's most fundamental reason for existence).

CONTEXT

In *A Business and Its Beliefs*, published in 1963, Thomas Watson Jr. observed, "Consider any great organization—one that has lasted over the years—I think you will find it owes its resiliency not to its form of organization or administrative skills, but to the power of what we call beliefs and the appeal these beliefs have for its people."

In the early 1980s, Tom Peters and Robert Waterman thought corporate values important enough to warrant an entire chapter in *In Search of Excellence*.

FOR MORE INFORMATION

Collins, James, and Jerry Porras. *Built to Last*. Rev. ed. New York: HarperBusiness, 2004.

A Business and Its Beliefs
THOMAS WATSON JR.

WHY READ IT?
A Business and Its Beliefs: The Ideas That Helped Build IBM was written by the son of the founder of IBM's commercial greatness, who himself led the company into the computer age. It describes the origins of one of the world's most successful corporations and shows how its achievements were built on a strong corporate culture and a passionate commitment to customer service.

GETTING STARTED
Thomas Watson Jr. went to work for IBM in 1946 as a salesman. He was appointed chief executive in 1956 and retired in 1970, after presiding over IBM's rise to preeminence at the beginning of the computer age.

IBM's origins lay in the Computing-Tabulating-Recording Company, which Thomas Watson Sr. joined in 1914. The company initially made everything from butcher's scales to meat slicers, gradually concentrating on mechanical tabulating machines. It became International Business Machines in 1924.

IBM's development was helped by the 1937 Wages-Hours Act, which required U.S. companies to record hours worked and wages paid. The existing machines couldn't cope, so Watson Sr. developed a solution, the Mark 1, followed by the Selective Sequence Electronic Calculator in 1947. By then IBM's annual revenues were $119 million, and it was set to make the great leap forward to become the world's largest computer company.

As far as management thinking is concerned, what IBM stood for is more important than what it did. Thomas Watson Jr. took on a hugely successful company with a strong corporate culture built around salesmanship and service. Thomas Watson Sr. had obsessively emphasized people and service. IBM was a service star in an era of machines that performed badly. Therein lies the message of this book.

> The secret I learned early on from my father was to run scared and never think I had made it.

CONTRIBUTION
1. Core Values Are Critical
Success, in Watson's view, comes through a sound set of beliefs, on which the corporation premises all its policies and actions. Beliefs must always come before policies, practices, and goals. The latter must always be altered if they are seen to violate fundamental beliefs.

Not only should the beliefs be sound, they should be stuck to through thick and thin. The most important single factor in corporate success is faithful adherence to those beliefs. Beliefs never change. Change everything else, but never the basic truths on which the company is based.

However, Watson argued for flexibility in all other areas. He asserted that if an organization is to meet the challenges of a changing world, it must be prepared to change everything about itself except its beliefs as it moves through corporate life. The only sacred cow in an organization should be its basic philosophy of doing business.

2. Develop a Corporate Culture

The beliefs that mold great organizations frequently grow out of the character, the experience, and the convictions of a single person. In IBM's case that person was Thomas Watson Sr.

The Watsons created a corporate culture that lasted. IBM, Big Blue, became the archetypal modern corporation and its managers the ultimate stereotype, with their regulation somber suits, plain ties, zeal for selling, and company song.

3. A Passion for Competing

Behind the corporate culture lay a belief in competing vigorously and providing quality service. Later, competitors complained that IBM's sheer size won it orders. This was only partly true. Its size masked a deeper commitment to managing customer accounts, providing service, building relationships, and adhering to the original values laid out by the Watsons.

4. People Matter

The real difference between success and failure in a corporation can very often be traced to the question of how well the organization brings out the great energies and talents of its people. Giving full consideration to the individual employee was one of the enduring beliefs on which IBM's success was built.

CONTEXT

In this book, the author codifies and clarifies what IBM stands for. The book is a statement of business philosophy, an extended mission statement for IBM.

Though it was published in the same year as Alfred P. Sloan Jr.'s *My Years with General Motors*, it could not be more different. Where Sloan sidelines people, Watson celebrates their potential; where Sloan espouses systems and structures, Watson talks of values.

Business guru Gary Hamel commented on this book, "Never change your basic beliefs, Watson argued. He may be right. But the dividing line between beliefs and dogmas is a fine one. A deep set of beliefs can be the essential pivot around which the company changes and adapts; or, if endlessly-elaborated, overly-codified, and solemnly worshipped, the manacles that shackle a company to the past."

FOR MORE INFORMATION

Watson, Thomas, Jr. *A Business and Its Beliefs: The Ideas That Helped Build IBM*. Rev. ed. New York: McGraw-Hill, 2003.

Capital
KARL MARX

WHY READ IT?

In the capitalist world, human labor itself becomes a commodity. *Capital*, the major work by the social philosopher Karl Marx (1818–1883), is a thoroughgoing critique of capitalism. Marx recognized the dynamics of the economic process, foresaw economic cycles, and developed a closed theory of economic activity. He was also the first economist to bring economics and history into relation with each other, and *Capital* was the book in which he did it.

GETTING STARTED

Marx describes the capitalist method of production in its overall context. He follows Ricardo in positing that only labor can produce value, then develops a theory of added value as the difference between the use value and the exchange value of labor as a commodity. Workers do only a portion of their work for themselves; a large portion goes to create added value, which falls entirely to the capitalist. Capitalists, Marx suggests, attempt to increase added value either by making their workers work longer or by reducing the amount of work time necessary for their workers' subsistence. Workers, therefore, have to earn their livelihoods in a shorter time, so that they can produce more added value. This leads to the exploitation of the working class.

CONTRIBUTION
1. Volume One: The Production Process of Capital

Volume one deals with the development of the laws of added value production. This is the part of *Capital* that has always played the largest role in often heated public discussion of the book.

Capitalist production, for Marx, is the production of goods, that is, production for the market. It is not conducted by small independent producers such as craftspeople, but by nonworking entrepreneurs, who control the means of production and therefore have the ability to make others work for them and to exploit them.

Every commodity, Marx argues, has two characteristics: usefulness (equivalent to its use value) and the property of being produced by human labor. Use value varies, depending on persons, time, and circumstances, so it cannot be the basis of price. Labor must therefore be the criterion of value.

With the development of the exchange of goods, Marx continues, trade emerges as an independent function. In trade, profit, not consumption, is the purpose of the act of exchange.

The following paradox, according to Marx, then emerges. The law of value regulating the exchange of goods knows only the exchange of equal values. But in exchange transactions in trade, an inequality must come into play. This can only stem from production. For this to be possible, the capitalist must discover a commodity whose use value is that it creates more value than it actually possesses. That commodity is labor.

2. Volume Two: The Circulation Process of Capital

In the second volume, Marx deals with the circulation of capital as it passes through various stages. Capital must, he says, continually take on and then divest itself of three separate forms to be able to function and be of use: money capital, productive capital, and commodity capital. Money capital constantly transforms itself into the elements of the production process—labor and the means of production—and the result of its functioning appears in the form of commodities, endowed with added value, which are once again transformed into money. Acts involving the circulation of commodities take place continually; sales and purchases are always being transacted; and goods and money are constantly brought into conjunction. But, says Marx, it is the fact that these acts are transition stages in the circulatory process of capital that makes them functions of capital; it is precisely that which transforms a sum of money into money capital, which makes commodities either productive capital or commodity capital. It is not their material nature that gives them this character, but rather the economic and historical conditions under which the process takes place. Commodities are not by nature capital, any more than workers are.

Capital is dead labor.

3. Volume Three: The Overall Process of Capitalist Production

In this volume, Marx brings volumes one and two into unity. The theoretical category of value, he asserts, is of interest to the capitalist. What the capitalist looks at is the capital advance that must be made to bring about production of a particular commodity. The advance is made up of constant and variable capital and represents, for the capitalist, the cost of the commodity. Capitalists do not calculate added value achieved in relation to the capital used; they simply calculate the surplus achieved against aggregate costs when the goods are sold: the profit.

Added value, says Marx, interests capitalists as little as does value per se. They expect a gain not on the variable capital they advance, but on aggregate capital. The added value on aggregate capital is profit; the numerical relationship of the one to the other is the profit rate.

CONTEXT

Marx came to economics after his political party failed to achieve power in the revolution of 1848–1849. *Capital*, published in 1867, became the cornerstone of Marxism, the political doctrine and system named after him. It is, of course, more than pure economic theory. It is a mighty intellectual construct made up of historical, sociological, and economic ideas and propaganda. It was to provide the groundwork for socialism and give a theoretical basis to Marx's other major work, the *Communist Manifesto*. Marx's guiding light was the classless society, communism. As a result, while some honor him as the prophet and advocate of the working class, others refuse to take him seriously as an economist. He has also been criticized for the fact that although he was concerned in theory with the working class, he avoided actual contact with the object of his investigations and never once saw a factory from the inside.

FOR MORE INFORMATION

Marx, Karl. *Capital: A Critique of Political Economy* (trans. Fernbach). New York: Penguin USA, 1992.

The Caring Economy
GERRY MCGOVERN

WHY READ IT?

This is a practical book on the importance of people in the new economy. While it is easy to assume that technology is the most important thing, the author shows that empowerment and other people-focused strategies are vital for success. The book also includes valuable advice on the importance of branding and customization on the Internet.

GETTING STARTED

People are impacted by, and have an impact on, new technologies and issues. New attitudes, rules, and business principles are needed for success in the digital age. The fundamental principle for success in the digital age is to think network.

What drives the Internet is not technology; it's the human touch—so put people first, because they provide a unique competitive advantage.

Among these people-centered rules for success are to empower people; focus on niches; focus on value, not costs; use information quickly and gain value from the momentum it creates; keep communication simple; learn to play; protect and build one's brand and good name; and have a long-term vision.

> What drives the Internet is not technology, it's the human touch.

CONTRIBUTION
1. A Perspective on the New Economy

We all need new attitudes, rules, and business principles for success in a digital age economy and society. Community and commerce are inherently intertwined; we can't have one without the other. What drives the Internet is not technology, it's the human touch.

2. Internet Business Principles

The book includes ten points that are intended to help guide the reader's thinking and actions in the new economy. The fundamental principle for success in the digital age is to "think network."

3. The Importance of Care

Care about customers, staff, and all those connected with you. Put people first, because people are where you will find your unique competitive advantage.

4. Empower People

Empower all those connected with you. Where appropriate, create communities that allow you to organize around the consumer, rather than around a product or service offering.

5. Focus on Niches

Champion and focus on old people, women, and children. Focus on niches and communities of interest, on delivering unique products and services. In the digital age, it will pay to specialize.

6. Focus on Value, Not Costs

Focus on the value you deliver, not just the costs you save. The Internet is not cheap to develop for. It requires quality brands, quality people, and substantial ongoing investment.

7. Let Your Information Flow

Focus on the three properties of information: content, structure, and publication. Use information quickly and gain value from the momentum it creates.

8. Keep Communication Simple

Keep the communication of information as simple as possible. Cut through the hype and don't fall into the trap of being complicated in a complex age.

9. Think Digital

Study the lessons that are being learned in software development and the Internet. The best way to succeed on the Internet is to imitate how the Internet itself became a success. This means thinking network.

10. Learn to Play

Challenge the unchallengeable, think the unthinkable, and encourage the heretic. Evangelize and bring other people with you. Embrace change and flow with the age.

11. Protect and Build Your Brand and Good Name

Trust is not easy to establish on the Internet. Those who gain the consumer's trust will reap long-term rewards.

12. Have a Long-term Vision

Don't forget the information-poor consumer. Remember that we are citizens of an increasingly connected world.

CONTEXT

The Caring Economy is a book about people (businesspeople and consumer people) and how we all interact on the Internet. It explains that we all need new attitudes, rules, and business principles for success in a digital age economy and society. The book analyzes a range of issues, including the history of the Internet, the nature of cyberspace, truths and myths about the information society, globalization, and the strengths and limitations of computers. It also offers advice on making the best use of the Internet, including a section on building brands online.

FOR MORE INFORMATION

McGovern, Gerry. *The Caring Economy*. Aberdeen, WA: Silver Lake Publishing, 2001. Web site: www.thecaringeconomy.com

The Change Masters
ROSABETH MOSS KANTER

WHY READ IT?

This book is regarded as an authoritative work on the factors behind successful corporate change. Kanter's work takes a human relations perspective and was one of the earliest books to focus on the importance of empowerment.

GETTING STARTED

According to the author, "change masters" are necessary for leading productive change. Companies with a commitment to human resources are significantly ahead in long-term profitability and financial growth.

Kanter suggests that growth problems in U.S. companies are due to suffocation of the entrepreneurial spirit. Innovation is the key to growth. New skills are required to manage effectively in innovation-stimulating environments: power skills, the ability to manage employee participation, and an understanding of how change is managed. Empowerment is critical to corporate success.

CONTRIBUTION
1. The Nature of Change Masters

Change masters are those people and organizations adept at the art of anticipating the need for, and leading, productive change. Change resisters are those who remain intent on reining in innovation.

2. The Importance of Managing People

A research program asked 65 human resource directors in large organizations to name companies that were progressive and forward thinking in their systems and practices, in relation to people. Forty-seven companies emerged as leaders in the field. They were then compared to similar companies. The companies with a commitment to human resources were significantly ahead in long-term profitability and financial growth.

The message is that if a company manages its people well, it is probably managing its business well.

3. Innovation as the Key to Growth

Kanter places responsibility for company growth problems on the quiet suffocation of the entrepreneurial spirit in segmentalist companies. She identifies innovation as the key to future growth. The way to develop and sustain innovation is to adopt an integrative approach rather than a segmentalist one.

Three new sets of skills are required to manage effectively in such integrative, innovation-stimulating environments:

- the compelling ability to persuade others to invest information, support, and resources in new initiatives driven by an entrepreneur
- the ability to manage problems associated with increased use of teams and employee participation

- an understanding of how change is designed and constructed in an organization: how the microchanges introduced by individual innovators relate to macrochanges or strategic reorientation

4. The Importance of Empowerment

The extent to which individuals are given the opportunity to use power effectively influences whether a company stagnates or innovates. In an innovative company, people are at center stage.

CONTEXT

Rosabeth Moss Kanter began her career as a sociologist before her transformation into international business guru. Her work is a development of the human relations school of the late 1950s and 1960s. Through *The Change Masters* (1983) and *When Giants Learn to Dance* (1989), she was partly responsible for the increased interest in empowerment, if not its practice.

> The companies with a commitment to human resources were significantly higher in long-term profitability and financial growth.

The Economist (October 15, 1994) commented, "Kanter-the-guru still studies her subject with a sociologist's eye, treating the corporation not so much as a micro-economy, concerned with turning inputs into outputs, but as a mini-society, bent on shaping individuals to collective ends." *The Change Masters* has been called "the thinking man's *In Search of Excellence*."

Gary Hamel said about this book:

> In a turbulent and inhospitable world, corporate vitality is a fragile thing. Yesterday's industry challengers are today's laggards. Entropy is endemic. Certainly *The Change Masters* is the most carefully researched, and best argued, book on change and transformation to date. While Rosabeth may not have discovered the eternal fountain of corporate vitality, she certainly points us in its general direction.

FOR MORE INFORMATION

Kanter, Rosabeth Moss. *The Change Masters*. New York: Simon & Schuster, 1983.

The Changing Culture of a Factory

ELLIOT JAQUES

> I'm completely convinced of the necessity of encouraging everybody to accept the maximum amount of personal responsibility.

WHY READ IT?

This book is based on an extensive study of industrial democracy in practice at the Glacier Metal Company in the United Kingdom, between 1948 and 1965. The company introduced a number of highly progressive changes in working practice that were ahead of their time and set a pattern for future practice.

GETTING STARTED

The Glacier Metal Company introduced a number of highly progressive changes in working practice, resulting in a form of industrial democracy that was ahead of its time. According to the study, the emphasis was on granting people responsibility and giving them a say in addressing every problem they encountered. The project highlighted the shortcomings of conventional industrial relations practice and showed that managers should be measured by the long-term impact of their decisions.

CONTRIBUTION

1. Introducing Industrial Democracy

The Glacier Metal Company introduced a number of highly progressive changes in working practice:

- A works council was introduced. This was far removed from the usually toothless attempts at worker representation.
- No change of company policy was allowed unless all members of the works council agreed. Any single person on the council had a veto.
- "Punching in," the traditional means of recording whether someone had turned up for work, was abolished.

Contrary to what experts and observers anticipated, the company did not immediately grind to a halt.

2. Increasing Personal Responsibility

The emphasis was on granting people responsibility and on understanding the dynamics of group working. Everybody should be encouraged to accept the maximum amount of personal responsibility and should be allowed to have a say in every problem in which they could help.

3. Anticipating Organizational Developments

The project was a decade ahead of any form of organizational development. It highlighted a number of issues:

- the redundancy of conventional organization charts;
- the potential power of corporate culture (a concept then barely understood); and
- the potential benefits of running organizations in a fair and mutually beneficial way.

4. Theory of the Value of Work

"The manifest picture of bureaucratic organization is a confusing one," according to Jaques. "There appears to be no rhyme or reason for the structures that are developed, in number of levels, in titling, or even in the meaning to be attached to the manager–subordinate linkage."

A solution, labeled "the time span of discretion," contended that levels of management should be based on how long it was before the managers' decisions could be checked. Managers should be paid in accordance with that time and measured by the long-term impact of their decisions.

CONTEXT

The practices introduced at the Glacier Metal Company were almost a decade ahead of their time. However, they did not ensure the company's survival.

The study's progressive views on the importance of motivation at work have undoubtedly influenced other management writers and practitioners, such as Mary Parker Follett and Frederick Herzberg. Jaques's work was based on long-term scientific observation, in contrast to what he terms the "fantasy fads," the "waffle and fiddling around" of management consultants.

FOR MORE INFORMATION

Jaques, Elliot. *The Changing Culture of a Factory.* Rev. ed. New York: Routledge, 2003.

The Clickable Corporation
JONATHAN ROSENOER, DOUGLAS ARMSTRONG, AND J. RUSSELL GATES

> More than a hundred million people are already online.... If that isn't a mass market, what is?

WHY READ IT?

This book was written by a group of Arthur Andersen consultants and represents valuable strategic advice. It provides practical advice and guidance on making money from the Internet using case studies and a self-assessment process.

GETTING STARTED

Clickable corporations maximize their Internet advantage, focusing on eight value propositions, which they deliver through their Web sites.

CONTRIBUTION
1. Capturing the Internet Advantage

Clickable corporations pursue strategies to maximize their Internet advantage. There are eight value propositions that a company must offer through its Web site:

1. knowledge
2. choice
3. convenience
4. customization
5. savings
6. community
7. entertainment
8. trust

Knowledge Customers can retrieve information about products and services that was previously inaccessible or available only at some cost and trouble.

Choice A well-designed Web site helps customers sift through the choices available and make an optimal decision.

Convenience The Internet removes barriers of time and space. Customers can act when it suits them and deal with providers from anywhere in the world.

Customization As Amazon has shown, it yields dividends to offer customers personalized attention and the opportunity to shape the Web site's service to their specific needs.

Savings The Internet can be used to streamline processes, eliminate barriers, and provide better control of the supply chain. In this way, costs can be reduced and consequent savings passed on to customers.

Community Online communities focus on customers' interests and needs. Communities provide an opportunity to offer products and services to an audience that is already predisposed to the offering.

Entertainment The Internet's capacity for providing fun experiences and interactivity can leverage customer attraction.

Trust It is vital to dispel customer doubts by offering high levels of service and security.

2. Making Money on the Web

The media's frequent stories about the Internet's profitless companies typically overlook the fact that many currently spend more than they earn. They are building infrastructures from scratch.

Many Internet start-ups boast stock-market valuations in significant multiples of their revenues, giving them easy access to the capital they need to grow.

3. Don't Hesitate

Many companies prefer to let others in their industry break ground and cope with the headaches that Internet leaders sometimes encounter. For example, Barnes & Noble simply watched an Internet-only bookseller, Amazon.com, seize a strong first-mover advantage.

4. The True Cost of Doing Business on the Web

The Internet isn't cheap, but many companies say the benefits far outweigh the costs. Cisco Systems, for example, attributes $500 million savings in annual operating expenses to its networked business model. Cisco also reports that online sales have resulted in about a 15 percent increase in account executive and sales engineer productivity.

5. Dealing with Security Concerns

Many companies fear losing customers, who worry that Internet intruders will steal their credit card data. This problem is controllable. Major companies are conducting millions of credit card transactions, safely and smoothly, round the clock, every day of the week.

6. Web Sites and Competitors

There is a perceived fear that a site may be picked clean by competitors poaching proprietary information about customers, products, or services. This isn't the case. Some Internet companies hope their competitors do check their Web sites.

7. The Internet Is Big Enough

More than 100 million people are already online. At the current growth rate, that number will reach one billion within five years—an order of acceleration and connectivity never seen before. However, in five years the vast majority of the world's people still won't yet own computers, much less have gone online, ensuring future Internet growth for years to come.

CONTEXT

The Clickable Corporation is based on research by consultants at Arthur Andersen and draws on evidence from 25 companies, including Federal Express, Amazon, and Dell.

The book sets out to offer an accessible guide for businesspeople who are looking to make optimal and profitable use of the Web. The authors provide examples and suggest a process that a company should go through to assess its readiness for online trading.

Critics feel that the book lacks depth, and its case-study approach means that the contents are liable to date quickly.

FOR MORE INFORMATION

Rosenoer, Jonathan, Douglas Armstrong, and J. Russell Gates. *The Clickable Corporation: Successful Strategies for Capturing the Internet Advantage.* New York: Free Press, 1999. Web site: www.arthurandersen.com/clickable

Clicks and Mortar
DAVID S. POTTRUCK AND TERRY PEARCE

WHY READ IT?
The title of this book is misleading. It's not about traditional companies adapting to the Internet; it's about the importance of people in any organization, traditional or online. The authors argue that it is important to build the right culture, and that takes passionate leadership. The book is a useful reminder that people are just as important as technology in the new economy.

GETTING STARTED
Internet businesses can access similar technology, and business models can be easily copied. According to the authors, the only sustainable advantage is people with passion. Passionate companies support individual contribution, teamwork, and risk taking. They generally have passionate leaders with a genuine desire to succeed.

The new economy rewards constant innovation, which is derived from the minds of people. Innovation requires people's passion to contribute, but diminishing loyalty makes it difficult to maintain passion.

A passionate corporate culture is key, and good management practices can generate success for the passion-driven company. Technology makes an important contribution, but building and reinforcing culture takes time, which to some seems wasteful when business puts a premium on speed.

CONTRIBUTION
1. Sustainable Advantage through People
Internet businesses all have access to similar technology. Models for online businesses can be copied easily, often within a matter of days. It is difficult to achieve a sustainable advantage over competitors. The answer is people—not just ordinary people, but those with passion.

2. The Passionate Organization
Passionate companies have cultures that are intentionally created and sustained. They support individual contribution, teamwork, and risk taking. Their business practices are anchored in the principles that helped the company become successful in the first place.

Passionate companies are more likely to have on board passionate leaders, who are themselves driven by a strong set of values. The leaders also have a genuine desire for their organization and the people who work there to succeed.

3. People Drive Constant Change and Improvement
Technological doors have opened wide to a new global, electronic economy. The new economy is built on a central premise of continuous change. It rewards constant improvement and innovation, and these are derived from the minds and imaginations of people.

4. Building Passion
The end of long-term employment and the growing need for innovation and imagination involve a culture clash. Innovation requires people's passion; this passion is fed by a certain loyalty to a compelling cause or purpose that will be advanced by ideas. When loyalty to a

company is seen as a thing of the past, it can be difficult to maintain that passion.

5. Culture at the Core

Corporate culture is the key driver of growth. A passionate culture is created on purpose, drawing on the vision and values of the company. Cultural sustainers such as story, image, and ritual can improve and sustain a meaningful culture. Diversity can be harnessed to play a positive role.

> Investing time in alignment is like tuning an engine; it creates efficiency that will not only pay off in results, it will make the whole journey smoother and more fulfilling.

6. Leadership Practices Inspire Passion-driven Growth

A specific leadership style is required in passion-driven cultures to sustain and build on what is already there. Personal integrity and open communication are vital leadership skills. The leader must also act as a role model for others, to inspire the "breakthrough thinking" needed to thrive.

7. Good Management Practices

The right use of core business tools and skills, including measurement, marketing, and customer relations, can generate success for the passion-driven company.

8. The Contribution of Technology

Without technology, many tasks would be harder. But without the passion of caring people, these tasks wouldn't get done at all.

9. Building Culture Takes Time

Building and reinforcing culture takes a lot of time, and it can seem like a waste or a luxury in a world that sets a premium on speed. But ignoring cultural construction breeds discontent and actually slows progress. Investing time in alignment creates efficiency that will not only pay off in results, it will make the whole journey smoother and more fulfilling.

CONTEXT

The fact that the authors employed the principles and ideas in their book during their involvement in the meteoric rise of the Charles Schwab Corporation is a clear indication that their ideas have value. Their belief is that in any business endeavor, clicks or bricks, the factor that makes the difference is the centrality of the human heart.

The book is about organizational transformation, and its findings contrast with the views of Champy and Hammer, whose drive to reengineer corporations put people very low on the list of priorities.

FOR MORE INFORMATION

Pottruck, David S., and Terry Pearce. *Clicks and Mortar: Passion-driven Growth in an Internet Driven World*. San Francisco: Jossey Bass, 2000.

Competing for the Future
GARY HAMEL AND C. K. PRAHALAD

WHY READ IT?
Competing for the Future, named the best management book of 1994 by *Business Week*, is regarded as the definitive book on strategy for contemporary business. It criticizes the narrow, mechanistic view of strategy and calls for a broader approach that recognizes a company's core competencies.

GETTING STARTED
This book argues that traditional strategy is too narrow in its perspective. Far from being a simple annual exercise, strategy is multifaceted; emotional as well as analytical; and concerned with meaning, purpose, and passion. Few managers spend enough time looking to the future. They should adopt "strategizing"—a new approach for developing complex, robust strategies, focusing on core competencies.

Today the onus is on transforming not just individual organizations, but entire industries. The true challenge is to create revolutions when a company is large and dominant. Downsizing is an easy option—growth comes from creating a difference, and vitality comes from within the organization, if only executives would listen.

CONTRIBUTION
1. The Narrow Focus of Traditional Strategy
The authors assert that strategy has tied itself into a straitjacket of narrow, and narrowing, perspectives:
- A huge proportion of strategists, perhaps 95 percent, are economists and engineers with a mechanistic view of strategy.
- Strategy is multifaceted; emotional as well as analytical; and concerned with meaning, purpose, and passion.
- Strategy should be regarded as a learning process.

2. Strategy Is Not Simple
In the authors' view, executives perceive that the problem with strategy is not creating it, but implementing it. Strategy is not a ritual or a once-a-year exercise. Managers are bogged down in the nitty-gritty of the present—spending less than 3 percent of their time looking to the future.

3. Adopt Strategizing
Instead of discussing strategy or planning, companies should ask, "What are the fundamental preconditions for developing complex, variegated, robust strategies?"

4. Focus on Core Competencies
Core competencies represent the collective learning in the organization, especially how to coordinate diverse production skills and integrate multiple streams of technologies. Organizations should see themselves as a portfolio of core competencies as opposed to business units. Core competencies are geared to growing opportunity share, whereas business units are narrowly focused on market share.

5. Different Approaches to Strategy

There is a thin dividing line between order and chaos. Neither Stalinist bureaucracy nor Silicon Valley provides an optimal economic system. Silicon Valley is extraordinarily good at creating new ideas, but in other ways is extraordinarily inefficient.

> A company surrenders tomorrow's businesses when it gets better without getting different.

6. Small or Large Organizations?

Small entrepreneurial offshoots are not the route to organizational regeneration. They are too random, inefficient, and prone to becoming becalmed by corporate indifference. Smaller companies have had a revolutionary impact (IKEA, Body Shop, Swatch, and Virgin), but the true challenge is to create revolutions when a company is large and dominant. The world is moving toward more democratic models of organization, to which U.S. corporations appear more attuned. In Europe and Japan there is a more elitist sense of knowledge residing at the top: a hierarchy of experience, not of imagination.

7. Rules for Success

- A company surrenders today's businesses when it gets smaller faster than it gets better.
- A company surrenders tomorrow's businesses when it gets better without getting different.
- Downsizing is an easy option.
- Growth (the authors prefer to speak of vitality) comes from difference, though there are as many stupid ways to grow as there are to downsize.
- The pressure for growth is usually ignited by a crisis.
- Vitality comes from within, if only executives would listen.
- Companies pay millions of dollars for the opinions of McKinsey's bright 29-year-olds, but ignore their own bright 29-year-olds.

CONTEXT

The debate on the meaning and application of strategy is long running. The 1960s gave us the analytical Igor Ansoff; the 1970s, Henry Mintzberg with his cerebral crafting strategy; and the 1980s, Michael Porter's rational route to competitiveness.

Nominations for the leading strategic thinkers of the 1990s would certainly include Gary Hamel and C. K. Prahalad. *Competing for the Future* has been called the blueprint for a new generation of strategic thinking. The surge of interest in core competencies has tended to enthusiastic oversimplification. They are a very powerful weapon, but can encourage companies to get into businesses simply because they see a link between core competencies rather than ones about which they have an in-depth knowledge.

The authors' strategic prognosis falls between two extremes. At one extreme are the arch-rationalists, insisting on a constant stream of data to support any strategy. At the other is the thriving-on-chaos school, with its belief in freewheeling organizations in which strategy is a moveable feast.

FOR MORE INFORMATION

Hamel, Gary, and C. K. Prahalad. *Competing for the Future*. Boston: Harvard Business School Press, 1996.

The Competitive Advantage of Nations
MICHAEL PORTER

WHY READ IT?

Many consider *The Competitive Advantage of Nations* to be one of the most ambitious books of our times. Said to do "for international capitalism what Marx did for the class struggle," it reexamines the nation-state, suggesting that its basic role today is an economic one, and that even in a global economy, it has a key role to play by ensuring the success of the companies operating within its borders, who are the actual wealth producers for the population.

GETTING STARTED

Michael Porter, author of the modern business classic *Competitive Strategy*, has extensive experience as a consultant to national governments. *The Competitive Advantage of Nations* emerged from his work on Ronald Reagan's Commission on Industrial Competitiveness. The research for the book encompassed ten countries: the United Kingdom, Denmark, Italy, Japan, Korea, Singapore, Sweden, Switzerland, the United States, and Germany (then West Germany).

The book can be read on three levels, as

- a general inquiry into what makes national economies successful;
- a detailed study of eight of the world's main modern economies; and
- a series of prescriptions about what governments should do to improve their countries' competitiveness.

The book asks crucial questions. What makes a nation's businesses and industries competitive in global markets? What propels a whole nation's economy to advance? Why is one nation often the home for so many of an industry's world leaders?

At its heart is a radical new perspective on the role of nations. From being military powerhouses, they are now economic units whose competitiveness is the key to power.

> Productivity is the prime determinant in the long run of a nation's standard of living.

CONTRIBUTION
1. Nations, Competition, and Productivity

According to the author, "Nations don't compete. Companies compete. Nations can make it hard or easy for them to do so." When governments deliberately set out to help companies compete, however, their efforts are often counterproductive. The principal economic goal of a nation is to produce a high and rising standard of living for its citizens. The ability to do so depends not on the amorphous notion of competitiveness but on the productivity with which a nation's labor and capital resources are employed.

2. The Paradox of Globalization

Companies and industries have become globalized and more international in their scope and aspirations than ever before. This would appear to suggest that the nation has lost its role in the international success of its firms. Companies, at first glance, seem to have transcended countries.

While the globalization of competition might appear to make the nation less important, instead it seems to make it more so. With fewer impediments to trade that shelter uncompetitive domestic businesses and industries, the home nation takes on growing significance because it is the source of the skills and technology that underpin competitive advantage.

3. The National Diamond

To make sense of the dynamics behind national or regional strength in a particular industry, Porter developed the concept of the national diamond, made up of four forces.

- Factor conditions: These would once have been restricted to natural resources and plentiful labor; now they embrace data communications, university research, and the availability of scientists, engineers, or experts in a particular field.
- Demand conditions: If there is strong national demand for a product or service, it can give the industry a head start in global competition.
- Related and supporting industries: Industries that are strong in a particular country are often surrounded by successful related industries.
- Company strategy, structure, and rivalry: Domestic competition fuels growth and competitive strength.

Together, these four factors determine whether a nation has competitive advantage.

4. Clusters

"Nations succeed not in isolated industries, but in *clusters* of industries connected through vertical and horizontal relationships." Groups of interconnected companies, suppliers, and related industries arising in particular locations contribute substantially to national success. Porter shows how such clusters come into being.

CONTEXT

According to *The Economist* (October 8, 1994), this was "the book that projected Mr. Porter into the stratosphere, read by aspiring intellectuals and despairing politicians everywhere." Not everyone, however, agrees with Porter on the relationship between the nation and the globalized economy. Kenichi Ohmae believes that the nation-state is on its way out, and Gary Hamel commented that Porter's book was backward-looking and does not address the future of competitiveness.

Yet on balance, readers around the world have embraced the challenges outlined in Porter's book, and its status and impact as a classic business text cannot be overestimated.

FOR MORE INFORMATION

Porter, Michael. *The Competitive Advantage of Nations*. Rev. ed. New York: Free Press, 1998.

Competitive Strategy
MICHAEL PORTER

WHY READ IT?
Competitive Strategy is a modern classic. It claims to provide a solution to a long-standing strategic dilemma and has put strategy at the forefront of management thinking.

GETTING STARTED
In 1973 Michael Porter became one of the youngest professors ever at the Harvard Business School. He has since acted as a strategy counselor to many leading U.S. and international companies and as an adviser to foreign governments.

Competitive Strategy bases its message on significant numbers—in this case three and five, the three generic strategies (every company must adopt one or lose out to its competitors) and the five competitive forces (which determine what a company must do to remain competitive). More than 20 years after its first publication, the critical consensus seems to be that the competitive forces are truer to reality than the generic strategies.

CONTRIBUTION
1. Resolving the Strategy Dilemma
Competitive Strategy presents a rationalist's solution to a long-standing strategic dilemma. At one end of the spectrum are the pragmatists, who contend that companies have to respond to their own specific situations. Competitive advantage emerges from immediate, fast-thinking responsiveness. There is no formula for achieving sustainable competitive advantage.

At the other end are those who think that market knowledge is all-important. Any company that masters the intricacies of a particular market can reduce prices and increase market share. Porter proposes a compromise, arguing that there are three strategies for dealing with competitive forces: differentiation, overall cost leadership, and focus.

- *Differentiation* entails competing on the basis of value added to customers (quality, service, differentiation), so that customers will pay a premium to cover higher costs. It requires creative flair, research capability, and strong marketing.
- *Cost-based leadership* involves offering products or services at the lowest cost.
- *Focus* involves combining elements of the previous two strategies and intensively targeting a specific market.

2. Combining the Strategies
Companies with a clear strategy outperform those whose strategy is unclear or that attempt to achieve both differentiation and cost leadership.

Sometimes the company can successfully pursue more than one approach, though this is rare. Effectively implementing any of these generic strategies usually requires total commitment, and organizational arrangements are diluted if there is more than one primary target.

3. The Risks of Ignoring Generic Strategies

Strategy is a choice on how to compete.

If a company fails to focus on any of the three generic strategies, it is liable to encounter problems. The company stuck in the middle is almost guaranteed low profitability. It either loses the high-volume customers who demand low prices or must bid away its profits to get this business away from low-cost companies. It also loses high-margin businesses, the cream, to the companies that are focused on high-margin targets. In addition, it will also probably suffer from a blurred corporate culture and a conflicting set of organizational arrangements and motivational systems.

4. The Five Competitive Forces

In any industry, whether domestic, international, product or service oriented, the rules of competition are embodied in the following forces:

- The entry of new competitors. These necessitate some competitive response, which will inevitably use resources and reduce profits.
- The threat of substitutes. If there are viable alternatives to a product or service in the marketplace, the price the company can charge will be limited.
- The bargaining power of buyers. If customers have bargaining power, they will use it. This will reduce profit margins.
- The bargaining power of suppliers. Given power over a company, suppliers will increase their prices and adversely affect its profitability.
- The rivalry among existing competitors. Competition leads to the need to invest in marketing or R&D, or to price reductions, which will reduce profits.

The collective strength of these five competitive forces determines the ability of companies in an industry to earn rates of return on investment in excess of the cost of capital.

CONTEXT

When *Competitive Strategy* was published, it offered a rational and straightforward method for companies to extricate themselves from strategic confusion. The reassurance proved short-lived. Less than a decade later, companies were having to compete on all fronts. They had to be differentiated through improved service or speedier development and be cost leaders, cheaper than their competitors.

Porter's other contribution proved more robust. The five forces are a means whereby a company can understand its particular industry. Initially passively interpreted as statements of the facts of competitive life, they are now usually seen as the rules of the game, which may have to be challenged if an organization is to achieve any impact.

FOR MORE INFORMATION

Porter, Michael. *Competitive Strategy: Techniques for Analyzing Industries and Competitors.* Rev. ed. New York: Free Press, 1998.

Complexity

M. MITCHELL WALDROP

> Species evolve for better survival in a changing environment—and so do corporations and industries.

WHY READ IT?

The science of complexity is now recognized as important to the development of economics and business strategy. This book is regarded as one of the most influential in the field. Complexity is based on mathematical theories that show how random events can quickly organize into complicated structures. In business, the theory can be used to gain an insight into the interdependencies of an organization and the potential impact of change.

GETTING STARTED

The science of complexity shows how, in any system, there are a vast number of independent agents interacting with each other in various ways. In many cases, the author claims, individual elements are interdependent. In a simple model of a market, for example, there may be thousands of buyers and sellers.

According to the author, complexity theory also indicates that these systems are self-organizing and adaptive. In the market example, groups or sectors will emerge, and these groups will change or adapt to external conditions. Waldrop explains that the order emerging from these groupings can be contrasted with a state of chaos, in which there is no interaction or dependency.

CONTRIBUTION

1. Complexity in Economics

An economy is a web of transformations among goods and services. A producer extracts raw materials and converts them into a product. As an economy grows more complex, the author explains, the number of possible combinations expands.

New technologies can accelerate the process even more. However, economies that depend on a single industry are likely to stagnate and decline. The author also describes a process called "economic take-off," whereby an economy reaches a critical point of complexity. Trade and mergers, he explains, can stimulate the complexity of different organizations.

2. The Problem of Predictability

Waldrop introduces game theory and chess analogies to describe economics. Players in a market, he explains, will not necessarily take predictable positions. They may change their roles. He points out that this runs counter to traditional economic theories that players make decisions based on analytical reasoning.

Traditional theory suggests that stock exchange behavior should be predictable. Prices should move up and down in line with the laws of economics. On that basis, he argues, crashes and booms should not occur. The complexity theory of economics says that the stock market is a living thing. It adapts to new pricing levels.

3. The End of Equilibrium

The author argues that it is difficult to follow economic theory when things are not in equilibrium, because change is occurring all the time. This means that

- problems are not well defined,
- the environment is not well defined,
- the environment might be changing, and
- changes are totally unknown.

The implication is that an economy can never be in equilibrium. The real world, he claims, is never that well defined.

4. A New Approach to Economics

Waldrop uses the terms "evolutionary economics" and "increasing return economics" to describe a new approach based on complexity theory. He points out that traditional economic theory is based on equilibrium, the balance of supply and demand in the marketplace. New economics looks at the phenomenon of increasing returns.

5. Increasing Returns

The author cites examples of increasing returns such as Silicon Valley, Microsoft Windows, or VHS video technology. Silicon Valley attracts more technology start-ups because the early technology companies are established there. Companies build to the Microsoft Windows standard because it is so widely adopted by computer users. VHS eliminated the technically superior Betamax video format because more people were buying VHS.

This is also known as positive feedback. Waldrop shows how new technology developments emerge from an interconnected web of dependencies. A new technology spawns other new developments, and the market becomes a self-organizing entity.

CONTEXT

Complexity theory has many other applications beyond economics. However, it is beginning to be accepted as part of mainstream management thinking.

Richard Pascale is another author who applies the theory to business. In a *Sloan Management Review* article, "Surfing the Edge of Chaos," he examines the challenges posed to organizations by continuous change. Pascale uses complexity theory to explain why it is important for companies to increase the number of winning strategies they pursue.

Pascale seeks to explore the process of change by trying to understand its complexities and interrelationships. He argues that

- complex adaptive systems cannot be directly controlled,
- a complex adaptive system is at risk when it is interfered with and controlled, and
- complex adaptive systems are capable of self-organization and of generating new methods of operating.

Kevin Kelly's 1994 book, *Out of Control: The New Biology of Machines*, explores the organic nature of human-made systems. Kelly's view is that our technological future is headed toward a "neo-biological" civilization.

The concept of positive feedback and the interdependencies among technology companies is also explored in *Information Rules* by Carl Shapiro and Hal R. Varian. The authors describe the development of networks fueled by positive feedback, though they base their views on observation, rather than on complexity theory.

FOR MORE INFORMATION

Waldrop, Mitchell M. *Complexity*. New York: Simon & Schuster, 1992.

FURTHER READING

Kelly, Kevin. *Out of Control: The New Biology of Machines*. Reading, MA: Addison-Wesley, 1994.

Shapiro, Carl, and Hal R. Varian. *Information Rules: A Strategic Guide to the Network Economy*. Boston: Harvard Business School Press, 1998.

Co-opetition
BARRY J. NALEBUFF AND ADAM M. BRANDENBURGER

WHY READ IT?
The authors claim that this is the first book to adapt game theory to business strategy. Combining cooperation with competition to produce "co-opetition" is, they claim, an innovative business strategy that will give companies a winning advantage. It is a technique for making the right strategic business decisions in complicated business situations.

GETTING STARTED
The authors explain why game theory provides a valid basis for thinking about business. The theory states that nothing is static; markets are dynamic and evolutionary. Companies can create new models or take on different roles to succeed. Nothing is taken as given. According to the authors, players in the game of business can change the rules to succeed. *Co-opetition* uses game theory to show how companies that cooperate can influence each other's success. Software, for example, becomes more valuable when a complementary company produces more powerful computers. Co-opetition strengthens the interdependence between companies.

CONTRIBUTION
1. The Game of Business
Nalebuff and Brandenburger believe that co-opetition depends on complementary activities. When products stimulate demand for complementary products, companies should cooperate.

They show how the game of business includes customers, suppliers, competitors, and complementors. These organizations form part of a value net with integral dependencies. The value net expands the concept of a company's customers. By taking a multiple perspective, they argue, companies can redefine the role of a customer in a value net.

The authors explain that film companies initially saw video as a threat to their business. Now they recognize video as complementary to film distribution. Similarly, computers did not create a paperless office; they made it easier to create paper.

2. The Importance of Added Value
To succeed in a game, companies must be able to offer added value. However, say the authors, this must represent what a customer or competitor regards as valuable. If the value is not sufficient, the company can change the game by playing a different role or changing the rules. Perception therefore plays an important part in co-opetition; recognizing what other people believe is important.

Companies must recognize the boundaries of their business and be realistic about their ambitions. According to the authors, companies operating in a lower segment can easily harm their core business by attempting to move into a higher segment.

3. Changing the Rules
The authors suggest a number of ways to change the rules.

A company entering a monopoly market may create competition, but if the incumbent has strong brand values, the new entrant may not gain sales. In those circumstances the authors recommend "getting paid to play." The new entrant should gain some benefit from entering a market, rather than just acting as a makeweight competitor.

The authors suggest that a company needing sales of complementary products to boost its own sales can influence a market by negotiating favorable prices for its own customers.

As the authors point out, a dominant supplier can exercise a monopoly position; limiting development and supplies to keep customers and suppliers hungry strengthens its own position.

4. Changing the Game

Nalebuff and Brandenburger recommend an action plan for bringing about change:

- Look at your own value net.
- Identify opportunities for cooperation and competition.
- Change the players.
- Identify the implications if the players change.
- Identify added value.
- See how you can add further value.
- Identify the other players' added value.
- Determine which roles are hindering or helping you.
- Identify roles you would like to adopt.
- Work out whether you can change the rules.
- Work out how other players perceive the game.

> Business is cooperation when it comes to creating a pie and competition when it comes to dividing it up.

CONTEXT

Game theory emerged in the 1950s with the publication of the book *Theory of Games and Economic Behavior* by Neumann and Morgenstern. Their theories were applied to economics, military strategy, computer science, and evolutionary biology. Game theory has been used more widely in business since the 1990s.

Co-opetition is the first book to use game theory to demonstrate business strategy. Its publication is timely, as industry commentators from leading companies believe that the idea of complementary business is still not widely understood.

FOR MORE INFORMATION

Nalebuff, Barry J., and Adam M. Brandenburger. *Co-opetition*. New York: Doubleday, 1996.

Corporate-level Strategy
MICHAEL GOOLD, MARCUS ALEXANDER, AND ANDREW CAMPBELL

WHY READ IT?
Although large conglomerates claim to add value through synergy and economies of scale, the authors suggest this is not the case. They recommend that multibusiness organizations should aim for a tighter fit between individual company strategies and the overall corporate strategy. The book introduces the concept of heartland businesses and shows how it can help corporations improve their overall performance.

GETTING STARTED
The authors argue that most large companies are now multibusiness organizations. Research indicates that the benefits of economies of scale and synergy do not, in reality, exist.

While individual businesses within the organization often have strategies, the corporation as a whole may not. Only a tight fit between the parent organization and its businesses will add value.

CONTRIBUTION
1. The Value of Multibusiness Organizations
Multibusiness companies, by virtue of their size, should offer economies of scale and synergy among the various businesses, which can be exploited to the overall good. The authors' research suggests that in reality this is not the case.

They calculate that in over half of multibusiness companies, the whole is worth less than the sum of its parts. Instead of adding value, the corporation actually detracts from its value. Its influence, though pervasive, is often counterproductive.

This criticism is not restricted to conglomerates. The influence of the corporate parent is also felt in companies with portfolios in a single industry or in a series of apparently related areas.

2. Lack of Overall Strategy
A primary cause of this phenomenon is that while individual businesses within the organization often have strategies, the corporation as a whole may not. The proclaimed strategy is often an amalgam of the individual business strategies, given credence by general aspirations.

3. Need for a Tight Fit
According to the authors, if corporate-level strategy is to add value, there must be a tight fit between the parent organization and its businesses.

Successful corporate parents focus on a narrow range of tasks and create value in those areas, and align their own structures, processes, and central functions accordingly.

4. Success Factors for Multibusiness Organizations
From their analysis of 15 successful multibusiness corporations, the authors identify three corporate essentials:
- The role of the parent must be clear. If the parent does not know how or where it can add value, it is unlikely to do so.
- The parent must have distinctive characteristics of corporate culture and personality.

- It must be recognized that each parent will only be effective with certain sorts of business, described as its "heartland."

5. The Importance of Heartland Businesses

"Heartland businesses are well understood by the parent; they do not suffer from inappropriate influence and meddling that can damage less familiar businesses," say the authors. "The parent has an innate feel for its heartland that enables it to make difficult judgments and decisions with a high degree of success."

> The parent has an innate feel for its heartland that enables it to make difficult judgments and decisions with a high degree of success.

Heartland businesses are broad ranging and may cover different industries, markets, and technologies. Given this complexity, the ability of the parent to intervene on a limited number of issues is crucial.

6. Core Businesses

The concept of heartland businesses is distinct from core businesses. "A core business is often merely a business that the company has decided to commit itself to," say the authors. Though core businesses may be important and substantial, the parent may not be adding a great deal to them.

7. Building Parenting Advantage

The authors continue: "In contrast, the heartland definition focuses on the *fit* between a parent organization and a business: Do the parent's insights and behavior fit the opportunities and nature of this business? Does the parent have specialist skills in assisting this type of business to perform better?"

Corporate strategy should be driven by "parenting advantage" to create more value in the portfolio of businesses than would be achieved by any rival. To do so requires a fundamental change in basic perspectives on the role of the parent and the nature of the multibusiness organization.

CONTEXT

Most large companies are now multibusiness organizations. The logic behind this fact of business life is generally assumed rather than examined in depth.

The authors' research runs counter to the findings of authors such as Alfred Chandler in *Strategy and Structure* and Peter Drucker in *The Practice of Management*.

Commenting on this book, Gary Hamel said:

> Chandler and Drucker celebrated large multidivisional organizations, but as these companies grew, decentralized, and diversified, the corporate center often became little more than a layer of accounting consolidation. In the worst cases, a conglomerate was worth less than its break-up value. In writing the definitive book on corporate strategy, Goold, Alexander, and Campbell gave hope to corporate bureaucrats everywhere.

FOR MORE INFORMATION

Goold, Michael, Marcus Alexander, and Andrew Campbell. *Corporate-level Strategy*. Hoboken, NJ: Wiley, 1994.

Corporate Strategy
IGOR ANSOFF

/

WHY READ IT?

In *Corporate Strategy*, Ansoff codified and generalized his experiences as a strategist at Lockheed. The book develops a series of concepts and procedures that managers can use to develop a practical method for strategic decision making within an organization.

GETTING STARTED

Corporate Strategy integrated strategic planning concepts invented independently in leading U.S. companies. The book provided a powerful, rational model for making strategic and planning decisions. Ansoff saw strategic planning as a complex sequence, or cascade, of decisions and defined two main concepts essential to understanding its nature and to implementing it successfully. The first was "gap analysis," the "gap" being the difference between the current position of an organization and its strategic objectives. The second was "synergy," the concept that 2 + 2 = 5.

CONTRIBUTION

1. Integrating Strategic Planning Concepts

Corporate Strategy integrated strategic planning concepts that were invented independently in a number of leading U.S. companies, including Lockheed.

Ansoff saw strategic management as a powerful applied theory, offering a degree of coherence and universality lacking in more traditional, functionally dominated management theorizing.

2. New Theoretical Concepts

The book presented several new theoretical concepts, such as partial ignorance, business strategy, capability and competence profiles, and synergy. One particular concept, the product-mission matrix, became very popular because it was simple and—for the first time—codified the differences between strategic expansion and diversification.

3. A Rational Model for Planning Decisions

Corporate Strategy provided a rational model by which strategic and planning decisions could be made. The model concentrated on corporate expansion and diversification, rather than on strategic planning as a whole. The Ansoff Model of Strategic Planning was a complex sequence, or cascade, of decisions, starting with highly aggregated ones and proceeding toward the more specific.

4. The Introduction of Gap Analysis

Central to the cascade of decisions is the concept of gap analysis, which can be summarized as see where you are, identify where you wish to be, and identify the tasks that will take you there. The procedure within each step of the cascade is similar:

- A set of objectives is established.
- The difference (the gap) between the current position of the organization and the objectives is estimated.
- One or more courses of action (strategy) is proposed.

- These are tested for their gap-reducing properties.

A course is accepted if it substantially closes the gap; if it does not, new alternatives are put forward and tested.

5. The Concept of Synergy

Corporate Strategy introduced the word *synergy* to the management vocabulary. Although the term has become overused, Ansoff's explanation (2 + 2 = 5) remains memorably simple.

> Paralysis by analysis.

CONTEXT

Corporate Strategy was published at a time of widespread enthusiasm for strategic planning, and an increasing number of organizations were joining the ranks of its users. Until its publication, strategic planning was a barely understood, ad hoc concept. It was practiced, but the theory remained largely unexplored. Ansoff also examined corporate advantage long before Michael Porter's dissection of the subject in the 1980s.

While *Corporate Strategy* was a remarkable book for its time, its flaws have been widely acknowledged, most honestly by Ansoff himself. It is highly prescriptive and advocates heavy reliance on analysis.

Some companies have encountered what Ansoff called "paralysis by analysis"—the more information they possess, the more they think they need. This vicious circle dogs many organizations that embrace strategic planning with enthusiasm.

Ansoff regarded strategic planning as an incomplete invention, though he was convinced that it was an inherently useful management tool. He spent 40 years attempting to prove it and that, rather than being prescriptive and unwieldy, strategic management can be a dynamic tool able to cope with the unexpected twists of turbulent markets.

Business guru Gary Hamel described Ansoff as "truly the godfather of corporate strategy," and went on to say that, "though Ansoff's approach may now appear overly-structured and deterministic, he created the language and processes that, for the first time, allowed modern industrial companies to explicitly address the deep questions of corporate strategy: how to grow, where to coordinate, which strengths to leverage, and so on."

FOR MORE INFORMATION

Ansoff, Igor. *Corporate Strategy*. New York: McGraw-Hill, 1965.

Digital Capital
DON TAPSCOTT, DAVID TICOLL, AND ALEX LOWY

WHY READ IT?
This book provides a wide-ranging insight into the growing importance of business webs, wherein companies come together to create new electronic marketplaces. It is a valuable guide for companies considering setting up or participating in business-to-business exchanges or other electronic alliances.

GETTING STARTED
Internet-based partnerships or alliances are known as "business webs," or "b-webs." Business webs open up new ways to create wealth. They enable companies to combine with like-minded partners, with complementary skills, in Internet-based partnerships. Business webs include suppliers, distributors, commerce services providers, infrastructure providers, and customers. The authors' eight stages for creating a business web are discussed below.

CONTRIBUTION
1. The Rise of Business Webs
Net and digital media open up new ways to create wealth. Companies like Schwab, eBay, Cisco, MP3, and Linux have transformed the rules of competition in their industries by making revolutionary offerings to their customers. They achieved this by combining with like-minded partners with complementary skills.

> Think of customers as part of your b-web and prospects as candidates for relationships, not as markets for your products.

2. The Structure of B-webs
A b-web is a distinct system of suppliers, distributors, commerce services providers, infrastructure providers, and customers that use the Internet for their primary business communications and transactions. Although alliance based, a b-web typically has an identifiable lead partner that formally orchestrates the strategies and processes.

There are five distinct types of b-web:

Agoras   The agoras of ancient Greece were centers for public intercourse and commercial transactions. In the digital economy, the term refers to markets where buyers and sellers meet to negotiate and assign value to goods freely. Price discovery mechanisms include one-to-one haggling, multiparty auctions, and exchanges. An example of an agora is eBay.

Aggregations   In an aggregation b-web, one company leads, positioning itself as a value-adding intermediary between producers and customers. The lead aggregator selects products and services, targets particular market segments, sets prices, and ensures fulfillment.

Value Chains   The lead organization structures a b-web network to produce a highly integrated value proposition. The output satisfies a customer order or market opportunity, and the seller has the final say in pricing.

Alliances   Alliances aim for high-value integration without a formal hierarchy of control. They include online communities, research initiatives, and shared experiences.

Distributive Networks   Distributive networks keep the new economy alive and mobile by supporting and enabling transactions.

3. Creating a B-web
There are eight stages to creating a b-web:
1. Describe the current value proposition from the customer's viewpoint.
2. Disaggregate: Consider the contributors and their strengths and weaknesses.
3. Compare the parts and capabilities of your business to those in other systems.
4. Envision b-web-enabled value through brainstorming and other techniques.
5. Decide what the new value proposition will be.
6. Reaggregate: Define what it will take to deliver the new value proposition, including processes, contributors, contributions, applications and technologies, and other success factors.
7. Prepare a value map: Design a visual map that depicts value exchanges in the b-web.
8. Do the b-web mix: Define a b-web typing strategy that will improve your competitive advantages.

4. A New Alphabet of Marketing
The A, B, C, D, and Es of marketing have replaced the four Ps:
A. Any place, any time, any way shopping replaces place. Companies must design integrated strategies for the market space and, if appropriate, the marketplace and market face. Customers want convenience.
B. B-web customers drive revenue. Relationship capital is reflected in a brand. Think of customers as part of your b-web and prospects as candidates for relationships, not as markets for your products.
C. Communication works, not promotion. One-way media, like broadcasting, can be part of the marketing mix, but the customer decides whether—and with whom—to engage in a one-, two-, or multi-way communication.
D. Discovery of price replaces fixed price. The days when companies unilaterally control prices are nearly over.
E. Experience replaces product. Customers pay for experiences, not products. Products must be bundled with enhanced, customized services.

CONTEXT
Digital Capital explores how the Net and digital media open up new ways to create wealth. It features companies like Schwab, eBay, Cisco, MP3, and Linux, which have transformed the rules of competition in their industries by making revolutionary offerings to their customers. Where this book differs from the majority is that it goes beyond mere description, beyond eye-catching but slight lists of key points. *Digital Capital* offers genuine insight and, even more important, some guidance on practical steps that can be put in place.

FOR MORE INFORMATION
Tapscott, Don, David Ticoll, and Alex Lowy. *Digital Capital: Harnessing the Power of Business Webs.* Boston: Harvard Business School Press, 2000.

Digital Darwinism
EVAN I. SCHWARTZ

WHY READ IT?
This book is part philosophy and part practical advice. It compares survival and success in the new economy with Darwin's theory of evolution and provides strategies for survival. While the philosophy may be of marginal interest to business executives, the strategies are based on sound thinking and offer useful advice.

GETTING STARTED
The Web is seen as an ecosystem in which players compete for survival and have to adapt to survive. There are seven breakthrough strategies for surviving in the Web economy:
- Build a solution brand.
- Allow prices to fluctuate freely with supply and demand.
- Let affiliate partners do the marketing and take advantage of viral marketing.
- Create valuable bundles of specific information and services.
- Sell custom-made products online, then manufacture them.
- Add new value to transactions between buyers and sellers.
- Integrate digital commerce with everything.

CONTRIBUTION
1. The Concept of Digital Darwinism
This is a different way of looking at the Web economy and how it is co-evolving with the larger business world around it. There are parallels with Darwin's theory of evolution: The Web is an ecosystem in which players are scrounging for money, and they are competing as if they were species in a natural environment.

2. Applying Darwinism to the Digital Economy
Brutal market forces lead to new strategies for economic survival. The Web has given birth to entirely new species of start-ups and enterprises that could not have existed previously. The new economic organisms are in turn forcing older corporate species to evolve in new ways.

3. Surviving in the Digital Economy
In the natural world, it can take thousands of years for major or even slight changes to become apparent. In the digital world, companies can change their appearance and switch their survival plans in a matter of weeks. However, successful evolution requires a more significant time frame to produce results, effects, and lessons learned the hard way.

> The Web is in the throes of an especially frenetic evolution. As an environment that can sustain economic life, the Web has given birth to entirely new species of start-ups and enterprises that could not have existed previously.

4. Build a Solution Brand
A solution brand stands for solving problems. Selling products cheaply over the Web doesn't guarantee survival, so companies need to identify specific issues faced by customers and put in place interactive services that address those problems. This creates a "solution brand," a unique, comprehensive solution that is resilient against aggressive competition.

5. Allow Prices to Fluctuate Freely with Supply and Demand

Online auction houses like eBay are bringing dynamic pricing to the masses. Shopbots are roaming the Net, seeking out the best deal on any given item and feeding that information to customers.

6. Let Affiliate Partners Do the Marketing

Companies should recruit affiliate partners to sell their products and spread their marketing messages. As competing affiliate networks increase, companies will have to boost commissions to the most successful partners.

7. Create Valuable Bundles of Information and Services

Subscribers who pay for information services have a financial incentive to return to a site regularly. Companies should concentrate on a specific information niche. The more general a service, the more likely that it will be available somewhere else at no cost.

8. Sell Custom-made Products Online, Then Manufacture Them

The economics of sell and build are inherently superior to build and sell. The Dell Computer model demonstrates this.

9. Add New Value to Transactions between Buyers and Sellers

Intermediaries are under some threat from the Web, but they can add value. One way is to develop a neutral meeting space where buyers and sellers can find each other and place and receive orders efficiently.

10. Integrate Digital Commerce with Everything

Setting up effective feedback loops among various business channels allows companies to share best practice and enables cross-promotional initiatives.

11. Survival of the Fittest

Marketing and technology, which can account for at least 50 percent of the cost of goods at dot-coms, eat into cash reserves, and many Web companies do not yet earn enough revenue to cover these costs. Profit soon, rather than profit eventually, has become the key to survival.

CONTEXT

In *Digital Darwinism*, the author notes some interesting parallels between Darwin's theory of evolution and the online world. On a practical level, he includes seven strategies for survival that outline what any business should be doing to achieve Web success. These provide a set of tools to help create, expand, or enhance an online business, with relevant case studies to support the argument.

PWC's May 2000 report suggested that survival of the fittest was a valid theory. The report came in the same month as the high-profile collapse of boo.com and triggered a real crisis of confidence in dot-com businesses.

FOR MORE INFORMATION

Schwartz, Evan I. *Digital Darwinism: Seven Breakthrough Business Strategies for Surviving in the Cut-throat Web Economy.* New York: Broadway Books, 1999. Web site: www.digitaldarwinism.com

Direct from Dell
MICHAEL DELL

WHY READ IT?
Books like this can be dismissed as a "corporate puff," but they can also provide inspiration and insight for someone who is trying to build a business. The book provides extensive coverage of the principles that made Dell Computer successful, and the principles of selling direct and exploiting the Internet can be adapted by other businesses.

GETTING STARTED
Dell Computer Corporation redefined the industry with its direct-sale approach. Michael Dell provides a series of guidelines for building a successful business.

CONTRIBUTION
1. Redefining the Industry
Dell Computer Corporation—formed in 1985 with $1,000—has become one of the most successful computer businesses in the world. It has redefined the industry with its direct-sale approach and the customer support model it pioneered.

2. Sell Direct
Dell eliminates the middleman by custom-building IBM clones and selling them directly to consumers. This reduces overhead costs and eliminates dealer mark-ups.

3. Value and Manage Inventory
This is a direct consequence of Dell's sell and build approach to manufacturing PCs.

4. Don't Grow for Growth's Sake
In the early 1990s, Dell Computer experienced several expansion problems, including failure of a line of low-quality laptops. Growth is good, but it has to be controlled growth.

5. Make Gradual Improvements to Each Product Line
This reduces risk and allows the company to take advantage of rapid technological developments.

6. Practice Market Innovation
Dell was the first firm to market PCs by phone, but now actively encourages business via the Web. Be alert to opportunities outside traditional distribution channels.

7. Think and Act Globally
Michael Dell took his firm abroad almost a decade before most other technology companies did.

8. Don't Focus on Computers; Focus on Customers and Their Needs
Dell believes in going to where customers do business to understand their needs. Think about the customer, not the competition. Competitors represent your industry's past; customers are your future, representing new opportunities, ideas, and avenues for growth.

9. Ally with Employees

Hire those who can generate ideas, train people to be creative, and create an environment that allows ideas to be tested. Work to maintain a healthy sense of urgency and crisis, but don't fabricate deadlines or keep people so stressed that they quickly burn out.

10. Ally with Suppliers

Highest quality comes from outsourcing. Leave the manufacture of components to suppliers with the most expertise, experience, and quality in producing that part.

11. Turn your Competition's Greatest Strength into a Weakness

Every great athlete has an Achilles' heel; so, too, do all great companies. Study the competition's "game" and exploit its weakness by exposing its greatest strength.

12. Be Opportunistic, but Also Be Fast

Look to find opportunity, especially when it isn't readily apparent. Focusing on the customer doesn't mean that you should ignore the competition. If something that your competition did or didn't do provided you with an opportunity today, would you recognize it and be able to act on it immediately?

> Business is like baseball. Go for the highest batting average rather than trying to hit a home run every time.

13. Stay the Course

If the formula works, don't mess with it. Dell has been called a "methodical optimizer," a company that comes up with a good idea, recognizes it as such, then tirelessly pursues it.

14. Be the Best as Often as You Can

There's no such thing as a grand slam product or technology that lasts forever. Your competitive edge must come from strategic execution and from gaining knowledge. Study the economics of your business and ensure the flow of information throughout your organization.

15. Stay Focused

Success is a dangerous thing, as it makes us at once invincible and vulnerable. Keep your team focused on growing the business and on winning and acquiring new business.

CONTEXT

Dell Computer has become one of the most successful computer businesses in the world, redefining the industry with its direct-sale approach and the customer support model it pioneered. The book is a useful reiteration of Dell's business philosophy.

The main elements—eliminate middlemen, build machines to order rather than hold a stockpile, and focus on making cheap but high-quality PCs—remain sound principles for any direct-sale organization setting up in the new economy.

Michael Dell has undoubtedly played his part in building the global PC market. However, *Direct from Dell* can be seen as an exercise in corporate spin. A question remains whether the book will be as significant to the future of the new economy.

FOR MORE INFORMATION

Dell, Michael. *Direct from Dell: Strategies That Revolutionized an Industry*. New York: HarperBusiness, 1999.

The Discipline of Market Leaders
MICHAEL TREACY AND FRED WIERSEMA

WHY READ IT?

The authors suggest that no company can become a market leader until it learns certain key disciplines. They provide a broad variety of examples of winning companies that used these disciplines to reinvent the rules of competition in their chosen markets. This book, they claim, will make it impossible for companies to compete on the old terms.

GETTING STARTED

The authors have identified three value disciplines that they believe are essential to success: operational excellence, product leadership, and customer intimacy. By focusing on the most suitable discipline for its marketplace, a company can achieve leadership in its chosen field. That discipline, say the authors, should shape all the company's other plans and activities.

CONTRIBUTION
1. Improving Value

According to the authors, market leaders don't excel at everything. They have achieved a level of excellence in one value discipline that puts them ahead of competitors.

Treacy and Wiersema believe that there are now new rules of competition. Successful companies must change customer expectations. They explain that customers buy different types of value, such as product quality, expert advice, or personalized service.

> In today's economic environment, you've got to reinvent the rules of competition.

The authors advise companies to continue improving value year after year to meet rising customer expectations. However, producing ever-increasing value requires a superior operating model that can deliver results.

Winners, they suggest, concentrate on the competencies that are core to their value proposition. This determines their operating model.

2. Product Leadership

Product leaders, say the authors, focus on investment, product development, and market exploitation. They tend to have a loose-knit organizational structure that encourages enterprise.

They believe that companies who compete on premium product performance need to have a good basis of design and quality management. Such companies also educate and prepare the market for new products, reducing risk and uncertainty for customers.

The authors demonstrate how product leadership companies are driven by vision and concept. Such companies cultivate talent who can turn ideas into marketable products. Talent is their most important asset, so they spend a great deal of time recruiting and retaining the right people. They create a culture for innovation by giving their people personal challenges.

Despite product leadership, they argue, companies have to adjust prices to market conditions. Brand leadership no longer provides price protection. If price is a chosen weapon, it requires an integrated system to sustain the advantage.

3. Service-driven Organizations

Treacy and Wiersema show how service-driven organizations recognize and reward employees, get the supply position right, and deliver first-class service. Time, they believe, is critical to a market leader. Customers are no longer prepared to wait for slow service. They expect support as well as an excellent product, and that, the authors argue, makes service an integral part of any market-leading offer.

4. Leadership through Customer Intimacy

The authors explain that companies that lead through customer intimacy build strong relationships and aim to achieve high levels of customer lifetime value. Their employees are empowered to deliver great levels of personal service to customers throughout the relationship.

These companies, they argue, focus on a hierarchy of customer needs. They go beyond the product and basic service to discover underlying problems and contribute to customer success. They leverage their understanding of customer problems and offer a variety of support services.

Frequently, they manage customers' problems for them and mold their own organizations to those of their customers. The authors believe that customer intimacy requires the focus of all employees so that deep relationships can be formed throughout an organization.

5. Building on Operational Strengths

According to Treacy and Wiersema, companies that build on their operational strengths demonstrate a number of important characteristics. They offer standard products, services, and operating procedures. They have developed tried and tested formulas for success, and they simplify transactions. They also make extensive use of information technology to improve their efficiency.

CONTEXT

The book is one of many that look at successful companies and try to identify a formula for success. Many of the companies given as examples are similar to those found in other "success books."

Tom Peters and Robert Waterman first brought the technique to prominence with the publication of *In Search of Excellence*. Unfortunately, many of their excellent companies failed in subsequent years, but that did not prevent other authors from following similar investigations.

Treacy and Wiersema focus on three strands—operational excellence, product leadership, and customer intimacy. The themes of product leadership and customer intimacy are well covered by other authors.

Operational excellence is less of a recurring theme. However, the authors acknowledge a debt to Hammer and Champy's *Reengineering the Corporation* for examples of operational excellence at work.

FOR MORE INFORMATION

Treacy, Michael, and Fred Wiersema. *The Discipline of Market Leaders: Choose Your Customers, Narrow Your Focus, Dominate Your Market.* Cambridge, MA: Perseus, 1997.

Dynamic Administration
MARY PARKER FOLLETT

WHY READ IT?
The book provides one of the earliest perspectives on business from the point of view of human relationships. It was written at a time when workers were seen simply as part of the mass-production process. It provides useful background on the development of concepts such as empowerment and visionary leadership.

GETTING STARTED
In the author's view, management is a social process and should have a special human dimension. The process is based in human emotions and in the interrelations created by working. The working environment has human problems, with psychological, ethical, and economic dimensions.

She went on to say that workers should be given greater responsibility, which is the great developer of people. Successful leaders must offer a vision of the future and train followers to become leaders.

Relationships, not just transactions, are important in organizations. Knowing this involves recognizing that conflict is a fact of life that we should use to work for us—but integration is the only positive way forward.

CONTRIBUTION
1. Management as a Social Process
"We can never wholly separate the human from the mechanical sides," said Follett. The study of human relations in business and of the technology of operating are bound up together. The everyday incidents and problems of management reflect the presence or absence of sound principles.

Management has a special human character. Its nature as a social process is deeply embedded in the emotions of human beings and in the interrelations to which the everyday working of industry necessarily gives rise—both at the managerial and worker levels and, of course, between the two.

2. Toward Empowerment
Mary Parker Follett believed that, "we should undepartmentalize our thinking in regard to every problem that comes to us." She continued, "I do not think that we have psychological and ethical and economic problems. We have human problems, with psychological, ethical, and economical aspects, and as many others as you like."

Follett advocated giving greater responsibility to people at a time when the mechanical might of mass production was at its height. "Responsibility is the great developer of men," she said.

3. Leadership through Vision
The most successful leader of all is one who sees another picture not yet actualized—who sees the whole rather than the particular, organizes the experiences of the group, offers a vision of the future, and trains followers to become leaders.

Leading should be a two-way, mutually beneficial process. "We want worked out a relation between leaders and led which will give to each the opportunity to make creative contributions to the situation," Follett wrote.

4. Relationships Matter

Relationships, not just transactions, are important in organizations. The reciprocal nature of relationships means that a mutual influence is developed when people work together, however formal authority is defined.

Conflict is a fact of life that we should use to work for us. There are three ways of dealing with confrontation: domination, compromise, or integration. Integration is the only positive way forward. This can be achieved by first uncovering the real conflict and then taking the demands of both sides and breaking them up into their constituent parts.

Outlook is narrowed, activity is restricted, and chances of business success are largely diminished when thinking is constrained within the limits of what has been called an either–or situation. "We should never allow ourselves to be bullied by an either–or," said Follett. There is often the possibility of something better than either of two given alternatives.

CONTEXT

Published eight years after her death, *Dynamic Administration* is a collection of Mary Parker Follett's papers on management gathered from 12 lectures given between 1925 and 1933. Her work stands as a humane counterpoint to that of Frederick Taylor and the proponents of scientific management. Follett was a female, liberal humanist in an era dominated by reactionary males intent on mechanizing the world of business.

Bearing in mind that she was speaking of the United States in the early 1920s, her thinking can be described as little less than revolutionary, and certainly a generation ahead of its time. Mary Parker Follett's thinking on management was generally ignored during her lifetime, although in Japan there was a great deal of interest in her perspectives.

> We should remember that we can never wholly separate the human from the mechanical sides.

Leading commentator Gary Hamel said of her, "The work of Mary Parker Follett is refreshingly different from that of her peers. She was the first modern thinker to get us close to the human soul of management. She had the heart of a humanist, not an engineer."

To some, Follett remains a utopian idealist, out of touch with reality; to others, she was a torchbearer of good sense whose ideas have sadly not had significant impact on organizations.

Henry Mintzberg commented, "Integration requires understanding, in-depth understanding. It requires serious commitment and dedication. It takes effort, and it depends on creativity. There is precious little of all of these qualities in too many of our organizations today."

FOR MORE INFORMATION

Follett, Mary Parker. *Dynamic Administration*. Rev. ed. New York: Buccaneer Books, 1982.

Emotional Intelligence
DANIEL GOLEMAN

WHY READ IT?
Goleman describes the evolution of the brain and explains how the two main brain functions that influence behavior—emotion and intelligence—are situated in different parts of the brain. The part of the brain that controls emotions receives external signals before the intelligence functions, and that means that initial reactions to events may be emotional rather than rational. Goleman explains that the brain still retains a primitive "survival mode" that may trigger inappropriate reactions and responses. To succeed, he advises, we need to understand those reactions and learn how to control them.

GETTING STARTED
In this international best seller, Daniel Goleman challenges the traditional view that a high IQ is essential for success. He provides examples of people with high IQs and considerable academic achievement who have failed in business and in life; conversely, he also shows how those who are apparently less intellectually gifted were able to manage and harness their emotional intelligence to succeed. Although the book does not specifically relate to behavior in a business setting, its conclusions highlight patterns that can be used to improve personal performance at work. Emotional intelligence is also one of the "soft skills" that are increasingly regarded as important in commercial life, particularly for people in sales, supervisory, or customer service roles.

CONTRIBUTION
1. Overcoming Impulses
According to Goleman, emotions have a wisdom of their own that can be harnessed. Although our natural reaction is to respond emotionally, it is important to make use of emotional intelligence to develop more appropriate responses.

2. A Framework of Emotional Intelligence
Goleman has developed a framework that explains emotional intelligence in terms of five elements:
- self-awareness
- self-regulation
- motivation
- empathy
- social skills

Self-awareness   According to Goleman, this element enables us to develop a better understanding of the way emotions affect our performance. We can also use our values to guide our decision making. By looking at our strengths and weaknesses and learning from our experiences, we can gain self-confidence and certainty about our capabilities, values, and goals.

Self-regulation   Goleman describes how this element can help us control our tempers and reduce stress by acting in a more positive and action-oriented way. This enables us to retain our composure and improves our ability to think clearly under pressure. Through self-regulation, he claims, we can handle our impulses effectively and exercise self-restraint.

Motivation   According to the author, by harnessing this aspect of emotional intelligence, we can enjoy challenge and stimulation and strive for achievement. We will be committed to the cause and seize the initiative. We will also be guided by our personal preferences in following one set of goals rather than another.

> The ability to control impulse is the basis of will and character.

Empathy   Empathy is the characteristic that enables us to understand other points of view and behave openly and honestly.

Social Skills   Goleman describes how social skills such as persuasion, communication, listening, negotiating, and leading can be honed.

3. Emotional Intelligence and Management
Goleman claims that people with a higher degree of emotional intelligence are more likely to succeed in senior management. He also believes that emotional intelligence can be developed over a period of time, although this has been disputed.

CONTEXT
Daniel Goleman has built on the work in this book to research leadership styles based on various characteristics of emotional intelligence. These styles range from coercive leaders, who are self-motivated and driven to succeed; to democratic leaders, who are good at communication and listening; to coaching leaders, who listen well and motivate others. The research was reported in the March–April 2000 issue of the *Harvard Business Review*.

Commentators have pointed out a possible contradiction in Goleman's work. He claims that emotional intelligence is inherent, yet suggests that it can be developed.

Other studies of leaders have pointed out the relationship between high achievement and characteristics such as self-awareness and empathy. In *Emotional Intelligence*, Goleman does not specifically deal with the direct relationship between leadership and emotional intelligence. His subsequent research does, however, analyze the relationship further.

FOR MORE INFORMATION
Goleman, Daniel. *Emotional Intelligence: Why It Can Matter More Than IQ*. New York: Bantam, 1997.

FURTHER READING
Goleman, Daniel. "Leadership That Gets Results." *Harvard Business Review* (March–April 2000).

Goleman, Daniel. *Working with Emotional Intelligence*. New York: Bantam Doubleday Dell, 2000.

The E-myth Revisited
MICHAEL E. GERBER

WHY READ IT?

Since its publication in 1995, *The E-myth Revisited* has been an international best seller, providing insight into how to turn an entrepreneurial dream into a successful and profitable reality. By means of his lively, readable, and occasionally anecdotal style, Michael E. Gerber guides the reader through the journey of becoming an entrepreneur, from the skills that are needed initially, to what is needed to ensure that a successful business emerges in its final, "mature" stage. Gerber's insight, gained as a consultant for small businesses, has made this an entertaining, enlightening, and effective guide to creating the modern small business.

GETTING STARTED

The "E-myth" is the entrepreneur myth, the belief that simply having an in-depth knowledge of the product or service is all that is needed for a successful business. The author argues that this just isn't enough, and he outlines the other skills necessary to create a successful business. In his view, the key principles any entrepreneur should be aware of include working *on* the business, rather than *inside* it, as well as lessons that can be learned from highly successful business franchises, such as providing consistent quality and exceeding customers' expectations. In addition, Gerber offers advice on how to establish effective marketing, work well with others, and reach one's "life-goals."

CONTRIBUTION
1. The Entrepreneur Myth

The "E-myth" is the assumption that because a person is a good "technician" within a particular area of expertise, he or she will be successful in owning a business in that field. Although being a good technician with a large knowledge base of the product *is* important, Gerber argues that it is only a starting point to becoming a successful entrepreneur.

2. The Characters

Success depends on having a product or a service that catches the consumer's imagination.

A successful business starter must assume the roles of three necessary but diverse characters: the *technician*, the *manager*, and the *entrepreneur*.

The *technician* provides the labor and delivery of the product. While these are vital skills, many technicians start their businesses without knowledge of how to be a manager or entrepreneur. The important fact for technicians to note is that, to produce a successful business, managerial and entrepreneurial knowledge is vital.

The *manager* provides the design of the business and organizes it into an efficient company operating at maximum performance and productivity.

The *entrepreneur* provides the vision, the audacity, and the drive to support and build the business. The entrepreneur lives in the future and is happiest when allowed to construct images of "what if? . . ." to explore possible strategies.

3. The Transitions among the Four Stages of Business

Gerber argues that a business typically undergoes four phases: *infancy, adolescence, comfort zone*, and *maturity*. To move successfully among these stages, the strengths of all three characters described above must be utilized. It is important to relinquish some responsibility for difficult tasks to appropriately skilled individuals.

This, in Gerber's view, will allow the business to move from *infancy* to *adolescence*. Qualified, external help will support the integration of the skills of the technician, manager, and entrepreneur to create a *comfort zone*. This zone inevitably ends when boundaries are pushed and the company becomes more disordered. If it is able to survive this period of turbulence, the author argues, the company can reach the last phase, *maturity*. Maturity, however, does not represent an end to the effort needed. Constant innovation and growth are required for a business to prosper.

4. Working *on* the Business

Gerber feels that it is important to spend more time working *on* a business than *inside* it. A common mistake is to assume the role of the technician, at the expense of the roles of entrepreneur and manager.

5. Standards for Franchise Prototypes

The author argues that a standardized business will deliver consistent success. The principles of standardization (sometimes also called systemization) are
- delivering a product or service that will continually match or exceed clients' expectations;
- allowing the work to be user-friendly and broadly accessible;
- making sure the business model is free from any potential problems;
- providing a clear, standardized operations manual;
- ensuring a predictable product or service; and
- ensuring that marketing, dress code, and facilities remain consistent with each other.

6. The Business Development Program

This is arguably the most important aspect of being an entrepreneur: developing a business that can survive and grow by itself, allowing the owner to step back from the business and focus on other projects or simply enjoy the rewards of the business.

A successful business development program consists of several factors:
- the Primary Aim
- the People Strategy
- the Strategic Objectives
- the Marketing Strategy
- the Organizational Strategy
- the Systems Strategy
- the Management Strategy

CONTEXT

The E-myth Revisited was published before the dot-com bubble burst in the late 1990s. While the title alludes to the cyber connection, it is most telling that this book challenges the flawed foundation of the dot-com dream, that only in-depth product knowledge is needed for a successful business.

As a business consultant, Michael Gerber has seen the mistakes he warns against. In *The E-myth Revisited*, these potential triumphs and pitfalls are shared with the reader, providing an eminently practical guide to becoming a successful entrepreneur.

FOR MORE INFORMATION

Gerber, Michael E. *The E-myth Revisited: Why Most Small Businesses Don't Work and What to Do about It.* New York: Collins, 1995.

The Entertainment Economy
MICHAEL J. WOLF

WHY READ IT?

Like Pine and Gilmore's *The Experience Economy*, this book argues that the best way to differentiate a commodity product or service is to add value that appeals to customers. The entertainment industry provides many good examples of this in action, and companies in more mundane markets can adopt these principles to support their own product development.

GETTING STARTED

According to Wolf, entertainment content has become a key differentiator in the consumer economy. Businesses compete primarily for the time and attention of customers, so content is critical, and the quality of the experience is what makes the difference.

Convenience is critical for simpler purchases. Consumers are saving themselves the trouble of going out at all by ordering products over the Internet, so retail will split into two paths: one headed toward entertainment venues, the other toward convenience.

Buying something is a multilevel experience, and a product or service can engage an audience at a number of different levels. The challenge to businesses is to move their products and services up the hierarchy; finding the reason why a consumer buys is essential to success. The phrase "unique buying proposition" can be used to differentiate products.

CONTRIBUTION
1. Entertainment Wins Customers

Wolf argues that media and entertainment have moved beyond mere culture to become the driving force of the global retail economy. Businesses compete primarily for the time and attention of customers, so entertainment content has become a key differentiator in virtually every aspect of the broader consumer economy.

All consumer businesses need to acknowledge the multilevel relationships that entertainment businesses set out to build with their customers.

2. Convenience Is Critical for Simpler Purchases

Not all businesses will, or should, adopt an entertainment-based approach. As consumers look to satisfy more complex emotional needs, they become increasingly reluctant to waste time on lower-order ones. Retail will therefore split into two paths, one leading to entertainment venues, the other to convenience.

For companies selling simpler purchases, convenience, price, and consistent quality rather than entertainment remain the key variables. To buy a regular, no-frills item like a T-shirt, most consumers will go for a low-hassle, low-cost solution that might involve spending a few minutes in a chosen store.

3. A Multilevel Buying Experience

There's no business without show business.

Going to watch a movie is an experience that can fall into a number of different categories. At one level, it might simply while away a couple of hours on a rainy day in a warm and comfortable environment. At another level, the movie might arouse curiosity or amuse us. It can also change the way we think or feel about something.

4. Moving Products up the Buying Hierarchy

Abraham Maslow's theory of motivation stated that people's needs fall into a hierarchy. Basic needs such as food, warmth, and shelter are at the bottom; more complex emotional needs are in the middle; and "self-actualization" is at the top. As each need is satisfied, people move up to the next one. The challenge to businesses is to move their products and services up the hierarchy.

The Starbucks coffee chain is a good example. It has created an entire experience out of drinking coffee within an industry that was increasingly commoditized and price-driven.

5. The High Concept

Hollywood has embraced the notion of "high concept"—a compelling idea expressed in one simple thought. "High concept" is similar to the term USP (unique selling proposition), used in advertising.

In the entertainment economy, it is more appropriate to use the term "unique buying proposition." What is the deep-down reason that a consumer buys a product? Find the reason, and we understand what creates a hit or even a phenomenon.

CONTEXT

The Entertainment Economy shows how a product's entertainment value creates a consumer experience that differentiates it from competitors.

The book has some valid and highly relevant messages for the business world. However, its lack of charts, tables, graphs, or even bullet points means that extracting these messages requires quite a bit of work on the business reader's part.

The book uses the example of a movie to show how a product or service can engage an audience at a number of different levels. The challenge to businesses is to move their products and services up the hierarchy. This is not a totally novel concept. The behavioral psychologist Abraham Maslow predicted this when he drew up his theory of motivation and stated that people's needs fall into a hierarchy.

The book also describes the Hollywood notion of "high concept," which is similar to the unique selling proposition or USP, an advertising concept that was put forward in 1961 by Rosser Reeves when he was chairman of Ted Bates & Company. In *Reality in Advertising*, Reeves stated that for a product to find its way in the marketplace, it was necessary to create a USP. According to Reeves, "The USP almost lifts itself out of the muck and wings its way to some corner of the mind. The USP leaps out at you!"

FOR MORE INFORMATION

Wolf, Michael J. *The Entertainment Economy: The Mega-Media Forces That Are Shaping Our Lives*. New York: Random House, 1999.

E-shock 2000
MICHAEL DE KARE-SILVER

WHY READ IT?

This is a highly practical guide to setting up an electronic retailing business. It includes analysis of the way the market is developing and a self-assessment tool that enables companies to determine whether their products are suitable for electronic retailing.

GETTING STARTED

According to the author, an unstoppable momentum will drive e-commerce forward. This will have a major impact on the shopping and retailing scene.

Direct-sell manufacturers bypass existing retail chains. Physical retail margins are very thin, and retailers are vulnerable to small shifts in all sectors. Retailers can survive and succeed if they follow the right strategic options. A clear strategy and new marketing skills will be needed, and significant upheaval and new investment in systems and skills will be essential.

The e-shopping test assesses a product's potential to be purchased electronically. The key factors are product characteristics, familiarity and confidence, and consumer attributes.

There are ten strategic options for entering e-shopping, from a minimal presence to separate electronic business, with options for mixed trading.

CONTRIBUTION
1. The Impact of E-shopping

Evidence indicates an unstoppable momentum that will drive e-commerce forward. It will be so pervasive and accessible that it will have a major impact on the shopping and retailing scene.

2. Changing the Face of Retailing

A drop of just 15 percent in store traffic can make stores unprofitable. Retail margins are very thin, and retailers are vulnerable to small shifts—so some shops are in danger of dying out.

Small shopping areas just won't be able to meet consumers' widening needs and expectations. The changes will affect all retail consumer sectors, with financial services one of the most vulnerable areas.

3. Surviving in the New Economy

Retailers can survive and succeed if they follow the right strategic options. Choices range from low-key response to aggressive investment in the new medium.

Manufacturers can establish their own direct consumer distribution and bypass existing retail chains.

> Given the way electronic commerce is moving and the speed of its development, there may be no choice.

4. Major Changes Needed

The electronic environment demands new marketing skills. The focus is on guiding consumers to a Web site and making it easy to shop.

Future success urgently requires the development of a clear long-term strategy. Players must immerse themselves in the marketplace and understand customers' needs. This may result in significant upheaval and new investment in systems and skills.

5. The E-shopping Test

The e-shopping test shows that a retailer's products or services have some potential to be purchased electronically. The test covers three elements: product characteristics; familiarity and confidence; and consumer attributes.

Product Characteristics   Does the product appeal to the senses? Does it need to be tried or touched before buying? Products that appeal in the realms of sight and sound are most naturally suited to e-shopping.

Familiarity and Confidence   To what extent does the consumer recognize and trust the product? Has the consumer used it before? Would the consumer be happy to repurchase?

Consumer Attributes   How does the consumer feel about the act of shopping? Would they prefer to visit a shop rather than purchase electronically? Is the consumer predisposed to shop electronically?

6. Strategic Options for Entering E-shopping

The book offers a range of strategic options:
- Having information only—establishing a minimal presence, as much to respond to consumer inquiries as to protect turf against competitors.
- Maintaining existing domestic retail outlets but using e-shopping to gain access to new markets and customers.
- Integrating into existing business without changing existing operations.
- Treating it as another channel, with e-shopping as an alternative means to reach a target group of existing customers.
- Setting up a separate business—recognizing that it is a fundamentally different business requiring different skills and competencies.
- Pursuing on all fronts—aggressively pursuing every sales channel that is available.
- Having a mixed system—maintaining flagship stores and adding online delivery.
- Switching fully—shifting away from physical retail sites to become a dedicated electronic trader.
- Having the "best of both worlds"—retaining most existing stores alongside a developed electronic presence.
- Revitalizing and bucking the trend—making sure that consumers will want to continue to shop at the physical store.

CONTEXT

When *E-shock* first came out in 1998, it was considered a landmark book. It analyzed the impact of the e-shopping revolution on retailers and manufacturers and the strategy for the future. Without the data and analysis that underpin its conclusions, the book's findings might appear a little glib and not terribly original. However, its findings derived from solid-looking research, and the intention was to provide a practical guide to companies that were wondering whether and how to enter the virtual selling marketplace.

FOR MORE INFORMATION

de Kare-Silver, Michael. *E-shock: The New Rules—Internet Strategies for Retailers and Manufacturers.* 2nd ed. New York: AMACOM, 2001.

The Experience Economy
B. JOSEPH PINE AND JAMES H. GILMORE

WHY READ IT?

The book shows how to differentiate what appear to be basic products and services by adding value. The result is a "consumer experience," which can be marketed at a much higher price than the core product. This is a very useful approach for anyone involved in product or service development, and the book provides many examples to illustrate the process.

GETTING STARTED

Depending on what a business does with it, a product can be one of three economic offerings: commodity, good, or service. Each offering has a distinct value for the customer. Where consumption embodies a heightened experience, customers pay even more, a fourth level of value. The most significant source of added value is the point at which the offering becomes an experience. It is also the level at which companies can differentiate themselves.

According to the authors, the key to success is a process that delivers a consistent, positive, and memorable experience for the customer. It is important to create a consistent and well-defined theme, and companies must introduce cues that affirm the nature of the experience and eliminate negative cues. Memorabilia provide a physical reminder of the experience. The more senses are engaged, the more memorable the experience.

CONTRIBUTION
1. Adding Value to a Commodity

A cup of coffee costs more from a trendy café than it does from a street vendor or when made at home. This is partly because of the inherent costs involved, but more significant is the nature of the experience and the value attached to it.

Depending on what a business does with it, coffee can be a commodity, good, or service, with three distinct ranges of value customers attach to the offering. Where consumption embodies a heightened ambience or sense of theater, consumers pay even more.

Businesses that ascend to this fourth level of value establish a distinctive experience that envelops the purchase of coffee, increasing its value by a massive order of magnitude over the original commodity.

2. Creating an Experience for the Customer

The product's journey goes from commodity, to good, to service, and finally to experience. The most obvious and significant source of added value in this journey is the point at which the offering becomes an experience for the consumer. This is the "fourth level of value." It is at the experience level that companies have their greatest opportunity to distinguish themselves from their rivals.

3. The Key to Successful Experiences

Disney is a model provider of experiences. The company's success can be attributed to its ability to sell indelible impressions, engage the senses to facilitate escapism, and create memories.

The key to success is a process that delivers a consistent, positive, and memorable experience for the customer. There are five design principles involved in creating a memorable experience:

Theme the Experience   Create a consistent and well-defined theme that resonates throughout the entire experience. For example, eat at the Hard Rock Café or TGI Friday, and you instantly know what to expect when you walk through the door.

Harmonize Impressions with Positive Cues   While the theme is the foundation of the experience, impressions are the "takeaways" that fulfill the theme. To create the right impressions, companies must introduce cues that affirm the nature of the experience to the customer. Even the smallest cue can aid in the creation of a unique experience.

For example, when a restaurant waiter says, "Your table is ready," no particular cue is given. But when a Rainforest Café host declares, "Your adventure is about to begin," it sets the scene for something special.

Eliminate Negative Cues   Crabby staff, long queues, unpleasant environments, and intrusive announcements are negative cues. Unfortunately, the easiest way to turn a service into an experience is to provide poor service, creating a memorable encounter of the unpleasant kind.

Mix in Memorabilia   Postcards, T-shirts, and other memorabilia provide a physical reminder of the experience. They might influence the customer to repeat the experience or to share stories about the good experience with friends and colleagues.

Engage the Five Senses   The more senses are engaged, the more memorable the experience.

4. Prospects for the Experience Economy

These principles do not repeal the laws of supply and demand. An overpriced experience will struggle to attract repeat customers, no matter how well it is delivered. Overcapacity will put pressure on demand and pricing.

A growth in the experience economy seems inevitable, because it represents the best opportunity for a company really to distinguish itself in the eyes of its customers.

> Unfortunately, the easiest way to turn a service into an experience is to provide poor service—thus creating a memorable encounter of the unpleasant kind.

CONTEXT

The Experience Economy is crammed with illustrations and intriguing insights. It offers another perspective from which to view the future of commerce.

From a new economy perspective, it would have been interesting to hear how the experience economy might operate in the online world.

FOR MORE INFORMATION

Pine, B. Joseph, and James H. Gilmore. *The Experience Economy: Goods and Services Are No Longer Enough*. Boston: Harvard Business School Press, 1999.

The Fifth Discipline
PETER SENGE

WHY READ IT?

This is the book that popularized the concept of the learning organization. More philosophical in tone than most business-oriented books, it adopts a holistic approach. Learning is both an individual and a group experience, Senge would claim, much deeper than just taking in information. He wrote: "It is about changing individuals so that they produce results they care about, accomplish things that are important to them."

GETTING STARTED

Peter Senge is director of the Center for Organizational Learning at MIT. *The Fifth Discipline* emerged from extensive research by Senge and his team, but Senge said the "vision that became *The Fifth Discipline*" came to him one morning during his meditation.

The "fifth discipline" of the title is systems thinking. Of the five building blocks of a learning organization, systems thinking connects the other four and enables them to work together for the benefit of business.

CONTRIBUTION
1. Learning Is Vital

In Senge's view, as business becomes more complex and dynamic, work must become more "learningful." It is no longer sufficient to have one person learning for the whole organization. It is no longer possible to figure things out from the top and have everybody else follow the orders of the grand strategist.

The organizations that will excel in the future are those that can tap the commitment and capacity to learn of people at all levels within them. Managers should therefore encourage employees to
- be open to new ideas,
- communicate frankly with each other,
- understand thoroughly how their companies operate,
- form a collective vision, and
- work together to achieve their goals.

2. The Five Disciplines

There are five components to a learning organization:
- systems thinking
- personal mastery
- mental models
- shared vision
- team learning

Systems Thinking Systems thinking is a conceptual framework to make patterns clearer, claims Senge. It requires a shift of mind to see interrelationships rather than linear cause and effect. It can help managers spot repetitive patterns, such as the way certain kinds of problems persist or the way systems have their own in-built limits to growth.

Personal Mastery   This idea is based on the familiar competencies and skills associated with management. But it also includes spiritual growth—opening oneself up to a progressively deeper reality and living life from a creative rather than a reactive viewpoint.

Shared Vision   Senge stresses the importance of co-creation and argues that shared vision can only be built on personal vision.

> The harder you push the system, the harder the system pushes you.

Team Learning   The discipline of team learning involves two practices: dialogue and discussion. Dialogue is characterized by its exploratory nature, discussion by the opposite process of narrowing down the field to the best alternative for the decisions that need to be made. The two are mutually complementary, but the benefits of combining them only come from having previously separated them.

3. Creating Learning Organizations

The author argues that transforming companies into learning organizations has proved problematical, principally because it involves managers surrendering their spheres of power and control to the people who are learning. If people are to learn, they must be allowed to experiment and fail. In a blame-oriented culture, this requires a major change in organizational attitude.

The learning organization demands trust and involvement, usually notable by their absence. Real commitment is rare in today's organizations. Experience indicates that nearly all of what passes for commitment is compliance. One man reported to Senge that by adopting the learning organization model, he made what he called "job-limiting choices." What he meant was that he could have climbed the corporate ladder faster by rejecting Senge's theories and toeing the company line.

CONTEXT

Although the learning organization sounds like a product, it is actually a process. Phil Hodgson of Ashridge Management College commented, "Processes are not suddenly unveiled for all to see. Academic definitions, no matter how precise, cannot be instantly applied in the real world. Managers need to promote learning so that it gradually emerges as a key part of an organization's culture."

The Fifth Discipline has proved highly influential. Though the learning organization has rarely been converted into reality, the idea has fueled the debate on self-managed development and employability and has affected the rewards and remuneration strategies of many organizations.

Gary Hamel observed that "while Professor [Chris] Argyris put organizational learning on the management agenda, Peter Senge married it with system thinking and created a language and approach that makes the whole set of ideas accessible to managers. Peter is no mere theorist, his organizational Learning Center at MIT has helped launch thousands of in-company learning experiments."

FOR MORE INFORMATION

Senge, Peter. *The Fifth Discipline: The Art and Practice of the Learning Organization*. Rev. ed. New York: Doubleday, 2006.

A Future Perfect
JOHN MICKLETHWAIT AND ADRIAN WOOLDRIDGE

WHY READ IT?
This book provides a wide-ranging discussion on the impact of globalization from a political and economic perspective. Although it considers the business implications of globalization, it is not intended to be a practical guide.

GETTING STARTED
Globalization has generated mixed reactions, from demonstrations against it at World Trade Organization meetings to being seen as a process both desirable and inevitable. In fact, it should be seen as a series of waves, rather like the Industrial Revolution.

According to the authors, globalization appears to lead to a more efficient use of resources, but it fails to confront the problem of the losers, such as U.S. car workers or the environment in Bangkok. Businesses and nations face the question, Should businesses go global?

Companies are struggling to find the secrets of business success in a global age. The three engines driving globalization are technology, the capital markets, and management.

Globalization is helping remove restrictions on where people can go; what they can buy; where they can invest; and what they can read, hear, or see. It brings down barriers and helps to hand the power to choose to the individual.

CONTRIBUTION
1. Contrasting Views on Globalization
Globalization has had a mixed press. It has been resented and denounced, most forcibly at the demonstrations during the World Trade Organization meeting in Seattle in November 1999. It has also been seen as desirable and is, in any case, inevitable.

Various myths have grown up around globalization:
- It is ushering in an age of global products.
- It has killed inflation and changed the rules of economics.
- Big, local companies will crush their smaller rivals.
- Geography means nothing in an age of rootless capitalism.

Globalization is not a single, great, coordinated movement. It should be seen as a series of waves.

2. The Case for Globalization
On the surface, globalization appears to make sense because it leads to a more efficient use of resources. However, that argument fails to confront the harsh questions about those people who lose on account of globalization, not just economically but socially and culturally.

That argument also undersells globalization: The process is concerned not just with economic efficiency; it has to do with freedom. Globalization offers the chance to fulfill the goals that classical liberal philosophers first identified several centuries ago and that still underpin Western democracy.

3. The Central Issues of the Globalization Debate
A number of major issues face companies and countries:

- Should businesses go global?
- What are the secrets of business success in a global age?
- Are we creating a winner-takes-all society?
- What should and what can be done about the losers from globalization?
- What will happen to one's career?

4. The Progress of Globalization

The first version of globalization (1890–1913) collapsed. The engines driving globalization now are technology, the capital markets, and management.

Globalization will create a new meritocratic global ruling class called "the Cosmocrats." It will also continue to create losers, from factory workers to local environments.

CONTEXT

The book reviews mixed opinions on globalization and provides wide-ranging examples of globalization in action. It joins a range of other books on the politics, business, and economics of globalization, but adds the element of technology and the impact of the new economy.

> Globalization offers the chance to fulfill . . . the goals that classical liberal philosophers first identified several centuries ago and that still underpin Western democracy.

On the political aspect, Gerald Segal, of the International Institute for Strategic Studies, argues, "Globalization has always primarily been a process of Westernization."

An article in the *International Herald Tribune* states, "The world welcomes America's cultural invasion," and explains the changing nature of globalization from a U.S. perspective: "America's biggest export is no longer the fruit of its fields or the output of its factories, but the mass-produced products of its popular culture—movies and music, television programs, books and computer software. Entertainment around the globe is dominated by American-made products."

John Naisbitt's book, *Global Paradox*, focuses on the cultural impact of globalization: "As the world becomes more universal, it also becomes more tribal. As people yield economic sovereignty and become economically interdependent, holding on to what distinguishes you from others becomes very important."

Francis Fukuyama, speaking at the Merrill Lynch Forum in 1998, argued that the process is not particularly advanced:

> I think that in many respects, globalization is still superficial. Although there is a great deal of talk about it currently, the underlying truth is that the global economy is still limited. It seems to me that the real layer of globalization is restricted to the capital markets. In most other areas, institutions remain intensely local. . . . Trade, for example, is still predominantly regional.

FOR MORE INFORMATION

Micklethwait, John, and Adrian Wooldridge. *A Future Perfect: The Challenge and Hidden Promise of Globalization*. Boston: Heinemann, 2000. Web site: International Institute for Strategic Studies, www.isn.eethz.ch/iiss/

Futurize Your Enterprise
DAVID SIEGEL

WHY READ IT?

The authors argue that most companies don't know how to approach the Internet. Because they apply traditional business thinking, they fail to take full advantage of the Internet. The book can help companies avoid that pitfall, outlining the most common e-commerce mistakes and giving practical examples of strategies that have succeeded.

> The limiting factor online isn't technology, branding or bandwidth— it's mind-set.

GETTING STARTED

Most companies understand that the Internet is changing business, but few understand how to approach the Web. The limiting factor online is mind-set. According to the authors, there are six common traps of e-commerce to avoid, discussed below.

Effective Internet companies reorganize around profitable customer groups so they can respond to customer needs faster. Customer-led companies use the Internet to benefit employees and customers equally. Re-creating the physical world online is a temporary, transitional, and often unnecessary strategy.

CONTRIBUTION
1. Developing an Internet Mind-set

Many companies fall into the six common traps of e-commerce.

They Don't Take the Internet Seriously   Companies treat the Web like a trade show or an extension of their paper catalogs.

They Try to Please Everyone   Packing the Web site with too many features can leave the customer baffled. In trying to please everyone, a Web site satisfies no one.

They Fall into the Technology Trap   Don't focus on technology rather than people. One measure of the technology trap is the length of time it takes to make a change on the site.

They Focus on Brands and Messages   When companies go down this route, the site is overcontrolled and carries too much bland content. Customer comments are discouraged in case they are critical.

They Have an Introverted Web Site   Make sure the site is not organized around internal issues rather than the needs of customers.

They Take the Site Too Seriously   Some companies are intent on putting in place content that they believe the customer ought to want to know about. The site then seems pompous and humorless. The real interests of customers are never known because nobody asks them what those interests are.

2. Reorganizing around Customer Groups

Companies like Microsoft and Dell have reorganized around customer groups, rather than product, content, or service offerings. This structure allows those companies to listen and respond to customer needs faster.

3. Supporting a Customer-led Web Site

Six actions are necessary to build a proper support system for a customer-led Web site: gain internal commitment; implement customer segmentation; actively listen to customers; develop appropriate measures; use customer modeling; and map out a strategy for implementation.

4. Success Factors

Properly aligned, customer-led companies use the Internet to benefit employees and customers equally. The keys to success seem to revolve around

- ongoing dialogue with customers,
- having employees who are empowered to respond to new demands, and
- putting in place processes that monitor customer behavior and needs.

5. Putting the Physical World Online

In the late 1990s, companies tried hard to re-create their familiar business environments online. They thought the World Wide Web would provide the new "front-end" to their existing business practices. Re-creating the physical world online is a temporary, transitional, and often unnecessary strategy.

6. Dell: A Model E-business

Michael Dell built an e-business before anyone coined the term. Rather than building new products in long planning cycles and having the products sit on the shelf, he started building customers' products as soon as they ordered them. Dell.com was a natural extension of the offline business.

Dell brings customers into the product-planning and manufacturing processes, not just the sales process. Management encourages everyone in the company to have contact with customers. That broad employee–customer interface prevents the communication bottleneck that occurs if only the Web team is in touch with e-customers.

CONTEXT

Futurize your Enterprise explains how companies can avoid the common traps of e-commerce and become meaningful players in the customer-led revolution that will connect almost two billion people to the Web by the year 2010.

The book is packed with insights and provocative assertions about the future shape of the Internet. It is a wake-up call for companies that think that the Internet is just starting to settle into recognizable business patterns, and that their online presence can be run using the same management mind-set that runs the bricks-and-mortar business.

FOR MORE INFORMATION

Siegel, David. *Futurize Your Enterprise: Business Strategy in the Age of the E-customer*. Hoboken, NJ: Wiley, 1999. Web site: *Futurize Your Enterprise* comes in seven parts. Four are in the book, and the other three are online at www.Futurizenow.com.

General and Industrial Management
HENRI FAYOL

WHY READ IT?
Fayol created one of the first systems that put management at the center of the organization. His system divides a company's activities into six groups, in which managerial activities are distinct from the other five. The book provides a systematic analysis of the process of management, in which he anticipated most of the more recent analyses of modern business practice. His brief résumé of what constitutes management largely held sway throughout the 20th century.

> To manage is to forecast and plan, to organize, to command, to coordinate and to control.

GETTING STARTED
Fayol created a system of management in which management was the foundation stone of the organization. His system focused on acceptance of, and adherence to, six functions. His view of forward planning was one of the first examples of business planning in practice.

CONTRIBUTION
1. A System of Management
Fayol created a system of management encapsulated in *General and Industrial Management*. "Management plays a very important part in the government of undertakings; of all undertakings, large or small, industrial, commercial, political, religious, or any other," he wrote.

2. Division by Function
Fayol's system was based on acceptance of, and adherence to, different functions. He said that all activities to which industrial undertakings give rise can be divided into six groups:
- technical activities
- commercial activities
- financial activities
- security activities
- accounting activities
- managerial activities

3. The Nature of Management
The management function is quite distinct from the other five essential functions. To manage is to forecast and plan, organize, command, coordinate, and control.

4. Principles of Management
From his observations, Fayol also produced general principles of management:
- division of work
- authority and responsibility
- discipline
- unity of command
- unity of direction
- subordination of individual interest to general interest

- remuneration of personnel
- centralization
- scalar chain (line of authority)
- order
- equity
- stability of tenure of personnel
- initiative
- esprit de corps

5. Forward Planning

Fayol discussed ten-yearly forecasts, revised every five years—one of the first instances of business planning in practice.

The maxim "managing means looking ahead" gives some idea of the importance attached to planning for the future in the business world. It is true that if foresight is not the whole of management, it is at least an essential part of it.

CONTEXT

Fayol created a system that put management at the center of the organization in a way never envisaged by contemporaries such as Frederick W. Taylor, author of *Scientific Management*.

Fayol's championing of management was highly important. While Taylor regarded managers as little more than overseers with limited responsibility, Fayol regarded their role as critical to organizational success.

In his faith in carefully defined functions, Fayol was systematizing business organization in ways that worked at the time, but proved too limiting and restraining in the long term.

In *The Principles and Practice of Management*, a 1953 study of early management thinking, E. F. L. Brech notes, "The importance of Fayol's contribution lay in two features: The first was his systematic analysis of the process of management; the second, his firm advocacy of the principle that management can, and should, be taught. Both were revolutionary lines of thought in 1908, and still little accepted in 1925."

Igor Ansoff has noted that Fayol anticipated imaginatively and soundly most of the more recent analyses of modern business practice. Fayol's view of what constitutes management was highly influential throughout the 20th century and has only recently been challenged.

An extrapolation of Fayol's methods was later exposed by Peter Drucker, who observed, "If used beyond the limits of Fayol's model, functional structure becomes costly in terms of time and effort."

FOR MORE INFORMATION

Fayol, Henri. *General and Industrial Management*. Revised by Irwin Gray. New York: IEEE Press, 1984.

The General Theory of Employment
JOHN MAYNARD KEYNES

WHY READ IT?

Should the state intervene to combat unemployment? Governments were already asking themselves this question during the 1930s. Keynes was the first to show convincingly why state intervention to boost employment is sensible and necessary. This book, first published in 1936, lays the foundations of Keynesianism, a demand-oriented doctrine that is still hotly debated and highly influential today.

GETTING STARTED

Keynes's *General Theory* shows how economic policy can overcome periods of stagnation. He argued in favor of investment being state directed to ensure full employment. In contrast to the exponents of classical economic theory, he did not believe in the self-healing power of the market. For him, demand was the lever of the economy, and in times of crisis it is the state that must operate the lever.

> Capitalism is the astounding belief that the wickedest of men will do the wickedest of things for the greatest good of everyone.

CONTRIBUTION
1. The Error in Classical Economics

According to Keynes, Adam Smith and David Ricardo started out from the assumption that the law of supply and demand regulates the price of goods and of labor. Workers, therefore, are only dismissed when their wages are too high. If they accept lower wages, they are re-employed. The classical economic model always returns to a state of balance: Anyone who is unemployed is so voluntarily.

The world economic crisis of the 1930s could not, however, be explained in this way, Keynes thought. Millions of workers were on the streets, although wages were sinking lower and lower. The "paradox of poverty in the midst of affluence" needed another explanation. Supply was not decisive in achieving economic success; demand was.

2. Aggregate Demand—Consumption and Investment

Demand across the entire economy—the sum of expenditure on consumer and investment goods—has one essential characteristic, Keynes argued: It is unstable. Expenditure on consumption depends on income: The higher the income, the more money is spent. But above a particular level of income, the tendency to increase consumption declines. Part of the additional income is saved.

Investments are the second element in aggregate demand, because they increase the potential of businesses to produce. Investments, according to Keynes, depend on the "marginal efficiency of capital." If this is higher than the standard rate of interest in the market, the investor has an incentive to use credit to implement investment plans. In the opposite case, the costs of credit would be higher than the profit, and the investment would not be made.

3. Imbalance between the Markets for Goods and Capital

The market interest rate for investments, said Keynes, results from the population's inclination toward liquidity; that is, their demand for cash. People save for many reasons: to purchase goods, protect themselves against hard times, or speculate. Speculators keep their savings in cash until prices become low and an opportunity arises to enter the stock market.

Harmonization between the goods and capital markets is the exception; equality of savings and investments is a rare and lucky chance. It is not the case, said Keynes, that savings decisions are solely dependent on the rate of interest and that the interest mechanism ensures that all savings are available to be loaned to businesses for the purchase of investment goods. Rather, he argued, businesses expand their production so long as they expect larger sales in the future. More and more investors try to attract the capital of the savers. Interest rates and production costs rise and reduce returns. The suppliers of capital get nervous. Panic grips the markets. The unrealistic expectations of the boom are followed by the hysteria of crisis. Investments fall, employment drops, purchasing power disappears, future prospects become more and more dismal. Businesses do not even invest when interest rates sink to zero. The national economy is caught in the "liquidity trap."

4. The State as Starter Motor of the Economy

To free the economy from this disastrous situation and turn it back in the direction of full employment, aggregate demand must rise, said Keynes, until increasing production by businesses offers all workers employment. If the demand for investment goods rises, this leads to more production, more work, and more income. Higher consumption boosts demand for goods and investment, which means that production and income rise further. A chain reaction begins, an "income multiplier"—an exogenous impulse, perhaps an extra boost to investment, gives rise to a multiple increase in income.

From this, Keynes drew the following conclusion. If entrepreneurs do not invest in sufficient quantities, the state must step forward as an investor to set the economy back in motion. To produce additional investment, the public purse accepts credit and uses it to finance, for example, roads, sewage systems, schools, or hospitals.

CONTEXT

The stock market crash of 1929, the crisis in the world economy, and the Great Depression of the 1930s brought forth a number of crucial economic and political questions, which Keynes attempted to answer in this book. It made him the most famous national economist of the 20th century and initiated one of the most influential strands in modern economic thought, Keynesianism. Keynesian ideas provided the framework for the recovery after World War II and held sway in many countries during the middle of the last century. Even President Richard Nixon remarked, "We are all Keynesians now." It was only in the 1970s that the "monetarist counterrevolution" began, eventually re-enthroning supply-side economics and the market forces whose fallibility it had been part of Keynes's purpose to demonstrate.

FOR MORE INFORMATION

Keynes, John Maynard. *The General Theory of Employment, Interest, and Money*. BNPublishing.net, 2008.

Getting Things Done
DAVID ALLEN

WHY READ IT?

When faced with a seemingly insurmountable workload, it is easy to feel intimidated. In *Getting Things Done*, David Allen presents a number of techniques designed to reduce stress and increase efficiency. With more than 20 years' experience as a management consultant, executive coach, and educator, David Allen has gained almost a cult following with this widely commended guide to "getting things off your mind and getting them done."

GETTING STARTED

The key principles in *Getting Things Done* center around moving "to-do lists," from the mind to actual, physical filing systems, and then making sure that prompt action is taken to deal with problems as soon as they become evident. Allen also emphasizes the importance of clear thinking and "horizontal control"—that is, coordinating among projects, tasks, and priorities.

Allen explains that "open loops" are the tasks that we do not tackle, which are often mismanaged and inappropriately prioritized. These act as a constant, often unconscious, source of distraction and stress. He provides three starting points to accomplishing tasks more effectively, to promoting better control of situations, and, consequently, to reducing stress:

- Rather than trying to keep all the information in your head, write it down so that you have a physical record of it.
- Decide actions and outcomes when things *first* emerge on your radar, instead of later.
- Regularly review and update the complete inventory of the "open loops" that exist in your life and work.

CONTRIBUTION

1. Coordinate Outcomes and Actions

When in a challenging situation, form a clear and concise picture of the ideal outcome of the situation. This will enable you to decide what action should be taken to achieve this result.

2. Exercise Horizontal Control

Make sure all projects are cohesive and consistent with each other. It is essential to maintain clarity about, and knowledge of, all necessary projects and tasks and how they will interact with each other.

3. Exercise Vertical Control

Ensure that there is a clear understanding of each *individual* task.

4. Understand the Five Phases of Workflow

To maintain horizontal control across all activities that require attention, the author believes that it can help to implement the following five stages:

- **Collect.** Gather and assess everything that requires action, either in an in-tray, computer, notepad, or other filing/collection system. Keep this filing system organized and make sure that you deal with it and empty it frequently.

- **Process.** Decide on the nature of the task. Is it possible to take action to complete the task? If it is, then either *do it*, *delegate it*, or *defer it*. If it is not actionable, then Allen suggests that you either *trash it*, *incubate it*, or *reference it* (that is, keep it in a filing system for easy reference in the future).
- **Organize.** Make sure that the results of the previous stages are kept organized.
- **Review.** Decide what options are available to deal with the task.
- **Do.** Complete the task.

5. Weekly Review

Over the course of a week, create lists to help you simplify thinking and organize workload. Allen believes that in addition, it is necessary to introduce processes to cope with new tasks as they arise. It is important to review and deal with new data on a weekly basis.

> Do it, delegate it, defer it, drop it.

This review should consist of
- collecting loose papers;
- reviewing notes;
- reviewing existing calendar data;
- creating new calendar data;
- keeping things out of your mind and in a more physical form—making lists of any new projects or activities; and
- reviewing any lists that have been made.

6. Create a Filing System

Allen believes that an efficient filing system is crucial to remaining organized and accomplishing goals. The ideal filing system is clear and easy to navigate. Label files alphabetically, unless a more specific method is required. They should not be grouped according to person, project, topic, or company. Remember to clear your files at least once a year.

CONTEXT

With stress now recognized as a major cause of illness and lost productivity, David Allen argues that it is vital to discover how it is possible for a person "to have an overwhelming number of things to do and still function productively with a clear head and a positive sense of relaxed control."

Allen's ideas build on his extensive experience as a management consultant and executive coach. They are perfectly tailored to people aiming to boost their productivity by simultaneously sharpening their competitive edge and slashing stress levels. The book's concepts are also effective for anyone struggling to deal with a large and stressful workload.

Although at times reminiscent of Eastern philosophies of clarity, inner peace, and allowing one's mind to flow "like water," *Getting Things Done* is based firmly in finding an effective and practical way to deal with today's fast-paced business culture.

FOR MORE INFORMATION

Allen, David. *Getting Things Done: The Art of Stress-free Productivity*. New York: Penguin Putnam, 2001.

Getting to Yes
ROGER FISHER AND WILLIAM URY

WHY READ IT?
Negotiation is an important skill in many aspects of business and personal life. The authors claim that people can become more effective negotiators by moving from adversarial haggling to constructive, joint problem solving, a solution they call "principled negotiation." Both Fisher and Ury have conducted negotiations at extremely high levels in business, politics, diplomacy, law, and international relations. They write with authority and have the experience to offer practical advice and insight into each stage of the negotiating process.

GETTING STARTED
The negotiating principles that the authors claim will lead to successful outcomes are
- don't bargain over positions;
- separate the people from the problem;
- focus on interests, not positions;
- invent options for mutual gain; and
- insist on objective criteria.

CONTRIBUTION
1. The Importance of Effective Negotiation
Negotiation involves everyone, the authors claim. People use negotiation to handle their differences at work and in personal life. However, they believe that standard negotiating strategies tend to leave one or both parties dissatisfied. They describe two types of negotiators:
- soft negotiators, who may make easy compromises to avoid conflict
- hard negotiators, who want to win at all costs

The authors propose a third type of negotiator, using what they call "principled negotiation." Its objective is to decide issues on their merits, rather than on the will of the parties involved.

2. Avoid Bargaining over Positions
Fisher and Ury point out that, traditionally, people take positions and defend them. Differences are only resolved through concessions. This approach can harm relationships and can be damaging to future negotiations. In this approach, emotions become entangled with logic, so it is important to separate people from problems.

3. Separate People from Problems
The authors prompt us to remember that negotiators are people with emotions. Negotiators are therefore just as interested in ongoing relationships as in dealing with the immediate problem. Understanding the emotions of the other side is important, because they can act as a barrier to rational discussion. It is important to understand the other person's perspective and find out what is important to him or her. Listening actively and acknowledging the other party's perspective is critical.

The authors explain how successful negotiators try to make the other party own the problem so that he or she fully participates in reaching a satisfactory conclusion. Communication is an important part of this process, helping to build constructive working relationships that can reduce the element of confrontation.

4. Focus on Interests, Not Positions

Fisher and Ury recommend looking for the underlying interest in negotiations. Interests may not conflict, although positions do. They suggest finding out or asking why the other side takes a particular position and acknowledging those interests as part of the problem.

> Separate the people from the problem.

5. Invent Options for Mutual Gain

The objective of negotiation is a single conclusion, say the authors. Introducing other options may appear to slow down the process, but it can actually make the outcome easier to achieve. Enlarging the pie can help to discover what appears to be mutual gain. The authors believe that brainstorming can help to determine the options because during brainstorming, no decisions have to be made and creativity is encouraged.

6. Insist on Objective Criteria

Finally, according to Fisher and Ury, it may be possible to decide on the outcome of negotiations by reference to an independent or objective authority. The standards adopted should be fair and must be acceptable to both sides. Comparable criteria from other negotiations may also be acceptable.

CONTEXT

Negotiation is a critical element of business. This book takes a detailed look at the process of negotiation independently of business processes such as sales, customer service, or union negotiations.

The authors build on their own experience of negotiations in politics, diplomacy, and the law. Although not every one of the examples relates directly to business, it is possible to apply the same principles to commercial situations of many types.

FOR MORE INFORMATION

Fisher, Roger, and William Ury. *Getting to Yes*. 2nd ed. New York: Penguin USA, 1991.

The Goal
ELIYAHU GOLDRATT AND JEFF COX

WHY READ IT?

What goes on in modern manufacturing businesses is highly complex and often very frustrating. Production problems and job delays are the order of the day, and attempts to improve the situation run into the existing organizational setup and come to grief. This may sound like the starting point for a textbook on process optimization, but Eliyahu Goldratt, famous for his use of the fictional format, takes an inefficient factory threatened with closure and makes it the setting for a novel as fast-paced and gripping as the average thriller. Many books are said to be entertaining as well as instructive, but Goldratt, here writing with Jeff Cox, does more than most to optimize the entertainment factor.

GETTING STARTED

Plant manager Alex Rogo is handed an ultimatum by his bosses: Either he makes a clear improvement in the profitability of his factory within three months, or the factory will close. For Rogo, it's then a race against time. In order not to fail, he has to change his ideas radically. He meets Jonah, the authors' spokesman in the novel, who helps him to break free of traditional ways of thinking and recognize what needs to be done. Jonah knows the solution to the factory's problems and enables Alex to discover it for himself by providing him with questions instead of guidelines. In this way the authors show that management can only learn by deductive insight.

CONTRIBUTION

Goldratt and Cox set out an important principle of product organization in their novel. The story deals with people who want to understand how business processes function. Because they think about their problems logically, they manage to establish cause-and-effect relations between their actions and the changes that result from them. From these they gradually derive the underlying principles that enable them to turn their factory around and finally achieve success.

Alex Rogo is the novel's narrator, the "I" of the story. It begins on the day when Bill Peach, the division vice president, walks into his factory and demands "to be shown the status of Customer Order Number 41427." It turns out that nobody knows anything about this order, which happens to be a fairly big one, which is also late. Rogo sums up the situation in the factory like this: "Everything in this plant is late. Based on observation, I'd say this plant has four ranks of priority for orders: Hot . . . Very Hot . . . Red Hot . . . and Do It NOW. We just can't keep ahead of anything."

Rogo meets Jonah, his former math teacher, who is now a specialist in production organization. When Jonah asks him whether productivity has risen in the plant since industrial robots were put in, Rogo says that it has—by 36 percent. In response to further questions, however, Rogo reveals that the 36 percent increase applies only to one section. Jonah then tells him that if he hasn't slimmed down his inventory and reduced his wage costs, and if the plant is not selling more product than before, the robots cannot have increased its productivity.

Rogo speaks to Lou, the plant controller. Together they establish benchmark figures for turning the business around. These should be the net profit, the return on investment, and cash flow, because negative cash flow would kill off the business.

But these figures are not enough in themselves. They are the ones that the people in division management use to measure progress. At the level of the individual factory, these figures do not make much sense. Jonah prompts Rogo to look at three more figures: throughput, inventory, and operating costs. Goldratt, speaking through Jonah, defines throughput as the amount of money per time unit that the system earns by sales, stressing the fact that sales are what counts, not production. Inventory, he says, is all the money that is invested in the system for the purchase of things that are intended for sale. And operating costs are all the money that the system spends to turn inventory into throughput.

Rogo starts thinking about what goes on in his factory in these terms. He then moves on to what is very much home territory for Goldratt, the exponent of the "Theory of Constraints." He decides that he has to find the *bottlenecks*, production units whose capacity is equal to or less than the market requirement allotted to them. He says he would like to organize everything so that the production unit with the smallest capacity has the top place in any work plans.

Eventually Rogo gets to the point where he can go to the managing director with a five-step program to save the plant:

1. Identify the regulating factor in the system.
2. Decide how the bottlenecks in the system can be used.
3. Make everything else subordinate to the above decision.
4. Free up the bottlenecks in the system.
5. Set the changed procedures in motion.

CONTEXT

The Goal is an economics textbook on the natural laws of business life in the form of a novel. It has attained cult status. Eliyahu Goldratt has been deemed an industrial guru and cultural revolutionary. He is an expert on production management. He created the mathematical and philosophical bases on which the OPT (Optimized Production Technology) system of planning and organizing production processes is built and leads a management organization, OPT Management Systems. Goldratt's appearances as a speaker are feared by many in business, because he tends to pillory firms and their practices in public.

FOR MORE INFORMATION

Goldratt, Eliyahu, and Jeff Cox. *The Goal: A Process of Ongoing Improvement.* 2nd ed. Great Barrington, MA: North River Press, 1994.

High Stakes, No Prisoners
CHARLES H. FERGUSON

WHY READ IT?
Like *Direct from Dell*, this book provides the inside story on a new company launch, in this case the most successful technology company launch in the United States. It covers mistakes as well as success factors and can provide valuable insight for someone who is planning to launch a new venture.

GETTING STARTED
The book offers an insight into the workings of Silicon Valley and describes the problems of a start-up in difficult times.

Start-ups are extremely demanding on personal and business life. It's important to counter competitive products as well as develop your own, and you have to remember that investors are just as dangerous as competitors. Nondisclosure and secrecy are critical during the start-up period; timing is critical for a product launch.

CONTRIBUTION
1. A Start-up in Difficult Times
Charles Ferguson set up a company in Silicon Valley when the United States was emerging from a recession, the stock market was flat, and the Internet had yet to be taken seriously by those with money to invest.

Within two years he sold the company to Microsoft for $133 million, making a fortune for himself and his associates.

2. A Strategically Important Product
The company's key product was FrontPage, the first software product for creating and managing a Web site. The product is now bundled with Microsoft Office and has several million users worldwide.

3. Start-ups Are Extremely Demanding
Ferguson admits to many mistakes and personal shortcomings during the start-up.

In the preliminary period, he had to fight for months to raise $4 million, and his life went from being demanding but manageable to being completely, totally insane. The start-up period proved to be the most exciting yet punishing months of his professional life.

4. Counter Competitive Products as Well as Develop Your Own
Ferguson had to counter NaviSoft's product launch. Everyone seemed dangerous because his new company threatened them.

5. Investors Are Just as Dangerous as Competitors
The company's problems were not confined to the outside world. It had to defend itself against investors and a newly hired CEO as much as against external threats.

6. Nondisclosure and Secrecy Are Critical

Although everything was connected to everything else, there was nobody the company could talk to openly. Everything had to be secretive. The company spoke to potential partners, large customers, and analysts selectively, under nondisclosure agreements, and usually without revealing sensitive technology or strategic plans.

> Start-ups are the intellectual equivalent of driving a small, fast convertible with the top down.

7. Timing Is Critical for a Product Launch

Because the timing was perfect, the company had a very successful launch. Everyone had already heard of the company, but no one had ever seen the presentations or software before.

CONTEXT

Like *Direct from Dell*, the book describes how the author built a company from scratch. Charles Ferguson set up a company called Vermeer Technologies in difficult times for start-ups. The book is an account of how business really gets done in high technology.

Ferguson is very tough on himself, owning up to the mistakes his start-up made and detailing his own shortcomings as a person and a businessman.

FOR MORE INFORMATION

Ferguson, Charles H. *High Stakes, No Prisoners: A Winner's Tale of Greed and Glory in the Internet Wars*. New York: Times Business, 1999.

How to Win Friends and Influence People
DALE CARNEGIE

WHY READ IT?
Dale Carnegie was a highly successful public speaker and author of books on public speaking and confidence development. *How to Win Friends and Influence People* provides practical advice on the universal challenge of face-to-face communication. As the familiarity of the title proves, the book has had a great impact. The first edition had a print run of a mere 5,000, but the book has since sold more than 15 million copies.

GETTING STARTED
Carnegie held that it is essential to handle people effectively and to make them like you to ensure your own success. His book is littered with illustrative anecdotes from the lives of the famous—Clark Gable, Marconi, Franklin D. Roosevelt, Mary Pickford—and the not so famous.

CONTRIBUTION
1. Handle People Effectively
Carnegie presented these fundamental techniques in handling people:
- Don't criticize, condemn, or complain.
- Give honest and sincere appreciation.
- Arouse in the other person an eager want.

2. Make People Like You
He added advice on other ways to make people like you:
- Become genuinely interested in other people.
- Smile.
- Remember that a person's name is to that person the sweetest and most important sound in any language.
- Be a good listener.
- Encourage others to talk about themselves.
- Talk in terms of the other person's interests.
- Make the other person feel important, and do it sincerely.

> The application of these principles literally revolutionizes the lives of many people.

CONTEXT
How to Win Friends and Influence People is the original self-improvement book, and Carnegie was the first superstar of the self-help genre. Cashing in on his success, he wrote a plethora of other titles on similar themes, including *Public Speaking and Influencing Men in Business, How to Stop Worrying and Start Living, How to Enjoy Your Life and Your Job*, and *How to Develop Self-confidence and Influence People by Public Speaking*. His successors included Anthony Robbins and Stephen Covey, who studied U.S. success literature (of which Carnegie's body of work is a prime example) before coming up with *The Seven Habits of Highly Effective People*.

Carnegie had done much the same 50 years before, and his principles have a similar homely ring to those of Covey. Carnegie's books and his company's training programs continue to strike a chord with managers and aspiring managers, because they deal with the universal challenge of face-to-face communication.

Carnegie was notable in being the first to create a credible long-term business out of his ideas. In creating a flourishing enterprise, Carnegie ensured that his name and ideas would continue to live on and make money after his death.

FOR MORE INFORMATION

Carnegie, Dale. *How to Win Friends and Influence People.* New York: Simon & Schuster, 2009.

The HP Way
DAVID PACKARD

WHY READ IT?

David Packard was half of the partnership that created one of the business and management benchmarks of the 20th century—Hewlett-Packard. In 1937, with a mere $538 and a rented garage in Palo Alto, California, Bill Hewlett and David Packard created one of the most successful corporations in the world. This book tells the story behind the company.

GETTING STARTED

According to Packard, the HP secret lay in a simple approach to business. The HP way reflected the culture of the company and the management style used to run it. It was based on openness and respect for the individual, which was key to the company's success. Management was always available and involved, and conflict had to be tackled through communication and consensus rather than confrontation. Management's commitment to people fostered commitment to the company, and HP people at all levels show boundless energy and enthusiasm. The recipe for growth was to make products leaders in their markets. The company kept divisions small and didn't do anything too risky. These values worked to save the company when times were hard.

CONTRIBUTION

1. A Simple Approach to Business

HP's secret lay in the simplicity of its methods. From the very start, Hewlett-Packard was guided by a few fundamental principles:

- It did not believe in long-term borrowing to secure the expansion of the business.
- Its recipe for growth was simply that its products needed to be leaders in their markets.
- It got on with the job.

"Our main task is to design, develop, and manufacture the finest [electronic equipment] for the advancement of science and the welfare of humanity. We intend to devote ourselves to that task," said Packard in a 1961 memo to employees.

The duo eschewed fashionable management theory: "If I hear anybody talking about how big their share of the market is or what they're trying to do to increase their share of the market, I'm going to personally see that a black mark gets put in their personnel folder."

2. Respect for the Individual

> Management by wandering about.

The company believed that people could be trusted and should always be treated with respect and dignity. "We both felt fundamentally that people want to do a good job. They just need guidelines on how to do it."

HP believed that management should be available and involved—"management by wandering about" was its motto.

Rather than soliciting the administrative suggestions of management, Packard preferred to talk of leadership. HP's legacy, and Packard's proudest achievement, is a management style based on openness and respect for the individual.

3. Keeping It Small

Hewlett-Packard was a company built on very simple ideas. While competitors were turning into conglomerates, Hewlett and Packard kept their heads down and continued with their methods. When their divisions grew too large (around 1,500 people), they split them up to ensure that they didn't spiral out of control.

They didn't do anything too risky or too outlandish. For example, Packard was skeptical about pocket calculators, although, in the end, the company was an early entrant into the market. They didn't risk the company on a big deal or get into debt.

4. Strong Commitment to Values

HP's values worked to save the company when times were hard. During the 1970s recession, Hewlett-Packard staff hung on and took a 10 percent pay cut and worked 10 percent fewer hours.

As the book documents, if the company hadn't had a long-term commitment to employee stock ownership, perhaps employees wouldn't have been so willing to make sacrifices. Packard claims that commitment to people clearly fostered commitment to the company.

CONTEXT

Hewlett-Packard has pulled off an unusual double—it is admired and successful. When they were assembling their list of excellent companies in the late 1970s, Tom Peters and Robert Waterman included Hewlett-Packard.

When Jerry Porras and James Collins wrote *Built to Last*, their celebration of long-lived companies, there was no doubt that Hewlett-Packard was worthy of inclusion. In the same vein, in 1985, *Fortune* ranked Hewlett-Packard as one of the two most highly admired companies in the United States. The company is ranked similarly in virtually every other poll on well-managed companies or those that would be good to work for.

"Wherever you go in the HP empire, you find people talking product quality, feeling proud of their division's achievements in that area. HP people at all levels show boundless energy and enthusiasm," observed Tom Peters and Robert Waterman in *In Search of Excellence*.

According to Louise Kehoe in the *Financial Times*, "Their legacy, and the achievement that Packard was most proud of, is a management style based on openness and respect for the individual."

FOR MORE INFORMATION

Packard, David. *The HP Way*. New York: Collins, 1996.

The Human Problems of an Industrial Civilization

ELTON MAYO

WHY READ IT?

The author was part of the team conducting the Hawthorne Studies at Western Electric's Chicago plant between 1927 and 1932, early studies into motivation in the workplace. The book shows the important link between workforce morale and organizational performance and paved the way for policies and management theories based on teamwork and effective communication.

GETTING STARTED

The Hawthorne Studies offered important insights into the motivation of workers:
- People and their motivation are critical to the success of any business.
- There is a link between morale and output—changes in working conditions lead to increased output.
- It is important to restore humanity to the workplace.

Workers selected for a test felt that more attention was being paid to them. They felt chosen and so responded positively. The feeling of belonging to a cohesive group led to an increase in productivity. Informal organizations among groups are a potentially powerful force.

> The desire to stand well with one's fellows, the so-called human instinct of association, easily outweighs the merely individual interest.

CONTRIBUTION

1. The Hawthorne Studies

According to Mayo, the studies offered important insights into the motivation of workers. It was found that changes in working conditions led to increased output, even if the changes didn't obviously improve working conditions.

Whatever the dictates of mass production and scientific management, people and their motivation were critical to the success of any business.

2. The Link between Morale and Output

The researchers were interested in exploring the links between morale and output. The author documented how five women workers were removed to a test room and observed as they worked. The research was initially restricted to physical and technical variables. Sociological factors were not expected to be of any significance. The results proved otherwise.

Removed from their colleagues, the morale of the "guinea pigs" improved. By virtue of their selection, the women felt that more attention was being paid to them.

3. The Importance of Group Cohesion

Mayo reported that the feeling of belonging to a cohesive group led to an increase in productivity. He commented: "The desire to stand well with one's fellows, the so-called human instinct of association, easily outweighs the merely individual interest and the logic of reasoning upon which so many spurious principles of management are based."

Mayo championed the case for teamworking and improved communications between management and the workforce.

The Hawthorne research revealed informal organizations among groups as a potentially powerful force, which companies could make use of or ignore at their peril.

4. Restoring Humanity to the Workplace

Mayo's belief that humanity needed to be restored to the workplace struck a chord at a time when the dehumanizing side of mass production was beginning to be more fully appreciated.

"So long as commerce specializes in business methods which take no account of human nature and social motives, so long may we expect strikes and sabotage to be the ordinary accompaniment of industry," Mayo noted.

The research assumed that the behavior of workers was dictated by the "logic of sentiment," while the behavior of the bosses was dictated by the "logic of cost and efficiency."

CONTEXT

The author is known for his contribution to the famous Hawthorne Studies of the motivation of workers. The experiments were carried out in 1927–1932 at the Chicago division of Western Electric. Although they were celebrated as a major event, their significance lay not so much in their results and discoveries but in the statement they made—that people and their motivation were critical to the success of any business.

The findings influenced the human relations school of thinkers, including Herzberg, McGregor, and Maslow, which emerged in the 1940s and 1950s.

The work of the Hawthorne researchers redressed the balance in management theorizing, and the scientific bias of earlier researchers was put into a new perspective.

FOR MORE INFORMATION

Mayo, Elton. *The Human Problems of an Industrial Civilization.* Rev. ed. New York: Routledge, 2003.

The Human Side of Enterprise
DOUGLAS MCGREGOR

WHY READ IT?
McGregor was a key member of the Human Relations School of Management, whose work significantly influenced management styles from the 1960s on. His most famous concept is "Theories X and Y," which describe two extreme approaches to managing people. The book highlights the potential for a more enlightened approach to human relations management and paved the way for approaches such as empowerment.

GETTING STARTED
Management assumptions about controlling human resources determine an organization's character. Theory X assumes that workers are inherently lazy, needing to be supervised and motivated. Authority is the central, indispensable means of managerial control. Theory Y assumes that people want and need to work, and organizations should develop employees' commitment. McGregor argues that the average human being learns not only to accept but to seek responsibility.

CONTRIBUTION
1. The Importance of Human Resources
According to the book, the assumptions management holds about controlling its human resources determine the whole character of the enterprise.

2. Theory X—A Traditional Management Approach
The Assumptions behind Theory X
- People inherently dislike work and will avoid it if they can.
- People need to be coerced, controlled, and threatened into making adequate effort toward the organization's ends.
- People lack ambition, preferring to be directed and to avoid responsibility. Above all they want security.

The Influence of Theory X   The assumption that authority is the central, indispensable means of managerial control pervades U.S. industry. In the author's view, this is a consequence not of human nature, but of management philosophy, policy, and practice. It is not people who have made organizations, but organizations that have transformed the perspectives, aspirations, and behavior of people.

3. Theory Y—A Humanist Approach
The Assumptions behind Theory Y
- Work is as natural as play or rest.
- External control and threat of punishment are not the only means for bringing about effort.
- Commitment to objectives is a function of the rewards associated with their achievement.
- The most important reward is the satisfaction of ego, which can be the direct product of effort.

- The average human being learns not only to accept but to seek responsibility.
- The capacity to use imagination, ingenuity, and creativity in the solution of organizational problems is widely distributed in the population.

4. Toward the Learning Manager

McGregor suggests that four kinds of learning are relevant for managers:
- intellectual knowledge
- manual skills
- problem-solving skills
- social interaction

CONTEXT

Despite publishing little in his short life, McGregor's work remains significant. His classic study of work and motivation reflected the concerns of the middle and late 1960s, when the monolithic corporation was at its most dominant and the world at its most questioning. The common complaint against Theories X and Y is that they are mutually exclusive. To counter this McGregor was developing "Theory Z" when he died in 1964, a theory that synthesized the organizational and personal imperatives. William Ouchi later seized on the concept of Theory Z. In his book of the same name, he analyzed Japanese working methods. Here he found fertile ground for many of the ideas McGregor was proposing:

- lifetime employment
- concern for employees including their social life
- informal control
- decisions made by consensus
- slow promotion
- excellent transmittal of information from top to bottom and bottom to top with the help of middle management
- commitment to the company
- high concern for quality

> It is not people who have made organizations, but organizations that have transformed the perspectives, aspirations, and behavior of people.

Leading author Gary Hamel commented on McGregor:

> Over the last forty years, we have been slowly abandoning a view of human beings as nothing more than warm-blooded cogs in the industrial machine. People can be trusted; people want to do the right thing; people are capable of imagination and ingenuity—these were McGregor's fundamental premises, and they underlie the work of modern management thinkers from Drucker to Deming to Peters, and the employment practices of the world's most progressive and successful companies.

FOR MORE INFORMATION

McGregor, Douglas. *The Human Side of Enterprise*. Rev. ed. New York: McGraw-Hill, 2005.

In Search of Excellence
TOM PETERS AND ROBERT WATERMAN

WHY READ IT?

In Search of Excellence is one of the most popular management books of recent times. Appearing when Japanese competition had brought Western business low, it gave managers new heart and a new direction, reminding them, in Gary Hamel's words, "that success often comes from doing common things uncommonly well."

GETTING STARTED

This book emerged from research conducted by Peters and Waterman with the consulting firm McKinsey. They identified excellent companies, then sought to distill lessons from their behavior and performance.

The sample was eventually whittled down to 62 (which were not intended to be perfectly representative). The choices were largely unsurprising, including the likes of IBM, Hewlett-Packard, Wal-Mart, and General Electric. The emphasis was exclusively on big companies.

> Do it, fix it, try it, is our favorite axiom.

There is a certain irony here, however. Although it celebrated big manufacturing businesses, the book condemned the excesses of dispassionate modern management practice and advocated a return to simpler virtues. The authors later came to feel that their ideas were better embodied in smaller companies.

CONTRIBUTION
1. Success Builds on First Principles

The book attacks the excesses of the rational model and the business strategy paradigm that had come to dominate Western management thinking. It counsels a return to first principles:

- attention to customers
- an abiding concern for people (productivity through people)
- the celebration of trial and error (a bias for action)

"The excellent companies really are close to their customers. That's it. Other companies talk about it; the excellent companies do it," write the authors.

2. Achieve Productivity through People

The authors quote a General Motors worker laid off after 16 years making Pontiacs: "I guess I was laid off because I make poor quality cars. But in 16 years, not once was I ever asked for a suggestion as to how to do my job better. Not once."

Excellent companies encourage and nurture an entrepreneurial spirit among all employees.

3. The Management Role

The real role of the chief executive is to manage the values of the organization. Executives nurture and sustain corporate values. Rather than being distant figureheads, they should be there making things happen.

The word "manager" in lip-service institutions often has come to mean not someone who rolls up his or her sleeves to get the job done right alongside the worker, but someone who hires assistants to do it.

4. Keep Things Simple

Excellent companies "stick to the knitting." They remain fixed on what they know they are good at and are not easily distracted. One of their key attributes is that they have realized the importance of keeping things simple, despite overwhelming pressures to complicate things.

The authors explain what they call the "smart–dumb rule" as follows:

> Many of today's managers . . . may be a little bit too smart for their own good. The smart ones . . . shift direction all the time, based upon the latest output from the expected value equation [and] have 200-page strategic plans and 500-page market requirement documents that are but one step in product development exercises. Our dumber friends are different. They just don't understand why every customer can't get personalized service, even in the potato chip business.

5. Become Simultaneously Loose and Tight

The debate about how to become loose and tight (controlled and empowered; big yet small) has dominated much subsequent business writing. The authors recommend new management vocabulary. Each phrase turns the tables on conventional wisdom, implying both the absence of clear directions and the simultaneous need for action. They include the following:

- temporary structures
- fluid organizations
- product champions
- ad hoc groups
- internal competition
- skunk works

CONTEXT

Peter Drucker suggested that the book's simplicity explained its appeal: "The strength of the Peters book is that it forces you to look at the fundamentals. The book's great weakness—which is a strength from the point of view of its success—is that it makes managing sound so incredibly easy."

Gary Hamel said of the book, "The dividing line between simple truths, and simplistic prescription is always a thin one. For the most part, Peters and Waterman avoided the facile and the tautological. Indeed, the focus on operations research, elaborate planning systems, and (supposedly) rigorous financial analysis had, in many companies, robbed management of its soul—and certainly had taken the focus off the customer."

For such a trailblazing book, it is surprisingly uncontroversial. Peters and Waterman admit that what they have to say is not particularly original. They have commented that the ideas they were espousing had been generally left behind, ignored, or overlooked by management theorists.

The criteria for selecting excellence were debatable, as all criteria are, and set the authors up for a good deal of criticism when their excellent companies fell from grace. In 1984 *Business Week* revealed that some had speedily declined into mediocrity and, in some cases, abject failure. But Peters and Waterman had already provided a warning: "We are asked how we know that the companies we have defined as culturally innovative will stay that way. The answer is we don't."

In Search of Excellence created the impetus for the deluge of business books and, in the business world, established customer service as a key form of differentiation and advantage.

FOR MORE INFORMATION

Peters, Thomas, and Robert Waterman. *In Search of Excellence*. Rev. ed. New York: Collins, 2004.

The Information Age: Economy, Society and Culture

MANUEL CASTELLS

WHY READ IT?

This is another "big picture" book showing how the world is being changed by technology. It provides valuable insights into the impact of globalization and networked information, but would not rank as a practical business book.

GETTING STARTED

According to the author, globalization, networked organizations, and flexibility of work are the key characteristics of the Network Society. In some cases, globalization has marginalized countries and peoples. Despite a global communications revolution, there is no "global village." The multimedia world is increasingly populated by the "haves and have nots."

Megacities that function as nodes of the global economy are continuing to develop. Significant global social change will result from interaction between networks and identity. The information age will unleash unprecedented productive capacity by the power of the mind, although there is a gap between technological overdevelopment and social underdevelopment.

There is nothing that cannot be changed by conscious, purposive social action, provided with information and supported by legitimacy.

CONTRIBUTION

1. The Nature of the Network Society

The Network Society is characterized by

- the globalization of strategically decisive economic activities;
- the networking form of organization; and
- the flexibility and instability of work, and the individualization of labor.

2. The Marginalization of Countries

Globalization has marginalized whole countries and peoples by leaving them excluded from information networks. There is no systematic structural relationship between the diffusion of information technologies and the evolution of unemployment levels in the economy as a whole.

Although the communications revolution enables the global distribution of major events, we live in customized "cottages" globally produced and locally distributed.

The multimedia world is increasingly inhabited by two distinct populations:

- the interacting, who are able to select their communication options; and
- the interacted, who are provided with a restricted number of prepackaged choices.

3. A New Urban Form Emerging

According to Castells, the new global economy and the emerging information society are spawning a new urban form, megacities—cities with populations of anything from 10 to 20 million. Megacities will function as nodes of the global economy, concentrating media and political power, acting as magnets for regional resources and linking up the informational networks.

4. Globalization Shaping Social Change

Global social change will result from interaction between networks and identity. Significant trends that may configure society in the early 21st century include

> The 21st century will not be a dark age. Rather, it may well be characterized by informed bewilderment.

- the information technology revolution accelerating its transformative potential;
- technology achieving its potential to unleash productivity;
- the full flowering of the genetic revolution;
- the continuing and relentless expansion of the global economy;
- the survival of nation-states, but not necessarily their sovereignty; and
- the "exclusion of the excluders by the excluded."

Those who do not have the capability to participate in the information economy will become more tribal in outlook.

5. Unleashing the Power of the Mind

According to Castells, the information age will unleash unprecedented productive capacity by the power of the mind. The dream of the Enlightenment, that reason and science would solve the problems of humankind, is within reach.

6. Closing the Gap

There is an extraordinary gap between our technological overdevelopment and our social underdevelopment. Economy, society, and culture are built on interests, values, institutions, and systems of representation that, by and large, limit collective creativity, confiscate the harvest of information technology, and divert our energy into self-destructive confrontation.

The author believes that there is nothing that cannot be changed by conscious, purposive social action, provided with information and supported by legitimacy. Change will occur if

- people are informed and active and communicate throughout the world;
- business assumes its social responsibility;
- the media become the messengers, rather than the message; and
- political actors react against cynicism and restore belief in democracy.

CONTEXT

Manuel Castells has been described as "a sociologist with a European's bent for the large-scale sweep of history." *The Information Age* is a sprawling, literate, visionary, and densely argued piece of work that offers a catalog of evidence for the arrival of a new global, networked-based culture through linked investigations of contemporary global, economic, political, and social change.

Marshall McLuhan introduced the phrase "global village," referring to the impact of worldwide communications on national differences. Castells disagrees. Although the communications revolution enables the global distribution of information about major events, he claims we do not live in a global village. We live in customized cottages globally produced and locally distributed.

FOR MORE INFORMATION

Castells, Manuel. *The Information Age: Economy, Society and Culture.* Oxford: Blackwell Publishers Ltd. *Volume I: The Rise of the Network Society* (1996); *Volume II: The Power of Identity* (1997); *Volume III: End of Millennium* (1998).

Information Rules
CARL SHAPIRO AND HAL R. VARIAN

WHY READ IT?
Like Collins and Porras's *Built to Last*, this book argues that old-fashioned business principles are still vital to success in the new economy. It reminds anyone considering a start-up or rapid expansion that profits and long-term customer relationships still matter in the end. The book is a good balance to other works that argue speed is the only determinant of success.

GETTING STARTED
Technology changes; economic principles don't. Dot-com flotations seemed to indicate that the economic rules had changed, but falling markets and high-profile dot-com crashes confirm that profits still matter. Companies ignore basic economic principles at their own risk, as such principles still offer strategic value.

Information and analysis are critical to success, and pricing must be based on hard information. Information can also be used to differentiate products through personalization.

According to the authors, new economy business methods rely too much on forecasts and analogies. This can be a dangerous way to analyze strategies.

CONTRIBUTION
1. Technology Changes; Economic Principles Don't
Early in 2000, lastminute.com's flotation gave it the same market value as the long-established, bricks-and-mortar retailer, WH Smith. This seemed to confirm that the economic paradigm had been shifted by online businesses.

The message appeared to be, "Don't worry about this year's numbers, just imagine the potential a few years down the road." Share prices soared in line. Then the markets fell, followed by a series of high-profile dot-com crashes. This seemed to confirm that the Internet's period of grace was over.

The message is that profits still matter. Companies ignore basic economic principles at their own risk. Technology changes. Economic laws do not.

2. Classic Economic Principles Still Offer Strategic Value
Classic economic principles can still offer strategic value in a marketplace that depends on cutting-edge information technology. According to Shapiro and Varian, key issues include
- pricing and versioning information,
- rights management,
- recognizing and managing lock-in,
- switching costs, and
- factoring government policy and regulation into strategy.

3. Pricing in the New Economy
Analyze and understand how much you invest in producing and selling your product. If you are forced to compete in a commodity market, be aggressive but not greedy. Differentiate your product by personalizing the information and the price.

Invest in collecting and analyzing data about your market. Use the information about your customers to sell them personalized products at personalized prices.

Analyze the profitability of selling to groups, for example, site licenses.

4. The Risks of New Economy Business Analysis

Many books about the impact of technology are attempts to forecast the future, but the methodology for forecasting these trends is unclear. Typically, it is just extrapolation from recent developments.

Many authors use analogies like restoring an ecosystem, fighting a war, or making love to describe business strategy. Shapiro and Varian write that business strategy is business strategy, and though analogies can sometimes be helpful, they can be a dangerous way to analyze strategies.

Models, concepts, and analysis provide a deeper understanding of the fundamental forces at work in today's high-tech industries and enable companies to craft winning strategies for tomorrow's network economy.

CONTEXT

Information Rules sets out to show that, though technology changes, basic economic principles do not. Written by two Harvard economists, the book is rigorous in its analysis and convincing in its grip of the subject. It is not by any means an easy read, but it is accessible to the general reader who is prepared to concentrate.

The authors warn readers against new economy books that rely on trends. Their view is that the methodology for forecasting these trends is unclear; typically, it is just extrapolation from recent developments. They prefer forecasting to be based on durable economic principles that have been proven to work in practice.

They also caution against the overuse of analogies in business books. Analogies, they believe, can sometimes be helpful, but they can also be misleading.

They recommend models, not trends; concepts, not vocabulary; and analysis, not analogies. These traditional approaches provide a deeper understanding of the fundamental forces at work in today's high-tech industries and enable companies to craft winning strategies for tomorrow's network economy.

> We won't tell you that devising business strategy is like restoring an ecosystem, fighting a war, or making love. Business strategy is business strategy.

FOR MORE INFORMATION

Shapiro, Carl, and Hal R. Varian. *Information Rules: A Strategic Guide to the Network Economy*. Boston: Harvard Business School Press, 1999.

Innovation in Marketing
THEODORE LEVITT

WHY READ IT?

Levitt's views on the importance of marketing are highly regarded. His article "Marketing Myopia" (reprinted in the book) was one of the most popular *Harvard Business Review* articles ever published. It highlights how narrow perspectives result from companies focusing on production rather than customers.

GETTING STARTED

Historical success encouraged the belief that low-cost production was the key to success, but this inevitably leads to narrow perspectives. According to Ted Levitt's influential book, companies must broaden their view of the nature of their business and should be marketing-led rather than production-led. The emphasis is on providing customer-creating value satisfactions.

There is no such thing as a growth industry; success comes from being perceptive enough to spot where future growth may lie. Companies fail because they assume continued growth, believe that a product cannot be improved, and concentrate on improved production techniques to deliver lower costs. Mass-production industries aim to produce all they can, and marketing gets neglected.

CONTRIBUTION
1. A Focus on Customers

Levitt argues that the central preoccupation of corporations should be with satisfying customers rather than simply producing goods. Companies should be marketing-led rather than production-led. Management must think of itself not as producing products but as providing customer-creating value satisfactions. The lead must come from the chief executive and senior management.

2. Problems of Production-led Companies

Henry Ford's success in mass production fueled the belief that low-cost production was the key to business success. Ford continued to believe that he knew what customers wanted, long after they had decided otherwise.

Production-led thinking inevitably leads to narrow perspectives.

3. Narrow Perspectives

> The central preoccupation of corporations should be with satisfying customers rather than simply producing goods.

Companies must broaden their view of the nature of their business; otherwise their customers will soon be forgotten. The railroads are in trouble today not because the need was filled by others, but because it was not filled by the railroads themselves. They let others take customers away from them because they assumed they were in the railroad business rather than in the transportation business—they were product-oriented instead of customer-oriented.

The railroad business was constrained by a lack of willingness to expand its horizons. Similarly, the movie industry failed to respond to the growth of television because it regarded itself as being in the business of making movies rather than providing entertainment.

4. Taking Growth for Granted

Growth can never be taken for granted, asserts the author. History is filled with companies that fell undetected into decay because

- they assumed that the growth in their particular market would continue for as long as the population grew in size and wealth;
- they believed that a product could not be surpassed; or
- they put faith in the ability of improved production techniques to deliver lower costs and, therefore, higher profits.

5. Problems of Mass-production Industries

Mass-production industries are impelled by a great drive to produce all they can. The prospect of steeply declining unit costs as output rises is more than most companies can usually resist. The profit possibilities look spectacular, so all effort focuses on production.

Concentration on the product, in Levitt's view, also lends itself to measurement and analysis. The result is that marketing gets neglected.

6. Distinguishing Selling and Marketing

There is a distinction between the tasks of selling and marketing. Selling concerns itself with the tricks and techniques of getting people to exchange their cash for a product; it is not concerned with the values that the exchange is all about. It does not, as marketing invariably does, view the entire business process as consisting of a tightly integrated effort to discover, create, arouse, and satisfy customer needs.

CONTEXT

Ted Levitt's fame was secured early in his career with "Marketing Myopia," a *Harvard Business Review* article that enjoyed unprecedented success and attention, selling more 500,000 reprints. It has since been reproduced in virtually every collection of key marketing texts. "Marketing Myopia" is a manifesto rather than a deeply academic article. It embraces ideas that had already been explored by others (Levitt acknowledges his debt to Peter Drucker's book *The Practice of Management*).

In the 1980s, when marketing underwent a resurgence, companies began to heed Levitt's view that they were too heavily oriented toward production. Levitt's article and his subsequent work pushed marketing to center stage. In some cases it led to what Levitt called marketing mania, with companies obsessively responsive to every fleeting whim of the customer.

Influential writer Gary Hamel said:

> If Ted Levitt had done nothing else in his career—and he did plenty—he would have earned his keep on this planet with the article "Marketing Myopia." Managers get wrapped up inside their products (railroads) and lose sight of the fundamental benefits customers are seeking (transportation). Equally provocative was Ted's 1983 *Harvard Business Review* article, "The Globalization of Markets." While some argue that markets will never become truly global, there are few companies that are betting against the general trend.

FOR MORE INFORMATION

Levitt, Theodore. *Innovation in Marketing*. New York: McGraw-Hill, 1962.

The Innovator's Dilemma
CLAYTON M. CHRISTENSEN

There are times at which it is right not to listen to customers, right to invest in developing lower-performance products that promise lower margins, and right to aggressively pursue small, rather than substantial markets.

WHY READ IT?

This book faces up to a fundamental problem facing innovative companies—how to deal with breakthrough technologies when customers may not be ready for them. It argues that normal practice—focusing investment and development on the most profitable products, those that are in demand among top customers—may ultimately be damaging. The risk is that companies may reject innovative products that do not meet this criterion. Here Christensen explains how to overcome this problem and manage breakthrough products successfully.

GETTING STARTED

This book examines a variety of leading, well-managed companies that have failed to capitalize on innovative technologies. The dilemma is that it is often sound decisions by good managers that lead to failure. The author distinguishes between sustaining technologies, which foster improved performance, and disruptive technologies, which represent a breakthrough, but may initially lead to poorer performance. Examples of disruptive technologies include cellular telephones, digital photography, and online retailing.

Part of the problem, according to Christensen, is that the market may not be ready for the new technology. In other cases, leading customers may not be willing to risk a new product. Companies therefore focus on the safe bets, but may subsequently be overtaken by innovation.

CONTRIBUTION
1. Control by Customers

The disk drive industry shows the dilemma in action. The author explains how the major players in the industry used sustaining technologies to offer their customers improved performance.

New entrants introduced disruptive technologies, such as smaller floppy disks that required new computer architecture. These innovations, however, were initially rejected by customers, until they became a proven technology. The author concludes that, to a degree, the larger companies were controlled by their customers.

2. Value Networks

Christensen offers a possible explanation for failure in these cases—the concept of the "value network." This is a technique companies can use to assess the value of a new technology in relation to their current business and customer base. It asks what rewards the company would obtain from reallocating resources away from mainstream products.

The author believes that the problem is compounded by the scope of the company's suppliers and subcontractors. Each may have its own value network based on the needs of its own customers. Innovative ideas that come up from subcontractors may be stifled in the same way as internal ideas.

The author explains that the cost and profit structures in a value network can limit the attractiveness of an innovation. If profit margins are low, the emphasis will be on cost cutting across proven technologies. Innovation would be too risky. The other response from established companies is to move up market where they can earn more from existing products.

3. Avoiding Risk

Christensen points out that new entrants have frequently forced the pace of innovation with disruptive technologies. Established companies only moved in when there was a definite market. Disruptive technologies do not initially represent large, high-margin opportunities for established companies, and the decision-making structure may rule out innovative ideas.

The author cites five reasons successful companies fail to capitalize on disruptive technologies:

- Customers control the pattern of resource allocation.
- Small markets do not solve the growth needs of large companies.
- It can be difficult to identify successful applications in advance.
- Larger organizations rely on their core competencies and values.
- Technology supply may not equal market demand.

4. The Importance of Spinoffs

Christensen explains that companies that did harness disruptive technologies used a number of management techniques:

- Projects were handled within another "spinoff organization" that had customers who needed the new technology.
- Those same project organizations could get excited about small markets and small wins.
- Failure was an acceptable part of the process as companies proceeded by trial and error to the right solution.
- Companies looked for new markets and developed the market where the disruptive technology offered value.

The author provides examples of large corporations that have established spinoff companies to exploit new technology. Frequently, the corporation pulls the spinoff back into the core business when it proves successful.

CONTEXT

The book claims that overdependence on customer needs can affect a company's success. This argument runs counter to the marketing and customer service books that put customer focus at the top of the corporate agenda.

Books such as *When Giants Learn to Dance* by Rosabeth Moss Kanter (Touchstone, 1990) have pointed out the problems faced by larger corporations that compete in fast-moving technology markets. Christensen's book is unusual in highlighting the problems inherent in what appears to be sound decision making.

FOR MORE INFORMATION

Christensen, Clayton M. *The Innovator's Dilemma: The Revolutionary Book That Will Change the Way You Do Business Forever.* Rev. ed. New York: HarperBusiness, 2003.

Intellectual Capital
THOMAS STEWART

> You cannot define and manage intellectual assets unless you know what you want to do with them.

WHY READ IT?
The author is widely regarded as the world's leading authority on knowledge management, and his views are valuable to any organization that wants to improve the return on its "intellectual capital." The book is a useful guide to the strategic and practical issues of identifying, capturing, and using knowledge to improve a company's competitive advantage.

GETTING STARTED
Traditional capital had financial or physical characteristics. In the author's view, however, the emphasis now is on an intangible asset, intellectual capital, consisting of human, customer, and structural capital. The real value comes in being able to capture and deploy intellectual capital, Stewart argues.

CONTRIBUTION
1. The New Concept of Capital
Traditionally, capital could be viewed in purely financial or physical terms. It showed up in the buildings and equipment owned and could be found in the corporate balance sheets. The author suggests that in recent times, the emphasis has switched to an intangible form of asset, intellectual capital.

2. Human Capital
Human capital is the knowledge residing in the heads of employees that is relevant to the purpose of the organization. Human capital is formed and deployed when more of the time and talent of employees is devoted to activities that result in innovation. It can grow in two ways: when the organization uses more of what people know, and when people know more that is useful to the organization. Unleashing it requires an organization to minimize mindless tasks, meaningless paperwork, and unproductive infighting.

3. Customer Capital
This represents the value of a company's ongoing relationships with the people or organizations to which it sells. Indicators of customer capital include market share, customer retention and defection rates, and profit per customer. Customer capital is probably the worst managed of all intangible assets. Many businesses don't even know who their customers are.

4. Structural Capital
Structural capital is the knowledge retained within the organization. It belongs to the company as a whole and can be reproduced and shared. Structural capital includes technologies, inventions, publications, and business processes.

5. Managing Intellectual Capital

The real value comes in being able to capture and deploy intellectual capital. Knowledge assets exist and are worth cultivating only in the context of strategy. We cannot define and manage intellectual assets unless we know what we want to do with them.

There are ten principles for managing intellectual capital:

1. Companies don't own human and customer capital. Only by recognizing the shared nature of these assets can a company manage and profit from them.
2. To create usable human capital, a company needs to foster teamwork, communities of practice, and other social forms of learning.
3. Organizational wealth is created around skills and talents that are proprietary and scarce. Companies must see people with these talents as assets.
4. Structural assets are the easiest to manage but those that customers care least about.
5. Move from amassing knowledge "just in case" to having readily available information that customers need.
6. Information and knowledge can and should substitute for expensive physical and financial assets.
7. Knowledge work is custom work.
8. Every company should reanalyze its own industry to see what information is most crucial.
9. Focus on the flow of information, not the flow of materials.
10. Human, structural, and customer capital work together. It is not enough to invest in people, systems, and customers separately.

6. Knowledge Working and Individual Careers

Stewart argues that careers in the 21st century will have a number of characteristics:

- A career is a series of "gigs," not a series of steps.
- Project management is the furnace in which successful careers are made.
- Power flows from expertise, not position.
- Most roles in an organization can be performed by either insiders or outsiders.
- Careers are made in markets, not hierarchies.
- The fundamental career choice is not between one company and another, but between specializing and generalizing.

CONTEXT

Thomas Stewart pioneered the field of intellectual capital in a series of articles that earned him an international reputation, with the Planning Forum calling him in 1994, "the leading proponent of knowledge management in the business press."

Intellectual Capital has proved itself as the definitive guide to understanding and managing intangible assets. It not only explains why intellectual capital will be the foundation of corporate success but also offers practical guidance to companies about how to make best use of their intangible assets. Since it first appeared, there has been a flood of books on knowledge management.

FOR MORE INFORMATION

Stewart, Thomas. *Intellectual Capital: The New Wealth of Organizations*. New York: Doubleday, 1998.

Jack: Straight from the Gut
JACK WELCH AND JOHN A. BYRNE

WHY READ IT?

This book outlines what made former General Electric CEO Jack Welch successful. It explores the lessons he learned from leading. Without technical performance models, Welch knew "from his gut" what individuals needed to reach their potential. *Jack: Straight from the Gut* is both a textbook on leadership and competing and an entertaining and personal account of what made GE one of the most successful companies of the last century. Welch has been a role model for many leaders since becoming GE's youngest ever CEO in 1980, and his vision was critical to the business's success—from when he first addressed city analysts in his new role at GE, he maintained that vision was his main responsibility.

GETTING STARTED

Welch argues that the success of GE owed as much to the outstanding people he led as to his own skill as a leader. However, his intolerance of failure and mediocrity—which he calls "superficial congeniality"—and his ability to motivate and communicate an appealing vision were decisive. His evaluation of managerial talent produced unprecedented improvements in performance. He classified people into three categories: the best 10 percent, the critical 70 percent, and the worst 20 percent. His vision was to nurture and develop the top 10 percent, help the 70 percent meet their goals, and minimize the resources wasted on the bottom 20 percent. He did not differentiate among the most able 10 percent of managers, as this would waste perfectly capable talent—exemplifying Welch's policy of recognizing both the benefits and limitations of competition. This enabled Welch to develop people and reshape a massive company into achieving more.

> Every one of us must walk the talk.

In his efforts to destroy corporate bureaucracy, Welch created a culture of accountability and teamwork. Welch insisted on GE being either first or second in any market. If it wasn't, he would remove GE from, or downsize in, that market. Consequently, GE became more efficient and profitable. Unlike other successful entrepreneurs who believe in visionary thinking, Welch's management style is rooted in the real world. By using stock options as an incentive, he forced managers to relate their decisions to the reality of the marketplace.

CONTRIBUTION
1. Competing

Welch explains that a competitive spirit is fundamental to his own character as well as GE's organizational culture. It was a component of GE's success, motivating people to do better and to value excellence. He argues that competing effectively is about learning from one's mistakes, working as a team, and having confidence. Ambition is important when competing.

2. Motivating

Welch describes how, in 1963, after three years at GE, he blew up a factory. As the manager, he was responsible and took responsibility. Welch was not punished, however; instead he was encouraged to learn from his mistakes and be honest about them. Bearing this example in mind, Welch explains his view that when people make mistakes, the last thing they need is to be disciplined. Instead, their self-confidence needs to be restored so that they can improve. Motivation is a key theme in this book, and Welch is keen to emphasize that he always felt he was in the "people business." He feels that any company's greatest resource is its people, and at GE, motivating others enabled him to use his resources more effectively.

3. Focusing

According to Welch, a clear focus is essential to succeed in business. Winning requires a focus on what needs to be done and an elimination of waste. Welch explains how his policy of "fix, close, or sell" involved only operating in areas where GE was first or second in the market. If GE could improve its performance in a particular area to lead the market, it could "fix" itself; otherwise, it would either be closed or sold. This applied to staff as well; the best were rewarded, the majority were developed so that they could reach their full potential, and those who performed worst were "made redundant."

CONTEXT

In 1980 GE was a massive bureaucracy. The CEO was removed 12 levels from the factory floor. Having worked on the frontline, Welch had a strong prejudice against that type of bureaucratic culture. He brought significant change to GE by integrating innovative practices into many different areas of the business. Other companies were also developing some of these practices, such as e-commerce or cost-cutting, but GE under Welch's leadership was unique in focusing on the power of competition to develop people. Welch's search for the best talent to manage GE made a large company both efficient and good at creating new ideas. He created a meritocracy that was the foundation of GE's success.

FOR MORE INFORMATION

Welch, Jack, and John A. Byrne. *Jack: Straight from the Gut*. Rev. ed. New York: Headline, 2003.

The Knowledge-creating Company
IKUJIRO NONAKA AND HIROTAKA TAKEUCHI

WHY READ IT?
The book focuses on the development of organizational knowledge in Japanese companies. The authors explain how this knowledge forms the basis of innovations that have enabled Japanese companies to become world leaders in many different market sectors. They show that the ability to acquire and apply knowledge is becoming a key factor for success in the transition from an industrial economy to an information economy.

GETTING STARTED
Nonaka and Takeuchi believe that historical adversity has forced Japanese companies to pursue a policy of continuous innovation. Organizational knowledge, according to them, is the ability of a company to create new knowledge, disseminate it throughout the organization, and embody it in innovative products, services, and systems. They distinguish between explicit knowledge, such as rules or formulas, and tacit knowledge, which is gained from experience and can rarely be learned. The Japanese, they claim, are very effective at turning tacit knowledge into explicit knowledge that can be shared throughout an organization.

CONTRIBUTION
1. Characteristics of Knowledge Creation
According to the authors, there are three key characteristics of knowledge creation:
- metaphor and analogy;
- the transition from personal to organizational knowledge; and
- ambiguity and redundancy.

  The use of metaphor and analogy helps companies to visualize difficult concepts and explain them to other people within an organization. The transition from personal to organizational knowledge depends on the successful implementation of teamwork so that individuals can interact with each other. The concept of ambiguity and redundancy means that Japanese companies are happy to take a number of different approaches to innovation, some of which are bound to fail. They use redundancy to encourage creativity and identify what does not work in practical terms.

2. Knowledge Management
The authors review theories of knowledge from ancient times onward. They analyze recent management writing to identify attitudes toward the question of knowledge. They cite Peter Drucker's "knowledge worker" and Peter Senge's "learning organization" as important concepts in knowledge creation. They also discuss the concept of core competencies and argue that this can distract companies. Core competencies, they argue, suggest that knowledge is an existing, finite resource within a company. Knowledge creation, on the other hand, emphasizes the importance of acquiring and developing knowledge from as many internal and external sources as possible.

3. How Knowledge Creation Works
The authors claim that there are four key processes in knowledge conversion: socialization; externalization; combination; internalization.

An example of socialization is the brainstorming camps established by Honda to solve difficult production problems. Externalization is the process of using metaphors or analogies to communicate difficult concepts in product development. Combination is the process of sorting, adding, combining, and synthesizing various types of knowledge to create new knowledge. Internalization is like learning other people's experiences or learning by doing.

4. The Environment for Knowledge Creation

To create a suitable environment for knowledge creation, the authors stress the importance of vision to guide overall direction and autonomy to allow everyone in the organization to get involved in the process.

They describe a structure called "middle-up-down management" that underpins knowledge creation. This structure contrasts with the bottom-up or top-down management styles found in Western companies. The Japanese model puts middle managers at the heart of the process, acting between frontline workers and a visionary senior management team. The authors believe that this type of structure creates dialogue and builds positive relationships between the individual specialists who contribute to a development project.

> To these companies, change is an everyday event and a positive force.

5. Hypertext Organizations

Nonaka and Takeuchi refer to the concept of a "knowledge crew," consisting of knowledge engineers and knowledge practitioners. Underpinning this is what they call a "hypertext organization." This is an organization with multiple layers:

- a business system layer
- a project team layer
- a knowledge base layer

The business system layer and project team layer generate different types of knowledge, which are brought together in the knowledge base, which can be shared throughout the organization.

CONTEXT

A number of books have looked at the process of innovation, trying to identify the factors that distinguish a successful innovator. The authors offer both theoretical and practical insight into the way that Japanese companies use knowledge as the basis for innovation. Their findings are in contrast with the widespread Western view that Japanese success is based on access to cheap capital, lifetime employment, culture, or quality.

The authors draw on a wide variety of Western management sources to highlight the differences between Japanese and Western practice. Among others, they quote Peter Drucker and Alvin Toffler on the importance of knowledge, and Peter Senge on the concept of the "learning organization."

FOR MORE INFORMATION

Nonaka, Ikujiro, and Hirotaka Takeuchi. *The Knowledge-creating Company: How Japanese Companies Create the Dynamics of Innovation.* New York: Oxford University Press, 1995.

Leaders: Strategies for Taking Charge
WARREN BENNIS AND BURT NANUS

WHY READ IT?

Warren Bennis is an academic and presidential adviser who brought the discussion of leadership to a new mass audience. He is regarded as one of the most important contemporary thinkers. Burt Nanus is the founder and director of the Center of Futures Research at the University of Southern California. In this book the authors use an eclectic selection of U.S. leaders to offer the readers key lessons on how to become successful. Their message is that leadership is open to all.

GETTING STARTED

> None of us is as smart as all of us.

According to the authors, good leaders commit people to action and convert followers into leaders. They are usually ordinary people rather than particularly charismatic, as leadership is all-encompassing and open to all.

Successful leaders also have a vision that other people believe in and communicate it effectively. Instead of being individual problem solvers, they achieve greatness through working effectively with groups. Devising and maintaining an atmosphere in which others can succeed is the leader's creative act.

CONTRIBUTION
1. The Ordinary Leader

Leadership is not a rare skill—leaders are made rather than born. They are usually ordinary people, or apparently ordinary, rather than obviously charismatic. Leadership is not solely the preserve of those at the top of an organization; it is relevant at all levels. Leadership is not about control, direction, and manipulation.

2. Common Abilities of Leaders

From a survey of 90 U.S. leaders (including Neil Armstrong, the coach of the LA Rams, orchestral conductors, and businesspeople such as Ray Kroc of McDonald's), Bennis and Nanus identified four common abilities:

- management of attention
- management of meaning
- management of trust
- management of self

Management of Attention   This is a question of vision. Leadership is the capacity to create a compelling vision, translate it into action, and sustain it. Successful leaders have a vision that other people believe in and treat as their own.

Management of Meaning   A vision is of limited practical use if it is encased in 400 pages of wordy text or mumbled from behind a paper-packed desk. Effective communication relies on use of analogy, metaphor, and vivid illustration as well as emotion, trust, optimism, and hope.

Management of Trust   Trust is the emotional glue that binds followers and leaders together. In the authors' view leaders have to be seen to be consistent.

Management of Self   Leaders do not glibly present charisma or time management as the essence of their success. Instead, the emphasis is on persistence and self-knowledge, commitment and challenge, taking risks, and, above all, learning. The learning person looks forward to failure or mistakes, which means that the worst problem in leadership is basically early success. There's no opportunity to learn from adversity and problems.

3. A Positive Self-regard

Leaders have a positive self-regard, known as emotional wisdom. This is characterized by an ability to accept people as they are. They also have a capacity to approach things in terms of only the present and an ability to treat everyone, even close contacts, with courteous attention. They need an ability to trust others and to do without constant approval and recognition.

4. Leaders and Group Working

Greatness starts with superb people. Great groups don't exist without great leaders, but they give the lie to the persistent notion that successful institutions are the lengthened shadow of a great woman or man. It's not clear that life was ever so simple that individuals, acting alone, solved most significant problems. Instead of the individual problem solver, we have a new model for creative achievement.

5. Changing Leadership Qualities

According to Bennis and Nanus, the leader is a pragmatic dreamer, a person with an original but attainable vision. He or she knows that this dream can only be realized if others are free to do exceptional work. Typically, the leader is the one who recruits the others, by making the vision so seductive that they see it, too, and eagerly sign up.

Inevitably, the leader has to invent a leadership style that suits the group. Command and control simply don't work. The heads of groups have to act decisively, not arbitrarily. They have to make decisions without limiting the autonomy of other participants.

6. The Idealistic Leader

Individual leaders can create a human community that will, in the long run, lead to the best organizations. "A Great Group is more than a collection of first-rate minds. It's a miracle," say the authors. Every person wants to make a genuine contribution in his or her life, and the institution of work is one of the main vehicles to achieving this.

CONTEXT

With the torrent of publications and executive programs on the subject, it is easy to forget that leadership had been largely overlooked as a topic worthy of serious academic interest until it was revived by Bennis and others in the 1980s. Since then, leadership has become a heavy industry. Concern and interest about leadership development is no longer a U.S. phenomenon; it is truly global.

FOR MORE INFORMATION

Bennis, Warren, and Burt Nanus. *Leaders: Strategies for Taking Charge*. 2nd ed. New York: Collins, 2003.

Leadership
RUDOLPH W. GIULIANI

WHY READ IT?

Leadership covers the lessons former New York City Mayor Giuliani learned from his own experiences both during the September 11, 2001, terrorist atrocities in New York and from a lifetime of taking the helm effectively. The author describes how the leadership rules he practiced enabled him to gain control on September 11 as well as throughout his term as mayor. He compares the art of writing and researching to the art of politics—both are about persuading others to interpret things as you do. In *Leadership*, Giuliani explores the events and ideas that influenced him as a leader.

GETTING STARTED

Any leader, whatever the size of his or her business, may use Giuliani's rules for leadership to succeed. Giuliani demonstrated an important characteristic of good leaders during the events of September 11—emotional strength. With little experience in responding to a national emergency, Giuliani improvised. In his view, being able to learn and to be affected by circumstances is critical to good leadership. While we learn from personal experience, we can also learn entirely new ideas and incorporate them into our approach.

CONTRIBUTION
1. Be Accountable

When he was mayor of New York City, Giuliani had a sign on his desk saying "I'M RE-SPONSIBLE." He feels that leaders need to accept the blame if things go wrong—and expect similar standards from others. The accountability systems Giuliani established enabled the police to focus on and tackle crime more effectively. Giuliani instituted an accountability system for police command areas that won the 1996 Harvard Innovation in Government Award. Every week the leaders of the eight command areas would defend their performance to all the other leaders, which gave them a strong incentive to boost their performance and maintain standards. Giuliani recommends that reliable systems be put in place to provide data on performance, which can prevent disputes over blame.

> It's not a popularity contest.

2. Believe and Deliver

These two tools are about communicating a sense of authority and competence. Successful leaders manage expectations as well as results. This requires, as Giuliani puts it, "avoiding mentioning what you've done until you've actually accomplished something." Announce initiatives once you know they work. "Underpromising" focuses the internal team. The author cites as an example New York's budgeting process during his time in office. He often projected revenues to fall by up to 2 percent, to produce a frugal, lean culture. If revenues were higher than expected, the city gained a budget surplus, boosting the economy and the mayor's popularity at the same time.

Belief is also a powerful leadership tool, in Giuliani's view. Many people never develop strong beliefs at work, partly because they fear the consequences of rocking the boat. Consequently, things are done the way they were in the past, which is not necessarily the best way. This eliminates creativity. Inspirational leaders communicate positive beliefs to others and maintain firm beliefs themselves, while staying flexible only when uncertain. You can't lead people if you don't know *where* to lead them.

3. Think and Organize

Most organizational structures do not correspond to the organization's real purpose. Giuliani demonstrates the importance of "aligning the system with the purpose," using the example of the budget director's lack of visibility within the New York structure before he took office. The budget director controlled annual expenditures of $40 billion yet reported only to the deputy mayor. The budget director was rarely present at critical meetings, so financial constraints were rarely priorities. Giuliani made the budget director report to him directly and encouraged his participation in senior management meetings, which improved efficiency and team performance. Organizational structures must reflect the purpose, rather than generating alternative priorities that distract.

Giuliani argues that when you are making important decisions, it is advisable first to envision alternative scenarios. The longer you have to make a decision, the better chance you have of coming up with a mature and well-reasoned solution. When you are faced with a complex problem, the wisest approach is to reflect in more depth. Disasters occur when decisions are taken without enough thinking or when alternative scenarios are ignored. Giuliani explores how better organization and greater reflection—both part of a more rational decision-making process—produce spectacular success.

4. Funerals Are Mandatory

Difficult events in the lives of a team require leadership, strengthening the ties that bind people together. Giuliani argues that the real measure of a leader is taken during such tough times as funerals, when our fundamental responses are heightened. Emotional support is critical to effective leadership, and well-being is key to people's success. During difficult times, weak links break while strong ones are cemented, and as Giuliani explains, leaders who contribute during such times gain respect.

CONTEXT

Leadership, like parenthood, is something that many people aspire to. Yet isolating the characteristics of all great leaders is impossible. Different leaders exhibit different traits—the successful are, by definition, unusual. Giuliani's insight into the importance of leading during tough times derives from his experience on September 11, but his other achievements are well documented: Crime rates fell, while living standards and prosperity improved, during his tenure as mayor of New York City. *Time* magazine's "Person of the Year 2001" did not become a great leader on September 11, 2001, when he was soon to leave office; he had long understood the need to make hard decisions. Giuliani was often satisfied with being unpopular, writing "I thought I was doing a good job if anger was coming from a variety of sources—white collar criminals, mobsters, corrupt politicians, narcotic traffickers. It's not a popularity contest." Instead of chasing shallow popularity by avoiding confrontation, he faced problems head on with "zero tolerance" for failure, an important lesson for any leader to learn.

FOR MORE INFORMATION

Giuliani, Rudolph W. *Leadership*. New York: Miramax Books, 2002.

Leadership
JAMES MACGREGOR BURNS

> If we know all too much about our leaders, we know far too little about leadership.

WHY READ IT?

In *Leadership*, Burns makes an important contribution to management literature by refocusing interest on the nature of leadership. He brings practical insights from both business and politics and has used them to identify two key strands—transactional and transformational leadership.

GETTING STARTED

Burns believes we know too much about our leaders, but too little about leadership. Leadership is a structure for action, not the preserve of the few or the tyranny of the masses.

Burns identifies two vital strands of leadership—transformational and transactional leadership. Transactional leadership is built on reciprocity—the relationship between the leader and his or her followers develops from the exchange of some reward. The secret of effective leadership appears to lie in combining the two elements so that targets, results, and procedures are developed and shared.

CONTRIBUTION
1. Problems in Defining Leadership

There are literally hundreds of definitions of leadership and, as a result, the concept "has dissolved into small and discrete meanings," Burns claims.

2. Leadership as a Structure for Action

Leadership is exercised when people with certain motives and purposes mobilize—in competition or conflict with others—institutional, political, psychological, and other resources so as to arouse, engage, and satisfy the motives of followers. According to the author, the leadership approach tends often unconsciously to be elitist; it projects heroic figures against the shadowy background of drab, powerless masses. The followership approach tends to be populist or anti-elitist in ideology, perceiving the masses, even in democratic societies, as linked with small, overlapping circles of conservative politicians, military officers, hierocrats, and businesspeople.

Leadership is a structure for action that engages people, to varying degrees, throughout the levels and among the interstices of society. Only the inert, the alienated, and the powerless are unengaged. It is also intrinsically linked to morality—moral leadership emerges from, and always returns to, the fundamental wants and needs, aspirations, and values of the followers.

3. Transformational Leadership

This form of leadership occurs when one or more persons engage with others in such a way that leaders and followers raise one another to higher levels of motivation and morality. Their purposes, which might have started out separate but related, become fused. Power bases are linked, not as counterweights, but as mutual support for common purpose. Various descriptions are used for such leadership: elevating, mobilizing, inspiring, exalting, uplifting, exhorting, evangelizing.

It becomes moral in that it raises the level of human conduct and ethical aspiration of both the leader and the led, thus having a transforming effect on both. It is also dynamic, in the sense that the leaders throw themselves into a relationship with followers who will feel elevated by it and often become more active themselves, thereby creating new cadres of leaders.

Transformational leadership is concerned with engaging the hearts and minds of others. It works to help all parties achieve greater motivation, satisfaction, and sense of achievement. It is driven by trust, concern, and facilitation rather than direct control. The skills required are concerned with establishing a long-term vision, empowering people to control themselves, coaching and developing others, and challenging the culture to change. In transformational leadership, the power of the leader comes from creating understanding and trust.

4. Transactional Leadership

Transactional leadership is built on reciprocity. The relationship between the leader and his or her followers develops from the exchange of some reward, such as performance ratings, pay, recognition, and praise. It involves leaders in clarifying goals and objectives, communicating well in order to plan tasks and activities with the cooperation of their employees, so that wider organizational goals are met.

The relationship depends on hierarchy and the ability to work through the mode of exchange. It requires leadership skills such as the ability to obtain results, control through structures and processes, solve problems, plan and organize, and work within the structures and boundaries of the organization.

5. Combining Transformational and Transactional Leadership

In their apparent mutual exclusiveness, transformational and transactional leadership are akin to Douglas McGregor's Theories X and Y. The secret of effective leadership appears to lie in combining the two elements so that targets, results, and procedures are developed and shared.

CONTEXT

Burns's book provides an important link between leadership in the political and business worlds. The two have usually been regarded as mutually exclusive. His examination of transformational and transactional leadership also stimulated further debate on leadership at a time when it was somewhat neglected. In the 1980s it returned to prominence in management literature as a subject worthy of study.

Business guru Gary Hamel commented on this book: "There is no theme in management literature which is more enduring than leadership. Among the many contributions which Burns makes to our understanding of leadership, two seem central: leadership must have a moral foundation; and the responsibility for leadership must be widely distributed. Self-interested autocrats, whether political or corporate, ignore these truths at their peril."

FOR MORE INFORMATION

Burns, James MacGregor. *Leadership*. New York: HarperPerennial, 1982.

Leading Change
JOHN P. KOTTER

WHY READ IT?
Kotter is regarded as one of the world's leading figures in change management. This book sets forth the real problem of change management and includes dozens of examples of effective change management in action.

GETTING STARTED
Kotter believes that successful change is based on an eight-stage process:

1. establishing a sense of urgency
2. creating the guiding coalition
3. developing a vision and strategy
4. communicating the change vision
5. empowering employees
6. generating short-term wins
7. consolidating gains and producing more change
8. anchoring new approaches in the culture

CONTRIBUTION
1. Why Change Fails
Kotter opines that most business transformations fail because they do not meet the criteria set out in his eight-point plan. He believes that the pace of change is driven by forces such as technological development, international economic integration, and the globalization of markets and competition.

The result, according to Kotter, is that there are either more opportunities or more hazards, depending on whether an organization can adapt or not. He then explains how successful change goes through the eight-stage process. He adds, however, that it is essential to go through all the stages in sequence. He also believes that change must be led, not managed.

2. A Sense of Urgency
Establishing a sense of urgency helps to get the cooperation needed for change. A committed group, Kotter argues, can drive change through. He suggests a number of approaches for increasing the urgency level:

- creating a vision
- setting targets so high they cannot be achieved through business as usual
- getting staff to talk to customers
- showing that opportunities cannot be achieved by the present organization

3. Building the Guiding Coalition
Kotter's second stage is building the "guiding coalition." He believes that an isolated chief executive or a weak committee cannot cope with the pace of change. The coalition must comprise people with power, expertise, credibility, and leadership. Leadership is key, because change must be led, not managed. He explains why the coalition must be built on trust and a common goal, noting that team-building exercises can be an important part of that process.

4. Developing a Vision
According to Kotter, a vision clarifies the direction of change. Other decisions must be in line with the vision. Vision also helps to align individuals and motivate them in an efficient

way. He believes that a vision should be imaginable, desirable, feasible, focused, flexible, and communicable.

5. Communicating the Change Vision

Kotter argues that a vision has real power only when it is communicated effectively. Effective communication is vital because employees receive vast amounts of information, and communications about change can easily get lost. Kotter's advice is to keep it simple, use metaphors, keep repeating the message, listen, and lead by example.

6. Empowering Employees

Turning the vision into action means removing structural barriers to change so that employees are empowered, says Kotter. That may require training, reorganization, aligning information and systems to the vision, and confronting people who try to restrict change.

7. Generating Short-term Wins

According to Kotter, short-term wins are essential. They are visible and show that change is producing results. They also help to fine-tune the change process, build momentum, and reward the people who are delivering change. Pressure and challenging targets can help to deliver the gains.

8. Consolidating Gains

Kotter believes that all gains need to be consolidated to keep the process moving. This is particularly important in companies where there is a high level of interdependence. Maintaining momentum also requires strong leadership, effective project management, and support for the people who are effecting change.

9. Anchoring New Approaches

The final stage in Kotter's process is anchoring the new approaches in the corporate culture. He argues that the new behavior should become the norm. Ideally, everyone in the organization should have shared values. Kotter believes that achieving this level of acceptance depends on results. It may even require changing key people.

CONTEXT

The study of change has gained importance as competition has intensified and other structural factors impact the business environment. Kotter's work demonstrates the positive aspects of effective change. It also shows that strong leadership is essential if change is to succeed. On the other hand, in *Managing Transitions* (Perseus, 1991), William Bridges puts more emphasis on management of the personal consequences of change, highlighting the need to reduce anxiety and manage the process he calls "transition." Hammer and Champy's book *Reengineering the Corporation* (Collins, 2004) took change to a logical conclusion and showed how companies would have to transform themselves to compete effectively.

> If environmental volatility continues to increase as most people now predict, the standard organization of the twentieth century will likely become a dinosaur.

FOR MORE INFORMATION

Kotter, John P. *Leading Change.* Boston: Harvard Business School Press, 1996.

Liar's Poker
MICHAEL LEWIS

WHY READ IT?

Beyond economic history, *Liar's Poker* explores the characters and forces behind Salomon Brothers' bond-trading empire in the 1980s. This autobiographical account of the author's sojourn working for that company analyzes the costs and benefits of competition between individuals and between firms. He emphasizes how a culture of excessive competition contributed to Salomon's financial collapse, along with the recession following the crash of 1987–1988. An entertaining insight into human nature, *Liar's Poker* explores the drivers of success and failure in a complex, dynamic financial environment.

GETTING STARTED

The 1980s saw a boom in the U.S. mortgage market. *Liar's Poker* explains the drivers of that bubble but also explores the personal factors contributing to Salomon's (and the author's) changing fortunes. From his own experience at Salomon's rapidly developing mortgage bond desk, Lewis explains bond trading: buying and selling shares in debt. Salomon made mortgage debt tradable in a market with few buyers and only them trading, which proved to be a profitable monopoly. The sector reached maturity between 1983 and 1986, with the number of buyers rising; other firms entered the market, increasing competition. Together with worsening economic circumstances, this caused the bubble to collapse.

The book's title is particularly apt. The game of liar's poker is played on Wall Street. People form a circle, each holding a dollar bill to his or her chest and trying to fool others about its serial number. A player makes a "bid" suggesting, for example, "three sixes"— meaning all serial numbers contain three sixes. Players continue to bid as follows. The next player either makes a bid with higher numbers or challenges, in which case all players show their numbers. Bidding escalates until a challenge is made. Good players calculate probabilities of number combinations; great players read others' faces to gain critical information. Lewis feels that "in any market, as in any poker game, there is a fool." The person who doesn't know who the fool is probably is the fool! Salomon failed to use information to understand its competitors.

CONTRIBUTION
1. Culture and Loyalty

In *Liar's Poker*, the reader is shown how an organization's culture is critical to its success. In the 1980s, the culture of bond trading became increasingly competitive and ambitious. Weak traders were exposed by their failures, and the strong—"big swinging dicks"— commanded unprecedented salaries and bonuses. Salomon faced juxtaposing its hierarchical structure, culture, and outlook with a competitive, meritocratic environment. Rewarding successful traders became an issue. Lewis explains how most, including chairman John Gutfreund, were unwilling to pay substantial bonuses to successful young traders, despite their sizeable contribution to profits. Denied these benefits, the traders joined competitors, ultimately causing profits to fall. The author highlights how success relies on managing culture and cultural change and how he himself left Salomon, alienated by their undervaluing his efforts.

2. Communication and Information

Information is critical. In a poker game, reading others' expressions improves the likelihood of success. In a dynamic market, communicating with customers, competitors, and one's team is essential. At Salomon, communication was restricted, leaving bond salesmen on the floor below the main trading floor feeling distanced from the "big swinging dicks" above. This reinforced traders' unwillingness to share information and strengthened the culture of internal competition. Furthermore, it created clear winners and losers: Underperforming traders were marginalized, being unable to take credit for others' profits. Managing employees' access to information is important. In Lewis's view, the collapse of Salomon Brothers mortgage department was the result of poor communication between business units, a lack of market awareness, and dwindling employee loyalty.

> In any market, as in any poker game, there is a fool.

3. Competition and Customers

Actively competing with others is often key to success in a business environment, but competition at the expense of teamworking can be disastrous. Lewis attributes Salomon's difficulties after 1987 to its management's lack of focus and their behaving more like traders than managers—seeking to "manage by the numbers." He quotes a colleague: "Wall Street makes its best producers into managers. The best producers are cut-throat, competitive, and often neurotic and paranoid. You turn those people into managers, and they go after each other." Customers have to come first, and Salomon failed to maintain customer loyalty. Since their traders focused exclusively on commission-based bonuses, they appeared neither to value customers nor to show loyalty to their firm.

CONTEXT

In the 1980s, Paul Volcker's expansionist Federal Reserve drove the boom in the bond market. This policy of floating interest rates made the market volatile, providing traders with profitable opportunities. Another driver was rising debts for federal, municipal, corporate, and consumer borrowers. Trading exploded as traders moved $300 million in bonds each day, compared to $5 million per week in the 1970s. It was the age of greed and ambition. Salomon Brothers profited from structural economic change: Lewis transferred capital, in bonds, from savers outside the U.S. to consumers needing mortgages inside the country. This leveraging brought spectacular wealth.

Salomon's chairman, John Gutfreund, challenged chief trader Meriwether to liar's poker: "one hand, one million dollars, no tears." Beating his boss would be a "career-limiting move" for Meriwether; it was a lose-lose situation. Meriwether responded: "If we're going to play for those kind of numbers, I'd rather play for real money. Ten million dollars. No tears." He gambled that Gutfreund couldn't stomach the risk. Gutfreund declined. Here, Lewis highlights character traits of a successful trader: a fast, ambitious, and addicted gambler. Trading is about risk; the sole determinant of power is managing and defeating risk. Following the dot-com collapse of 2001, *Liar's Poker* has resonance: All good things must come to an end.

FOR MORE INFORMATION

Lewis, Michael. *Liar's Poker: Rising through the Wreckage of Wall Street*. New York: Norton, 1989.

The Living Company: Habits for Survival in a Turbulent Business Environment
ARIE DE GEUS

WHY READ IT?
This book looks at the problem of corporate failure, presenting alarming statistics on the relatively short life of European and Japanese enterprises. The author argues that short-term focus on profits, rather than nurturing people, is a key factor in failure. *The Living Company* is the testimony of someone who practiced the human side of enterprise and who believes that companies must be fundamentally humane to prosper.

GETTING STARTED
The author argues that corporations should last as long as two or three centuries, but the reality is that companies usually die young. Focus on profits rather than on human issues lies behind the high failure rate. However, like all organisms, the living company exists primarily for its own survival and improvement.

A successful company is one that can learn effectively, and senior executives must dedicate a great deal of time to nurturing their people.

CONTRIBUTION
1. The Problem of Corporate Mortality
Companies may be legal entities, but they are disturbingly mortal. The natural average lifespan of a corporation should be as long as two or three centuries—for example, the Sumitomo Group and the Scandinavian company, Stora.

The reality is that companies usually die young. A Dutch survey indicated 12.5 years as the average life expectancy of all Japanese and European firms. The average life expectancy of a multinational corporation—Fortune 500 or its equivalent—is between 40 and 50 years.

2. Reasons for Longevity
The author attributes the high company failure rate to the focus of managers on profits, rather than on the human community that makes up their organization.

In an attempt to get to the bottom of this mystery, de Geus and a number of his Shell colleagues carried out some research to identify the characteristics of corporate longevity. As one would expect, the onus is on keeping excitement to a minimum. The average human centenarian advocates a life of abstinence, caution, and moderation, and so it is with companies.

The research team identified four key characteristics. The long-lived companies were
- sensitive to their environment;
- cohesive, with a strong sense of identity;
- tolerant; and
- conservative in financing.

3. The Importance of People
There is more to a company and to its longevity than mere money making. The skills, capabilities, and knowledge of people are paramount; capital is no longer king.

4. The Learning Company

A successful company is one that can learn effectively. Learning means being prepared to accept continuous change, and a company can only change if its community of people changes.

Individuals change through learning, requiring senior executives to dedicate a great deal of time to nurturing their people. The author recalls spending around a quarter of his time on the development and placement of people; the CEO of GE, Jack Welch, claimed to spend half of his time on such issues.

According to de Geus, all corporate activities are grounded in two hypotheses:
- The company is a living being.
- The decisions for action made by this living being result from a learning process.

Like all organisms, the living company exists primarily for its own survival and improvement. It aims to fulfill its potential and to become as great as it can be.

CONTEXT

With its deep faith in learning, *The Living Company* represents a careful and powerful riposte to corporate nihilism. The book proposes that the wisdom of the past be appreciated and used, rather than cast out in the manner of a cultural revolution.

Contrast this with reengineering, which sought to dismiss the past so that the future could begin with a blank piece of paper. De Geus suggests that the piece of paper already exists, and notes are constantly being scrawled in the margins as new insights are added.

De Geus's arguments are probably at their weakest when he contemplates why companies deserve to live long lives. The average entrepreneur would probably accept a life expectancy of 12.5 years.

The Living Company is the testimony of someone who practiced the human side of enterprise and believes that companies must be fundamentally humane to prosper—whatever the century.

> Learning is tomorrow's capital.

FOR MORE INFORMATION

de Geus, Arie. *The Living Company: Habits for Survival in a Turbulent Business Environment.* Rev. ed. Boston: Harvard Business School Press, 2002.

The Long Tail
CHRIS ANDERSON

WHY READ IT?

In this book, Chris Anderson's rewriting of the laws of production ushers in a new perspective on innovation. Highlighting the profitability of niche products with small but significant markets over blockbuster ideas, *The Long Tail* argues that low barriers to entry enable firms to capitalize on the "endless demand curve." Evolving patterns of production mean that firms can now profitably supply products that have smaller levels of demand. For instance, cult music bands can now be profitable with much smaller audiences than before. The rules of innovation and marketing have changed; the "long tail" refers to the tail of the graph of business ideas, where a small number of products sell exponentially more than the overwhelming majority. Understanding that even products with small groups of potential customers in the global marketplace can be successful is critical to entrepreneurs looking to thrive.

GETTING STARTED

The popularity contest between products and services is increasingly becoming more symmetrical. Although 80 percent of the American population watched the television sitcom *I Love Lucy* in 1953, no television program has managed to capture a comparably large audience since. However, while markets are getting smaller, the expanding number of "niches" creates more opportunity for small distributors and for companies, such as Google and Amazon, who create a market in meeting the needs of specialist audiences. Anderson argues that demand is becoming infinite. Those producing products with small markets can compete more effectively than ever before. Large corporations, on the other hand, benefit from new ways of managing global distribution networks and the promise of a market, somewhere, for the products of their investments in research and development. However, understanding the corollary of this is critical—as markets have fractured into niches, it is increasingly difficult for any single product to achieve universal appeal.

CONTRIBUTION

Anderson identifies the three forces flattening the curve of popularity versus number of businesses, creating a flatter playing field—and a longer "tail."

1. **Democracy of production.** The flattening of access to the means of production, with improved technology and education, means more entrepreneurs and firms can develop and market their innovations. This is in contrast to times when economies of scale were fundamental to success.
2. **Democracy of marketing.** The democratization of marketing tools means that any firm with a Web site is a global company. It is no longer expensive to sell things; if a product is really good, customers will latch onto it. The smallest firms can compete with the largest multinationals in reaching specialized audiences, as information networks "flatten" the asymmetries of marketing budgets. Coca-Cola spends vast sums on its television advertising, but this is no longer fundamental to making sales. Viral marketing on the Internet can popularize a product with merit far more cheaply and effectively than more traditional methods.

3. **Connecting.** Connecting niche suppliers to niche markets has radically changed with the growth of the popularity of the Internet and Web sites that can market products with negligible margin costs. For example, while a book shop can stock only a limited number of books—its finite amount of shelf space means only the most popular products can be offered—Amazon.com can offer a far greater range at less cost. The long tail thrives as a consequence of the falling cost of connecting demand and supply.

CONTEXT

Anderson refers to the theories in James Surowiecki's *The Wisdom of Crowds* as critical to reinforcing the idea of the long tail. As word of mouth is essential in distributing any product, niche concepts must be able to captivate a crowd, even if it is a small one. In charting how "the many can be smarter than the few," Surowiecki's theory is important in "crowdsourcing" business models, where broad coverage is possible because of customers' participation in production. Wikipedia is able to offer such a broad coverage of encyclopedia entries—far greater than that of the *Encyclopaedia Britannica*—only because its users help generate content. By allowing the crowd to spread products, innovative ideas can reach niche markets without expensive, elite advertising strategies.

FOR MORE INFORMATION

Anderson, Chris. *The Long Tail: How Endless Choice Is Creating Endless Demand.* Rev. ed. New York: Hyperion, 2008.

The Machine That Changed the World
JAMES P. WOMACK, DANIEL T. JONES, AND DANIEL ROOS

WHY READ IT?

Lean production was Japan's secret weapon in the trade war, and it went on to conquer the world. In 1984 a team of researchers at the Massachusetts Institute of Technology (MIT) undertook a study of lean production. Within the framework of an analysis of the situation and problems of auto manufacturers worldwide, Womack, Jones, and Roos examined the differences between mass and lean production. This widely read and wisely praised book presents their findings.

GETTING STARTED

Lean production will supersede the mass production of goods, the authors announce. It can simultaneously double productivity, improve quality, and keep costs low. The book recounts the history of the rise of lean production, describes its essential elements, and presents the prospects for the spread of this revolutionary management initiative.

CONTRIBUTION
1. The Beginnings of Lean Production

In 1950 Eiji Toyoda, a Japanese engineer whose family had founded the Toyota Motor Company, and Toyota's production manager, Taiichi Ohno, visited the Ford motor works in Detroit, at that time the largest and most efficient production plant in the world. The basis of the Ford system was a complete division of labor among a wide variety of specialist operatives. The conveyor belt could never be halted; flaws were dealt with in postproduction.

Toyoda and Ohno felt that there was waste throughout this system: wasted labor, wasted materials, and wasted time. Apart from the assemblers, none of the specialists created any value for the car.

Upon his return to Japan, Ohno grouped his workers in teams, to whom he delegated more tasks and who were to work together on improvements. Each worker had a duty to halt the production line if a problem arose that he or she could not deal with. The whole team would then trace the fault back to its ultimate cause and think up a solution that would ensure it never happened again. The remedial work required before dispatch was thus reduced to zero, and lean production, the authors say, was born.

2. The Elements of Lean Production

The first element is the organization of the assembly works. A lean factory, the authors report, has two main organizational characteristics. First, it allots a maximum number of tasks and responsibilities to those workers who create actual value in the product on the line. Second, it has a fault detection system installed that quickly traces each fault back to its source.

The second element is product development. Lean production, the authors say, is quicker than mass production. The reason lies in basic differences in construction methods:

- Project leadership works on the *susha* system. The *susha* is the team leader, a position of great power in Japanese businesses. In mass-production companies the system is very different. The position of the development manager is too weak to push projects through. Top management often overrides his or her decisions.

- The *susha* creates a small, close-knit team, whose members are drawn from various specialist departments and who remain in contact with them. For the duration of the development project, however, they remain wholly under the control of the *susha*. In mass-production business, development teams consist of individuals on short-term loan from specialist departments.
- Communication, too, is different, say the authors. In Western mass production, it is only at a late stage in the project that there is any coordination of interests. In Japan, team members sign formal undertakings to do exactly what the team as a whole has decided. Any conflicts therefore show up at the very beginning of the crisis.

The third element in lean production is coordination of the supply chain. In the lean, *susha*-led product development process, all the necessary suppliers are carefully selected, not on the basis of their bids, but on the basis of earlier relationships and proven performance.

Customer relations form the fourth element. Japanese auto manufacturers, the authors point out, have comparatively few sales channels. These are differentiated in terms of their appealing to different types of purchaser. The objective is to establish a direct link between the production system and the customer. Employees in the sales channels are loaned to the development teams, and the dealers have a close relationship with the manufacturer.

The fifth major element in lean production is the way the lean company is managed. Various framework conditions have to exist:

- There must be money to finance development projects that last several years.
- Career ladders must be available for qualified and motivated employees.
- Decentralized activities must be coordinated worldwide.

CONTEXT

The MIT investigation was at the time the most comprehensive study of a single industry ever conducted. While it showed the undoubted successes of lean production, it also claimed to have uncovered certain deficiencies in the concept. Lean production, the authors suggest, overemphasizes the aspects of savings and mechanization and neglects categories such as know-how and innovation. Lean management brings a short-term improvement in efficiency, but not a long-term increase in productivity. In addition, the authors argue, it is unsuited to dismantling complexity. For example, anyone who wishes to reduce the complexity of serialized production steps through individualized manufacture must understand ever more expansive processes in their entirety. In theory, the highly innovative and flexible business organization with no hierarchy may count as the company of the future, but in everyday practice the weaknesses of lean production are clearly apparent.

> The whole world should adopt lean production, and as quickly as possible.

FOR MORE INFORMATION

Womack, James P., Daniel T. Jones, and Daniel Roos. *The Machine That Changed the World: The Story of Lean Production*. New York: HarperCollins, 1991.

Made in Japan
AKIO MORITA

WHY READ IT?
Made in Japan is the story of Sony and reflects the changes that took place in postwar business. Morita and Sony's story parallels the rebirth of Japan as an industrial power. When Sony was first attempting to make inroads into Western markets, Japanese products were sneered at as being of the lowest quality. Surmounting that obstacle was a substantial business achievement.

GETTING STARTED
This book charts the reemergence of Japan as an industrial heavyweight. It helped change the image of "Made in Japan" goods from shoddy to high quality. Sony invented new markets with a pioneering spirit by bringing out product after product, innovation after innovation. Its most famous success was the Walkman, the development of which was based on instinct, not research. Analysis and education do not necessarily help one reach the best business decisions; sometimes understanding must come before logic. "Japanese people tend to be much better adjusted to the notion of work, any kind of work, as honorable," says Morita. Recruitment is "management's risk and management's responsibility."

CONTRIBUTION
1. The Japanese Renaissance
Morita and Sony's story parallels the rebirth of Japan as a major industrial power. Together they helped change the image of items "Made in Japan" from shoddy to reputable and desirable. At the time, when Sony first tried to break into the Western electronics market, Japanese products were considered fifth-rate. Morita helped Sony, not only to overcome this prejudice, but to reverse it.

2. Inventing New Markets
Morita and Sony's gift was to invent new markets with a pioneering spirit. "Sony is a pioneer and never intends to follow others," says Morita. "Through progress, Sony wants to serve the whole world. It will always seek the unknown. Sony has a principle of respecting and encouraging one's ability . . . and always tries to bring out the best in a person. This is the vital force of Sony."

3. The Power of Innovation
While companies such as Matsushita were inspired followers, Sony set the pace with product after product, innovation after innovation.

Sony brought the world the handheld video camera, the first home video recorder, and the floppy disk. The blemishes on its record were the Betamax video format, which it failed to license, and color television systems.

4. Instinct and Research
Sony's most famous success was the Walkman, the brainchild of Morita. Morita noticed that young people liked listening to music wherever they went. He put two and two together and made—a Walkman. He did not believe that any amount of market research could have

told the company that this would be successful. As he famously said: "The public does not know what is possible. We do."

5. Analysis Doesn't Always Pay

Brilliant marketing by instinct was no mere accident. Morita believes that if you go through life convinced that your way is always best, all the new ideas in the world will pass you by.

Analysis and education do not necessarily help you reach the best business decisions. You can be totally rational with a machine, but if you work with people, sometimes understanding has to come before logic.

6. Japanese Culture Encourages the Work Ethic

Morita has emphasized the cultural differences in Japanese attitudes toward work. The Japanese tend to have a much stronger work ethic and see work as an honorable occupation.

In *Made in Japan*, Morita states his belief that management has ultimate responsibility for its staff. If a recession is looming, profit should be sacrificed rather than laying off employees.

> The public does not know what is possible, we do.

CONTEXT

The book tells the story of the rise of Sony and reflects the rise of Japan as a postwar industrial power. It looks at the role of quality and innovation as key factors in the success of Japanese companies. Many Western authors have focused on the role of quality in Japan, particularly the influence of people like Deming and Juran. Richard Pascale and Anthony Athos also look at the phenomenon in *The Art of Japanese Management*.

Morita and Sony took the attitude that global markets were important from the outset. Ken Ohmae writes on that subject from the Japanese perspective in *The Borderless World*.

FOR MORE INFORMATION

Morita, Akio. *Made in Japan*. New York: Dutton, 1986.

Management Teams: Why They Succeed or Fail
R. MEREDITH BELBIN

WHY READ IT?
Effective teamworking is now seen as key to the success of all types of organizations. Meredith Belbin identified the characteristics of people needed to make a successful team. His recommendations are still used, and the book can help anyone who needs to develop a team.

GETTING STARTED
Corporations have been preoccupied with the qualifications, experience, and achievement of individuals—however, it is not the individual but the team that is the instrument of sustained and enduring success in management.

Team performance is influenced by the kinds of people making up a group, and testing indicates that certain combinations of personality types perform more successfully than others. Nine archetypal functions (discussed below) make up an ideal team.

Unsuccessful teams can be improved by analyzing their composition and making appropriate changes.

CONTRIBUTION
1. The Preoccupation with Individuals
Corporations have been preoccupied with the qualifications, experience, and achievement of individuals, and have applied themselves to their selection, development, training, motivation, and promotion. However, commentators believe that the ideal individual for a given job cannot be found, because he or she does not exist. It is not the individual but the team that is the instrument of sustained and enduring success in management.

2. The Contribution of Individuals in Teams
Belbin was interested in group performance and how it might be influenced by the kinds of people making up a group. He asked members engaged in a business school exercise to undertake a personality and critical-thinking test and, based on the test results, discovered that certain combinations of personality types performed more successfully than others.

Belbin realized that given adequate knowledge of the personal characteristics and abilities of team members through psychometric testing, he could forecast the likely success or failure of particular teams. Unsuccessful teams can be improved by analyzing their team design shortcomings and making appropriate changes.

3. Identifying Team Characteristics
A questionnaire completed by team members was analyzed to show the functional roles the managers thought they performed in a team. From this research, Belbin identified nine archetypal functions that make up an ideal team.

4. Successful Team Composition
- Plant—creative, imaginative, unorthodox; solves difficult problems. Allowable weakness: bad at dealing with ordinary people.

- Coordinator—mature, confident, trusting; a good chairman; clarifies goals, promotes decision making. Not necessarily the cleverest member.
- Shaper—dynamic, outgoing, highly strung; challenges, pressurizes, finds ways around obstacles. Prone to bursts of temper.
- Teamworker—social, mild, perceptive, accommodating; listens, builds, averts friction. Indecisive in crunch situations.
- Completer—painstaking, conscientious, anxious; searches out errors; delivers on time. May worry unduly; reluctant to delegate.
- Implementer—disciplined, reliable, conservative, efficient; turns ideas into actions. Somewhat inflexible.
- Resource investigator—extroverted, enthusiastic, communicative; explores opportunities. Loses interest after initial enthusiasm.
- Specialist—single-minded, self-starting, dedicated; brings knowledge or skills in rare supply. Contributes only on narrow front.
- Monitor evaluator—sober, strategic, discerning. Sees all options, makes well-considered judgments. Lacks drive and ability to inspire others.

> It is not the individual but the team that is the instrument of sustained and enduring success in management.

CONTEXT

The explosion of interest in teamworking during the last decade has prompted greater interest in Belbin's work. The teamworking categories he identified have proved robust and are still used in a variety of organizations. Gary Hamel commented on this book, "High-performing companies increasingly believe that teams, rather than business units or individuals, are the basic building blocks of a successful organization. Belbin deserves much credit for helping us understand the basic building blocks of successful teams."

Antony Jay commented, "Corporations have been preoccupied with the qualifications, experience, and achievement of individuals . . . it is not the individual but the team that is the instrument of sustained and enduring success in management."

FOR MORE INFORMATION

Belbin, R. Meredith. *Management Teams: Why They Succeed or Fail*. 2nd ed. Burlington, MA: Butterworth-Heinemann, 2004.

The Managerial Grid
ROBERT BLAKE AND JANE MOUTON

WHY READ IT?
This book made an important contribution to the measurement of management performance. It challenged existing theories and provided organizations with a grid for assessing the types of manager they needed for various positions.

> Managers...don't produce nuts and bolts themselves, they organize others.

GETTING STARTED
In the early 1960s there was a sizeable gap in management theorizing, especially in terms of leadership and motivation. Douglas McGregor's Theory X and Y had a number of shortcomings in reality, and Blake and Mouton found that a management performance model with three axes was a more accurate representation of reality. The important axes were concern for productivity, concern for people, and motivation. Accurate measurement is important because of managers' capacity for self-deception and exaggeration.

CONTRIBUTION
1. Challenging Management Performance Theories
While acting as consultants for Exxon, Blake and Mouton concluded that there was a sizeable gap in management theorizing, especially in leadership and motivation. Popular among theories of the time was that of Douglas McGregor and his motivational extremes of X and Y. However, Blake and Mouton believed that many behaviors and motivations fell between these extremes. Theories X and Y were only a part of the overall picture of organizational behavior.

2. A New Model of Management Performance
Blake and Mouton's conclusion was that a model with three axes, rather than two, was a more accurate representation of reality. The three crucial axes they determined were concern for productivity, concern for people, and motivation.

Concern for production and people were both measured on a scale of one to nine, with nine being high. The reason a people axis was necessary is that managers achieve things indirectly. They don't produce nuts and bolts themselves; rather, they organize others so that the production line can be productive.

Motivation was measured on a scale from negative (driven by fear) to positive (driven by desire).

3. Flaws in Performance Measurement
Blake and Mouton found that, when left to rank themselves, some 80 percent of people give themselves a 9.9 rating. Once this is discussed and considered, this figure is routinely reduced to 20 percent. Given the capacity for self-deception, it is little wonder that change programs fail.

4. Key Management Styles
From the grid emerge five key managerial styles:

- 1 (production); 1 (people): The do-nothing manager. The leader exerts a minimum of effort to get the work done, with very little concern for people or production.
- 1 (production); 9 (people): The country club manager. This manager pays a lot of attention to people, but little to production. Can be seen in small companies that have cornered the market and some public sector organizations.
- 9 (production); 1 (people): This manager emphasizes production and minimizes the influence of human factors.
- 5 (production); 5 (people): Organization man or woman who diligently fosters mundanity.
- 9 (production); 9 (people): Managerial nirvana. The ultimate, with an emphasis on teamworking and team building. Personal and organizational goals are in alignment; motivation is high.

CONTEXT

When Blake and Mouton examined the behavior of people at Exxon, they found that many behaviors and motivations fell between Douglas McGregor's X and Y extremes. They observed that theories X and Y were only a part of the overall picture of organizational behavior.

Blake and Mouton's conclusion was that a model with three axes—concern for productivity, concern for people, and motivation—was a more accurate representation of reality.

FOR MORE INFORMATION

Blake, Robert, and Jane Mouton. *The Managerial Grid*. Houston, TX: Gulf Publishing, 1964.

Managing
HAROLD GENEEN

WHY READ IT?

Geneen joined the board of ITT in 1959 and set about turning the company into the world's greatest conglomerate. According to *Business Week*, along the way he became the legendary conglomerateur. The book relates the management style and culture that helped ITT to achieve that success. In particular, it highlights the importance of knowing the numbers in minute detail.

GETTING STARTED

Geneen's success was based on knowing every single figure possible. He did not invent the conglomerate, but he had an obsessive belief that it could be made to work. ITT bought 350 companies and appeared to be a managerial nightmare—yet Geneen made the nightmare work by fanatical attention to detail.

He only micromanaged the numbers; the people were generally overlooked. However, his success meant that people followed his methods without question. ITT devoted more than 200 days a year to management meetings held throughout the world.

Success was based on amassing all the facts so that decisions became self-evident—Geneen wanted no surprises.

CONTRIBUTION
1. A Rigorous Management Style

Geneen was the archetypal workaholic. His style was unforgiving, built on a degree of intellectual rigor that bordered on ruthlessness. He pinned his managerial faith on hard work and knowing every single figure possible. For Geneen, detail was everything. Once an accountant, always an accountant.

2. Making Conglomerates Work

> Putting deals together beats spending every day playing golf.

The conglomerate was not Geneen's invention. But he had an obsessive belief that it could be made to work. He believed that ITT could manage any business in any industry if it knew the figures.

His career with ITT, described in *Managing*, is a pageant of acquisition and diversification. Under Geneen, ITT bought companies as casually as a billionaire buys trinkets. One acquisition funded another. ITT bought 350 companies, including Avis Rent-A-Car, Sheraton Hotels, Continental Baking, and Levitt & Sons, among many others. By 1970 ITT was composed of 400 separate companies operating in 70 countries. With such huge numbers of companies in such vastly different fields, ITT was hopelessly diversified. To contemporary eyes, the company was a managerial nightmare. Yet Geneen made the nightmare work by fanatical attention to detail.

3. Managing the Numbers

Geneen micromanaged the numbers. "The very fact that you go over the progression of those numbers week after week, month after month, means that you have strengthened your memory and your familiarity with them so that you retain in your mind a vivid composite picture of what is going on in your company," he wrote.

4. Management Culture

Geneen inculcated a remarkable culture within ITT. His success meant that people followed his methods with the unquestioning faith of true believers.

Between 1959 and 1977, ITT's sales went from $765 million to nearly $28 billion. Earnings for the same period went from $29 million to $562 million, and earnings per share rose from $1 to $4.20.

As part of Geneen's formula, more than 50 executives flew every month to Brussels to spend four days poring over the figures. It was calculated that more than 200 days a year were devoted to management meetings held throughout the world.

5. Success Based on Facts

The point was to amass all the facts available so that the decisions became self-evident. If one knew everything, one would then know exactly what to do. Facts were the lifeblood of the expanding ITT.

"The highest art of professional management requires the literal ability to smell a real fact from all others," Geneen believed. "Managers should have the temerity, intellectual curiosity, guts and/or plain impoliteness, if necessary, to be sure that what they do have is indeed what we will call an unshakeable fact."

Geneen wanted no surprises. He also hoped to make people as predictable and controllable as the capital resources they must manage.

CONTEXT

Much of Geneen's managerial philosophy and rigorous practice would appear to be anathema to the contemporary executive. However, his fundamentalist style of management persists. Management consultants, for example, continue to espouse their rational models—pour in all the figures you can find and the right decision will emerge. There is still a temptation to manage by numbers rather than through and with people.

On the positive side, Geneen can be said to have elevated management to a new level. His system required a team of highly numerate, professional managers who had to take responsibility.

The Geneen legacy is most notable in the conglomerates that continue to survive. General Electric, under Jack Welch and now Jeff Immelt, may be the most lauded corporation of our age, but it is also a conglomerate with interests in everything from financial services to nuclear reactors and washing machines. Harold Geneen would have regarded the survival of such companies as vindication of his methods.

Others, however, point to the decline of ITT after his departure as a true measure of the long-term validity of Geneen's approach to management.

FOR MORE INFORMATION

Geneen, Harold. *Managing*. New York: Doubleday, 1985.

Managing across Borders
CHRISTOPHER A. BARTLETT AND SUMANTRA GHOSHAL

WHY READ IT?

Bartlett and Ghoshal map out the new business reality of globalization and the kinds of organizations a "borderless" business world requires. The book is regarded as a classic and has helped many companies focus on the type of organization they need for success in the global economy.

GETTING STARTED

According to the authors, changing patterns of international management have led to a new global model, in which enabling innovation and disseminating knowledge in globally dispersed organizations is an important challenge.

A number of organizational forms are now prevalent among global companies. Multinational companies offer a high degree of local responsiveness; global companies offer scale efficiencies and cost advantages; international companies have the ability to transfer knowledge and expertise to overseas environments that are less advanced; and the transnational company combines local responsiveness with global efficiency and the ability to transfer know-how better, cheaper, and faster.

Integration and the creation of coherent systems for value delivery are the new drivers of organizational structure.

CONTRIBUTION
1. Changing Patterns of International Management

The traditional international management model was simply to export one's own way of doing things elsewhere, and companies believed that global operations were simply a means of achieving economies of scale. Local nuances were overlooked in the quest for global standardization; *global* and *local* were mutually exclusive. In general, organizations either gave local operations autonomy or controlled them rigidly from a distance.

2. A New Global Model

Global presence with local responsiveness is now key. Companies face the challenge of enabling innovation and disseminating knowledge in globally dispersed organizations. Bartlett and Ghoshal identify a number of organizational forms prevalent among global companies.

3. Multinational Companies

The multinational or multidomestic organization offers a very high degree of local responsiveness. It is a decentralized federation of local businesses, linked together through personal control by expatriates who occupy key positions abroad.

4. Global Companies

Global organizations offer scale efficiencies and cost advantages. With global-scale facilities, the global organization seeks to produce standardized products. It is often centralized in its home country, with overseas operations considered as delivery pipelines to tap into global market opportunities. There is tight control of strategic decisions, resources, and information by the global hub.

5. International Companies

International companies have the ability to transfer knowledge and expertise to overseas environments that are less advanced. They are coordinated federations of local businesses, controlled by sophisticated management systems and corporate employees. The attitude of the parent company tends to be somewhat parochial, fostered by the superior know-how at the center of the organization.

> Integration and the creation of a coherent system for value delivery are the new drivers of organizational structure.

6. The Transnational Companies

Global competition is forcing many businesses to shift to a fourth model, which they call the transnational. This organization combines local responsiveness with global efficiency and the ability to transfer know-how better, cheaper, and faster. The transnational company is made up of a network of specialized or differentiated units, which focus on managing integrative linkages among local businesses as well as with the center. The subsidiary becomes a distinctive asset, rather than simply an arm of the parent company. Manufacturing and technology development are located wherever it makes sense, and there is an explicit focus on leveraging local know-how to exploit worldwide opportunities.

7. The Importance of Integration

Integration and the creation of a coherent system for value delivery are the new drivers of organizational structure. Companies cannot be left to their own devices, but have to be brought within the fold—while also keeping in touch with their local business environment.

What binds the companies together is a set of explicitly or implicitly shared values and beliefs that can be developed and managed effectively. There are three techniques crucial to an organization's psychology:

1. There must be a clear, shared understanding of the company's mission and objectives.
2. The actions and behavior of senior managers are vital as examples and statements of commitment.
3. Corporate personnel policies must be geared up to develop a multidimensional and flexible organizational process.

CONTEXT

Managing across Borders is one of the few business books of recent years that deserves recognition as a classic. When it was published in 1989, understanding of globalization was in its infancy. With its emphasis on networking across the global organization and transferring learning and knowledge, the book effectively set the organizational agenda for a decade and created a new organizational model.

The authors effectively signaled the demise of the divisional organization—which gives divisions independence—first developed by Alfred P. Sloan of General Motors.

FOR MORE INFORMATION

Bartlett, Christopher A., and Sumantra Ghoshal. *Managing across Borders: The Transnational Solution.* 2nd ed. Boston: Harvard Business School Press, 2002.

Managing on the Edge
RICHARD T. PASCALE

WHY READ IT?
This book challenges traditional management thinking, which Pascale feels is too complacent for an environment driven by change. He sets out a new perspective for "contention management," which seeks to harness the conflicting energies in an organization to achieve positive change. The book set the management agenda for a decade after its publication.

GETTING STARTED
Managerial history in the United States has been largely inward-focused and self-congratulatory. Change is a fact of business life, but complacency can cause problems. It is essential to change the management perspective. The incremental approach to change is no longer effective. The new emphasis should be on asking questions. Successful organizations undergo continual renewal by constantly asking questions.

The book argues that four factors (discussed below) drive stagnation and renewal. "Contention management" is essential to orchestrate tensions that arise among these four factors. Forces locked in opposition can be used to generate inquiry and adaptation, and the manager's job is to maintain a constructive level of debate.

CONTRIBUTION
1. The Dangers of Complacency
Nothing fails like success. Great strengths are inevitably the root of weakness. Of the companies listed in 1985's Fortune 500, 143 had been dropped by 1990.

2. The Need for Change
According to Pascale, change is a fact of business life. We are ill-equipped to deal with it, and the traditional approach to managing change is no longer applicable. The incremental approach to change is effective when the goal is to obtain more of the same thing. Historically, that has been sufficient. The U.S. advantages of plentiful resources, geographical isolation, and absence of serious global competition defined a situation in which U.S. companies competed with each other and everyone played by the same rules.

3. Growth of Management Fads
There have been more than two dozen management fads since the 1950s; a dozen emerged in the five years prior to 1990.

4. Driving Stagnation and Renewal
Four factors drive stagnation and renewal in organizations:
- *Fit* describes an organization's internal consistency (unity).
- *Split* describes a variety of techniques for breaking a bigger organization into smaller units and providing them with a stronger sense of ownership and identity (plurality).
- *Contend* refers to a management process that harnesses (rather than suppresses) the contradictions that are inevitable by-products of organizations (duality).
- *Transcend* alerts people to the higher order of complexity that successfully managing the renewal process entails (vitality).

5. Changing Management Perspective

Pascale calls for a fundamental shift in perspective. Managerial behavior is based on the assumption that people should rationally order the behavior of those they manage. That mindset needs to be challenged. Orderly answers are no longer appropriate, in his view, and the new emphasis should be on asking questions. Strategic planning, at best, is about posing questions, more than attempting to answer them. Successful organizations undergo a continual process of renewal. Central to achieving this is a willingness to ask questions constantly and to harness conflict for the corporate good, through systems that encourage questioning. To facilitate this, Pascale argues that companies must become "engines of inquiry."

6. Contention Management

Managers are ill-equipped to deal with the contention that arises when fundamental questions are posed. "Contention management" is essential to orchestrate tensions that arise. When contention arises, about half the time it is smoothed over and avoided.

The forces that we have historically regarded as locked in opposition can be viewed as apparent opposites that generate inquiry and adaptive responses. Pascale holds that each point of view represents a facet of reality, and these realities tend to challenge one another and raise questions. If we redefine the manager's job as maintaining a constructive level of debate, we are in effect holding the organization in the question. This leads to identifying blind spots and working around obstacles. Truth—personally and organizationally—lies in the openness of vigorous debate.

> Nothing fails like success.

In the final analysis, organizations are interactions among people.

CONTEXT

Managing on the Edge presents a formidably researched and argued challenge to complacency and timidity.

Pascale criticizes Peters and Waterman's *In Search of Excellence*, saying, "Simply identifying attributes of success is like identifying attributes of people in excellent health during the age of the bubonic plague."

Managing on the Edge set the tone for much of the management thinking of the 1990s. Its emphasis on the need for constant change has since been developed by Pascale. He now argues that the issue of managing the way we change is a competence rather than an episodic necessity. The capability to change is a core competence in its own right.

Influential critic Gary Hamel commented,

> In *Managing on the Edge*, Richard Pascale provides a number of useful observations on the sources of corporate vitality. One of the things I've always admired about Richard Pascale is that he focuses not on tools and techniques, but on principles and paradigms. While management bookshelves groan with the weight of simplistic how-to books, Pascale challenges managers to think, and to think deeply. Pascale forces managers to deconstruct the normative models on which they base their beliefs and actions.

FOR MORE INFORMATION

Pascale, Richard T. *Managing on the Edge: How Successful Companies Use Conflict to Stay Ahead.* New York: Simon & Schuster, 1990.

Managing Transitions
WILLIAM BRIDGES

WHY READ IT?

This book focuses on the human aspects of change management. Change is a situation. What the author calls "transition" is the psychological process people go through to come to terms with change. The book stresses that change involves people and that managers and leaders must help people deal with the transition. The author shows, through practical examples, how managers should make people feel comfortable and unthreatened during a period of change and offers advice, as well as case studies, on the best way to achieve this.

GETTING STARTED

> It isn't the changes that do you in, it's the transition.

The author believes that many companies try to impose change, but fail to manage the transition. Transition requires recognizing that things cannot be the same after an organizational change. People must get used to the new ways of doing things. They do this by going through a "neutral zone" before emerging into a new beginning.

CONTRIBUTION
1. Letting Go

The author explains that transition begins with a process of "letting go." However, many people in an organization find this difficult. They are comfortable with familiar, proven ways of doing things, and they fear the unknown.

The first stage, he suggests, is to identify who is losing what, by analyzing what is going to change and identifying the impact on various groups of people. Managers should be aware that people will react in different ways. They should acknowledge the effect of the change on people and, if necessary, make some compensation for their loss. Managers should also acknowledge what was good about the existing processes and emphasize the element of continuity in the most important aspects of the new proposals.

2. The Neutral Zone

Bridges believes that the "neutral zone" is the most difficult part of the transition process, because this is where people's uncertainties and anxieties about change are most acute. He advises managers to give people a clear sense of direction, as well as support to help them through this difficult stage. Moving from an existing routine to a new one can prove difficult without the right help.

Bridges argues that managers can reduce the damaging impact of the neutral zone by setting short-term targets that are achievable. He also believes that they should not expect or demand exceptional performance during a period of transition.

Communication is vital, claims Bridges, at this and every stage of transition. It is also important to encourage creativity during the neutral zone period, particularly when there is less pressure on people to perform. Creativity can help to overcome the sense of loss people feel about leaving old routines behind.

3. New Beginnings

According to Bridges, when people move to the new system, uncertainties can remain. There is always a risk in new ways of doing things. It is therefore essential to set out a clear plan, with timings and targets. Managers should ensure that everyone has a clear part to play in the new system.

He recommends clear, regular communications to explain the objectives and rationale for the new system. A vision of the future can help to paint a clear picture for people in the organization. To reinforce the new beginning, Bridges recommends that companies create a new identity and celebrate success.

The book also includes advice for readers on how to take care of themselves during a period of transition.

CONTEXT

This book is one of a number that deal with the subject of managing the process of change. John Kotter's *Leading Change* (Harvard Business School Press, 1996), for example, reflects on the themes of leadership, vision, and communication.

Bridges's book looks at the human perspective on change and includes a great deal of practical advice on ways of dealing with the personal issues that people face. It also contains a number of useful studies, case histories, and exercises that could be used in workshops.

The book may be more suitable for people in human resources or line management roles. Senior executives who are concerned with the strategic implications of change might find more value in an author such as Kotler.

FOR MORE INFORMATION

Bridges, William. *Managing Transitions: Making the Most of Change.* 2nd ed. Cambridge, MA: Perseus, 2003.

FURTHER READING

Bridges, William. *Transitions: Making Sense of Life's Changes.* 2nd ed. Cambridge, MA: Perseus, 2003.

Bridges, William. *Creating You and CO: Learn to Think like the C.E.O. of Your Own Career.* Cambridge, MA: Perseus, 1998.

Marketing Management
PHILIP KOTLER AND KEVIN KELLER

WHY READ IT?
Kotler is one of the leading authorities on marketing. This definitive marketing textbook covers the full scope of contemporary marketing. It is the most widely used marketing book in business schools.

GETTING STARTED
Marketing continues to evolve and expand its scope exponentially. The emphasis is shifting from transaction-oriented marketing to relationship marketing—retaining customer loyalty through continually satisfying their needs. Marketing management is the process of planning and executing functions that satisfy customer and organizational objectives. Customer-delivered value is the difference between total customer value and total customer cost. Organizations encounter three common hurdles to marketing orientation.

CONTRIBUTION
1. Marketing Continues to Evolve
The marketing discipline is redeveloping its assumptions, concepts, skills, tools, and systems for making sound decisions. Marketers must know when to
- cultivate large markets or niche markets;
- launch new brands or extend existing brand names;
- push or pull products through distribution;
- protect the domestic market or penetrate aggressively into foreign markets;
- add more benefits to the offer or reduce the price; and
- expand or contract budgets for sales force, advertising, and other marketing tools.

The scope of marketing is expanding exponentially:
- industry and competitor analysis;
- designing strategies for the global marketplace;
- managing product life cycle strategies; and
- retailing, wholesaling, and other physical-distribution systems.

2. The Change to Relationship Marketing
Good customers are an asset that, when well managed and served, will return a handsome lifetime income stream. In the intensely competitive marketplace, the company must retain customers' loyalty through continually satisfying their needs in a superior way.

3. Defining the Role of Marketing
Marketing is the social and managerial process by which individuals and groups obtain what they need and want through creating, offering, and exchanging products of value with others. A market consists of all the potential customers sharing a particular need or want who might be willing to exchange to satisfy that need or want.

Marketing management is the process of planning and executing the conception, pricing, promotion, and distribution of goods, services, and ideas to create exchanges with target groups that satisfy customer and organizational objectives.

4. Analyzing Products

A product is anything that can be offered to a market for attention, acquisition, use, or consumption that might satisfy a want or need. A product has five levels:

- the core benefit (marketers must see themselves as benefit providers),
- the generic product,
- the expected product (the normal expectations the customer has of the product),
- the augmented product (the additional services or benefits added to the product),
- the potential product (all the augmentations and transformations that this product might undergo in the future).

> Good companies will meet needs; great companies will create markets.

5. Customer Value

Customer-delivered value is the difference between total customer value and total customer cost. Total customer value is the bundle of benefits customers expect from a given product or service. It consists of product value, service value, personnel value, and image value. Total customer cost consists of monetary price, time cost, energy cost, and psychic cost. Combined, the two produce customer-delivered value.

6. Barriers to Marketing Orientation

To become marketing oriented, organizations must overcome three hurdles:

- Organized resistance—entrenched functional behavior tends to oppose increased emphasis on marketing, as it is seen as undermining functional power bases.
- Slow learning—most companies only slowly embrace the marketing concept.
- Fast forgetting—companies that embrace marketing concepts tend, over time, to lose touch with the principles. Various U.S. companies have sought to establish their products in Europe with scant knowledge of those different marketplaces.

7. Achieving Market Leadership

Good companies will meet needs; great companies will create markets. Market leadership is gained by envisioning new products, services, lifestyles, and ways to raise living standards. There is a vast difference between companies offering "me-too" products and those creating previously unimagined product and service values. In Kotler's view, marketing at its best is about value creation and raising the world's living standards.

CONTEXT

Marketing Management is the definitive marketing textbook. Tightly argued and all-encompassing, its content has been expanded and brought up to date through various editions. The eighth edition, published in 1994, maps out the emerging challenges to all those involved in marketing. The very size and scope of *Marketing Management* demonstrate the exponential expansion of marketing.

FOR MORE INFORMATION

Kotler, Philip, and Kevin Keller. *Marketing Management.* 13th ed. Des Moines, IA: Prentice Hall, 2008.

Megatrends
JOHN NAISBITT

WHY READ IT?
Megatrends was written in 1982, before the technology revolution took hold. It attempts to predict the key changes in business and society. Naisbitt correctly anticipated a number of factors, such as globalization and the rise of an information economy.

GETTING STARTED
We have changed to an economy based on the creation and distribution of information. Speed is a competitive weapon. We must now acknowledge that we are part of a global economy. The larger the world economy, the more powerful its smallest player—and in small organizations, we have rediscovered the ability to act innovatively and to achieve results from the bottom up. Economies of scale are giving way to economies of scope. The acceleration of technological progress has created an urgent need for a return to a human scale.

Empowerment, along with responsibility, has become more important for every individual in an organization. We are more self-reliant and less hierarchical. Society is moving toward much longer-term time frames.

CONTRIBUTION
1. Toward the Information Economy
Since the book was first published, we have moved away from being an industrial society and become an economy based on the creation and distribution of information.

In the early 1980s, however, traditional issues, such as production methods, still held sway. The technological possibilities in information exchange and transfer were contemplated by a small group in West Coast laboratories.

2. Technology with a Human Scale
We are moving in the dual directions of high tech/high touch, matching each new technology with a compensatory human response. High touch is about getting back to a human scale. All change is local and from the bottom up. If you keep track of local events, you can see the shifting patterns.

We can't stop technological progress, but by the same token, we can hardly go wrong with a high-touch response. FedEx has all the reliability and efficiency of modern electronics, but its success is built on a form of high-touch, hand delivery.

3. The Emergence of a Global Economy
We no longer have the luxury of operating within an isolated, self-sufficient, national economic system. We must now acknowledge that we are part of a global economy. We have begun to let go of the idea that the United States is the world's industrial leader. The global paradox is that the larger the world economy, the more powerful its smallest player will be.

4. A Longer Time Frame
We are moving away from a society governed by short-term considerations and rewards to one that deals with things in much longer-term time frames.

5. The Growth of Empowerment

We have rediscovered the ability to act innovatively and achieve results from the bottom up. Naisbitt anticipated the fashion in the late 1980s and early 1990s for empowerment, with responsibility being spread more evenly throughout organizations rather than centered on a small group of managers.

> The bigger the world economy, the more powerful its smallest player.

6. Greater Self-reliance

We are shifting from institutional help to more self-reliance in all aspects of our lives. Trends in working patterns suggest that this is becoming the case for a select few professionals with marketable skills.

7. Changing Framework of Democracy

We are discovering that the framework of representative democracy has become obsolete in an era of instantaneously shared information. Alvin Toffler suggested this in his 1970 book *Future Shock*.

8. Informal Networks Replacing Hierarchy

We are giving up our dependence on hierarchical structures in favor of informal networks. It has become one of the great trends of the last decade as networks are developed in a bewildering variety of ways—with suppliers, between competitors, internally, and globally.

Technology has enabled the creation of networks never previously anticipated, with important repercussions.

9. Speed as a Competitive Weapon

Linked to reliance on networks is the entire question of speed, which Naisbitt identified early on as a competitive weapon. Economies of scale are giving way to economies of scope, finding the right size for synergy, market flexibility, and above all, speed.

10. More Choice for Society

From a narrow "either/or" society with a limited range of personal choices, we are exploding into a free-wheeling, multiple-option society.

11. The Power of Small Businesses

Naisbitt championed the role of small business in generating the wealth of the future. Small companies, right down to the individual, can beat big bureaucratic companies every time. Unless big companies reconstitute themselves as a collection of small companies, they will just continue to go out of business. It's the small companies that are creating the global company.

CONTEXT

Megatrends identified ten critical restructurings. Some have proved accurate predictions of what has happened in intervening years; others have proved less accurate. Naisbitt predicted the rise of the information economy when the technology was still a laboratory product, and he identified the emergence of factors such as globalization and empowerment.

FOR MORE INFORMATION

Naisbitt, John. *Megatrends*. New York: Warner Books, 1984.

The Mind of the Strategist
KENICHI OHMAE

WHY READ IT?
This book illuminates the strategic thinking behind Japanese corporate success. The author shows how and why it differs from the Western approach to strategic thinking and explains that Western companies can adapt to this successful model.

GETTING STARTED
Kenichi Ohmae argues that to a large extent, Japanese success can be attributed to the nature of Japanese strategic thinking. Japanese businesses tend not to have large strategic planning staffs. The customer is at the heart of the Japanese approach to strategy. There are three main players in any business strategy, collectively called the strategic triangle. Just as events in the real world do not always fit a linear model, the Japanese approach to strategy is irrational and nonlinear.

CONTRIBUTION
1. Strategy Determines Japanese Success
Japanese success can be attributed to the nature of Japanese strategic thinking, according to Ohmae. This is basically creative and intuitive rather than rational, but the necessary creativity can be learned. Unlike large U.S. corporations, Japanese businesses tend not to have large strategic planning staffs. Instead they often have a single, idiosyncratic, naturally talented strategist. From the dynamic interaction of the company, customers, and competition, a comprehensive set of objectives and plans eventually emerges.

2. The Customer at the Center
In contrast to the West, the customer is at the heart of the Japanese approach to strategy and the key to corporate values.

3. Strategic Triangle
In the construction of any business strategy, three main players must be taken into account: the corporation itself, the customer, and the competition. This is the strategic triangle.

The job of the strategist, as Ohmae sees it, is to achieve superior performance. At the same time, the strategist must be sure that his strategy matches the strengths of the corporation with the needs of a clearly defined market. Otherwise, the corporation's long-term viability may be at stake.

4. Strategy Is Irrational
The central thrust of the book is that strategy as epitomized by the Japanese approach is irrational and nonlinear.

In strategic thinking, one first seeks a clear understanding of each element of a situation, then makes the fullest use of human brain power to restructure the elements in the most advantageous way.

Events in the real world do not always fit a linear model. Hence the most reliable means of dissecting a situation into its constituent parts, and reassembling them in the desired pattern, is not a step-by-step methodology, but the ultimate nonlinear thinking tool, the human brain.

True strategic thinking thus not only contrasts sharply with the conventional mechanical systems approach, but also with the purely intuitive approach, which reaches conclusions without any kind of breakdown or analysis.

5. Gaining Ground through Effective Strategy

An effective business strategy is one whereby a company can gain significant ground on its competitors at an acceptable cost to itself. There are four main ways of achieving this:

- focusing on the key factors for success (KFS),
- building on relative superiority,
- pursuing aggressive initiatives, and
- utilizing strategic degrees of freedom.

The principal concern is to avoid doing the same thing, on the same battleground, as the competition.

Focusing on Key Factors for Success   Certain functional or operating areas within every business are more critical for success in that particular business environment than others. If you concentrate effort into these areas and your competitors do not, this is a source of competitive advantage. The problem lies in identifying these key factors for success.

Ohmae argues that without exception, successful leaders began by bold deployment of strategies based on KFS.

> The job of the strategist is to achieve superior performance, relative to competition, in the key factors for success of the business.

Building on Relative Superiority   When all competitors are seeking to compete by focusing on the KFS, a company can exploit any differences in competitive conditions. For example, it can make use of technology or sales networks not in direct competition with its rivals.

Pursuing Aggressive Initiatives   Frequently, the only way to win against a much larger, entrenched competitor is to upset the competitive environment by undermining the value of its KFS. That means changing the rules of the game by introducing new KFS.

Utilizing Strategic Degrees of Freedom   The company should focus on innovation in areas that are untouched by competitors.

CONTEXT

The author is Japan's only successful management guru. The book was published in the West at the height of interest in Japanese management methods.

Ohmae challenged the simplistic belief that Japanese management was a matter of company songs and lifetime employment. Instead, Japanese success could be attributed to the nature of Japanese strategic thinking.

FOR MORE INFORMATION

Ohmae, Kenichi. *The Mind of the Strategist: The Art of Japanese Business*. Rev. ed. New York: McGraw-Hill, 1991.

Moments of Truth
JAN CARLZON

WHY READ IT?

Jan Carlzon is a Swedish businessman who rocketed to international prominence by leading a turnaround at the Scandinavian airline, SAS. The turnaround was based on excellence in customer service, and the book contains many practical examples of the way this can be applied. The SAS story is one of the most frequently used case studies in customer service training and literature.

GETTING STARTED

Carlzon used customer service as a vehicle for turning SAS around. He held that quality service is built around moments of truth—the critical transactions at each stage of the ownership or use cycle. Customer satisfaction and value are affected at different points in the cycle. They also vary by customer type.

This approach owes much to the Scandinavian management style—humane and people centered. Scandinavian companies embraced teamworking and employee participation before they became fashionable. Their leaders are anti-authoritarian, they make very effective use of coaching and mentoring, and they also communicate consistently and continually.

CONTRIBUTION
1. Making Customer Service Work

Carlzon actually made customer service work and used it as a vehicle for turning SAS—formerly an indifferent performer—into a world class organization.

Carlzon came up with the phrase, "moments of truth"—the sequence of critical transactions across each stage of the ownership or use cycle. Any time a customer comes into contact with any aspect of a business, however remote, is an opportunity to form an impression.

2. Identifying Moments of Truth

The critical transactions are broken down into:
- initial contact,
- first use,
- problem solving,
- ongoing support,
- further purchases, and
- recommendations to others.

The key to understanding customer behavior is first to evaluate the degree to which satisfaction and value are affected at these different points in the cycle and subsequently to understand how they vary by customer type.

Carlzon decided to dramatically prove the company's dedication to these moments of truth by sending tens of thousands of SAS managers on specially tailored training programs.

3. The Success of the Scandinavian Approach

Like most stereotypes, the image of highly motivated, well-rewarded, hardworking, and contented Scandinavians is only partly true. However, Scandinavian companies have a track record of managing their human resources in innovative ways. Their management style tends to be humane and people centered, and they were champions of teamworking and employee participation long before those practices became the height of managerial fashion.

Scandinavians have very stable political systems and fairly homogeneous societies, and problems typically are solved through negotiation. Historically there has been little unrest—but the counter to this is that often, without a crisis, advancement is not achieved.

Scandinavian business culture shares some characteristics with that of the Japanese. Saving face is important and, rather than direct frontal attack, Scandinavians prefer a more indirect and subtle approach.

4. A Scandinavian Leadership Style

Old-fashioned virtues are in. Typically, in one survey cited by Carlzon, U.S. executives rated honesty as the prime business virtue. Swedish executives did not include honesty at all—it was assumed.

The Scandinavian leader tends to be decidedly anti-authoritarian. Highly personal and practical theories, such as coaching and mentoring, find fertile ground; being up front and communicating openly is expected. With Carlzon and others there is a certain amount of showmanship—they play their roles to perfection. They stand in the middle of their strategy. They don't preach the strategy; they *are* the strategy. They communicate consistently and continually, and repeat the same messages again and again. But they never grow tired of saying them—there is no sign of boredom, no cynicism, no sarcasm. They give words real meaning. This appetite for communication is clearly linked to a more humane style of management.

> All business is show business.

CONTEXT

Carlzon set in train SAS's revival, which became a benchmark for international best practice in customer service. The achievement was celebrated by, among many others, Tom Peters in *A Passion for Excellence*.

After Carlzon left SAS the company's halo slipped a little, and Scandinavian role models were thin on the ground for a number of years. During the 1990s, however, there was a steady stream of corporate benchmarks. The new Scandinavian role models—IKEA, Skandia, Oticon, and ABB—remain indebted to Carlzon's example.

FOR MORE INFORMATION

Carlzon, Jan. *Moments of Truth*. New York: Collins, 1989.

Motion Study: A Method for Increasing the Efficiency of the Workman
FRANK GILBRETH

WHY READ IT?

Frank and Lillian Gilbreth made an art of measuring motion and, in doing so, helped to further lower the borders between measurement and management. The book is written by genuine enthusiasts for measurement. The Gilbreths, and Frank in particular, were committed to the principles of scientific management and were among the first to find practical applications of the key theories behind the movement. Frank was an advocate of the work of F. W. Taylor and founded the Society to Promote the Science of Management in the 1890s. After Taylor's death in 1915, the Society was renamed the Taylor Society.

GETTING STARTED

Analysis and measurement of work can identify inefficient practices. Through analysis of motion, the Gilbreths concluded that there were 16 units of movement. They asserted, "Fatigue elimination must increase Happiness Minutes."

CONTRIBUTION
Analysis of Motion

One of Frank Gilbreth's key concerns was integrating efficiency into everyday working life, benefiting at one stroke the employer (who saw an increase in productivity) and the employee (whose levels of fatigue were decreased and the risk of injury therefore lessened). Fatigue elimination, starting as it does from a desire to conserve human life and eliminate enormous waste, must increase what Gilbreth termed "Happiness Minutes," at the very least, or would be seen to have failed in its fundamental objective.

As a practical example of this concern, Frank Gilbreth examined bricklayers at work and found them to be inefficient. In response, he designed and patented scaffolding that reduced bending and reaching and increased output by over 100 percent.

The Gilbreths' analysis of motion was aided by photography, and to help in the analysis of their photographs, they developed the microchronometer, a device still used today. This was a clock that could record time to 1/2000 of a second, which was placed in the area being photographed.

The Gilbreths named the 16 units of movement "therbligs" (Gilbreth spelled backward and slightly altered for ease of pronunciation).

Henry Gantt developed the idea of what became known as a Gantt chart at around the time that the Gilbreths were conducting their research, and they made use of this new measurement tool. They also incorporated flow diagrams and process charts into their studies, which enabled them to see exactly which constituent subtasks were involved in the completion of one major task.

CONTEXT

The Gilbreths put scientific management to the test. They made an art of measurement and, in doing so, helped further blur the borders between measurement and management.

Though their methods were sometimes viewed as eccentric and their blind enthusiasm took them down some unusual avenues, the Gilbreths had a powerful effect on management thinking. They elevated measurement to an all-embracing credo and helped establish it as one of the central tasks of management.

Even though the influence of the concept of scientific management began to wane from the 1960s onward, the work of the Gilbreths should not be underestimated. They brought together the disciplines of motion study and industrial psychology and made a lasting contribution to both management thought and the ways in which we work today.

> Fatigue elimination, starting as it does from a desire to conserve human life and to eliminate enormous waste, must increase Happiness Minutes, no matter what else it does, or it has failed in its fundamental aim.

FOR MORE INFORMATION

Gilbreth, Frank. *Motion Study: A Method for Increasing the Efficiency of the Workman.* New York: D. Van Nostrand, 1911.

Motivation and Personality
ABRAHAM MASLOW

WHY READ IT?
Maslow introduced the concept of a hierarchy of needs, which has formed an integral part of marketing, human resource, motivational, and management literature ever since. The book makes an important contribution to the emergence of human relations as a professional discipline.

GETTING STARTED
There is an ascending scale of needs that provides the basis for motivation. Basic physiological needs come first; once these are met, other needs dominate. At the top of the scale is self-actualization, where individuals achieve their personal potential. Also high up are social or love needs and ego or self-esteem needs.

The hierarchy of needs provides a rational framework for motivation, and human nature determines that motivation is intrinsically linked to rewards. First presented over 65 years ago, it is a concept still found useful by managers today.

CONTRIBUTION
1. The Hierarchy of Needs
There is an ascending scale of needs, which must be understood if people are to be motivated. First are the fundamental physiological needs of warmth, shelter, and food. It is quite true that man lives by bread alone—when there is no bread.

But what happens when there is plenty of bread?

2. Emerging Needs
Once basic physiological needs are met, others emerge to dominate. These can be categorized roughly as the safety needs. If a person's state is sufficiently extreme and chronic, he or she may be characterized as living almost for safety alone.

Next in the hierarchy are social needs and self-esteem needs.

3. Self-actualization
As each need is satisfied, eventually self-actualization comes—the individual achieves his or her own potential.

4. From Motivation to Reward
While the hierarchy of needs provides a rational framework for motivation, its flaw lies in the nature of humanity. People always want more. When asked what salary they would be comfortable with, people routinely—no matter what their income—name a figure that is around twice their current income.

Instead of being driven by punishment and deprivation, motivation has become intrinsically linked to reward.

CONTEXT
Abraham Maslow was a member of the human relations school of the late 1950s, which also included Douglas McGregor and Frederick Herzberg.

Motivation and Personality is best known for its hierarchy of needs—a concept that was first published by Maslow in 1943. He argues that there is an ascending scale of needs, which must be understood if people are to be motivated.

Maslow's hierarchy of needs contributed to the emergence of human relations as a discipline, and to a sea-change in the perception of motivation.

Gary Hamel commented about Maslow's hierarchy:

> However subtle and variegated the original theory, time tends to reduce it to its most communicable essence: hence Maslow's hierarchy of needs, Pascale's seven Ss, Michael Porter's five forces, and the Boston Consulting Group's growth/share matrix. Yet there is no framework that has so broadly infiltrated organizational life as Maslow's hierarchy of needs. Perhaps this is because it speaks so directly to the aspirations each of us holds for oursel[ves].

> It is quite true that man lives by bread alone—when there is no bread.

FOR MORE INFORMATION
Maslow, Abraham. *Motivation and Personality*. 3rd ed. New York: Harper & Row, 1987.

The Motivation to Work
FREDERICK HERZBERG, BERNARD MAUSNER, AND BARBARA BLOCH SNYDERMAN

WHY READ IT?
Herzberg's work has had a lasting influence on human resource management. Concepts such as job enrichment, self-development, and job satisfaction have evolved from his insight that motivation comes from within the individual, rather than from a policy imposed by the company.

GETTING STARTED
According to the authors, employee motivation can be improved through greater emphasis on human relations. Research indicates that motivation at work takes two forms—hygiene factors and motivation factors (discussed below). Improvements in hygiene factors remove the barriers to positive attitudes in the workplace, although hygiene factors alone are not sufficient to provide true motivation to work. Employers should aim to motivate people through job satisfaction, rather than reward or pressure.

CONTRIBUTION
1. The Importance of Employee Attitudes
"People are our greatest assets" has become one of the most overused clichés in business. However, before Herzberg, "people issues" were a low priority in management literature. Management thinkers rarely sought the opinions of employees or considered them worthy of study. Herzberg and his colleagues, Mausner and Snyderman, highlighted the importance of employee attitudes through a study of 203 Pittsburgh engineers and accountants. By asking what pleased and displeased people about their jobs, they raised the wider question: "How do you motivate employees?"

2. Identifying Factors That Motivate Employees
Herzberg made a critical distinction between factors that cause unhappiness at work and factors that contribute to job satisfaction. This distinction was based on his earlier work in public health, where he had concluded that mental health was not the opposite of mental illness. Transferring that concept to the workplace, he suggested that the reverse of the factors that make people happy did not make them unhappy. His research indicated that motivation at work takes two forms—hygiene factors and motivation factors.

Hygiene Factors   Hygiene factors cover basic needs at work. They include working conditions, supervision levels, company policies, benefits, and job security. If these are poor or deteriorate, they lead to dissatisfaction with work. Conversely, improvements in hygiene factors remove the barriers to positive attitudes in the workplace. However, improvement in hygiene factors alone is not sufficient to provide true job satisfaction.

Motivation Factors   Herzberg discovered that the factors that lead to dissatisfaction are completely different from those that provide satisfaction. He called the positive factors "motivation factors." These meet uniquely human needs and include achievement, personal development, job satisfaction, and recognition. Improving these factors can make people satisfied with work.

3. Challenging the Reward Process

Herzberg concluded that organizations should aim to motivate people through job satisfaction, rather than reward or pressure.

This led to the concept of job enrichment, which would enable organizations to liberate people from the tyranny of numbers and expand the creative role of an individual within the organization.

CONTEXT

Herzberg belonged to the humanist school of management thinking, which emphasizes the human aspects of organizations. The humanist tradition also includes Mary Parker Follett, Elton Mayo, Douglas McGregor, Abraham Maslow, Charles Handy, and Tom Peters.

Maslow's hierarchy of needs, formulated in 1943, influenced industrial psychologists like Herzberg by showing that work can be made more satisfying by giving greater emphasis to affection, ego, and self-actualization needs.

Herzberg's breakthrough was to identify hygiene and motivation factors. His work has had a lasting influence on human resource management; concepts such as self-development and job satisfaction have evolved from his insight that motivation comes from within the individual, rather than from a policy imposed by the company. It has also influenced organizations' rewards and remuneration packages.

The trend toward "cafeteria benefits" reflects Herzberg's belief that people choose the form of motivation that is most important to them. Many organizations believe that money is the sole motivation for workers; Herzberg offers a more subtle approach. There has been much subsequent academic debate over the extent to which pay or other factors are the most important motivators.

Guru Gary Hamel commented: "Too many organizations believe that the only motivation to work is an economic one. Treating knowledge assets like Skinnerian rats is hardly the way to get the best out of people. Herzberg offers a substantially more subtle approach—one that still has much to recommend it."

Critics of Herzberg argue that pay plays an important part in the motivational equation and can be used to reinforce other motivational levers. Others point out that people frequently describe good work experiences in terms that reflect credit on themselves—success, greater responsibility, or recognition. Conversely, they will blame bad work experiences on factors that are outside their control, such as poor working conditions or a difficult boss.

> If you have someone on a job, use him. If you can't use him, get rid of him.

Recent commentators believe that the main application of Herzberg's theories has been to nonmanual workers, where the hygiene factors are normally well satisfied. They believe that employees who are well rewarded will tend to emphasize motivational factors as more important.

FOR MORE INFORMATION

Herzberg, Frederick, Bernard Mausner, and Barbara Bloch Snyderman. *The Motivation to Work.* Rev. ed. Somerset, NJ: Transaction, 2003.

My Life and Work
HENRY FORD

WHY READ IT?
My Life and Work is an account of Henry Ford's life and business philosophy. It provides unique insights into the man who took mass production to new levels and opened up mass markets through consistently low pricing and standardization. It also highlights the risk of a single-product strategy and the problems of autocratic control.

GETTING STARTED
Ford's policy was to reduce the price, extend the operations, and improve the item. He did not bother about the costs. Price forces the costs down. Ford reduced prices by 58 percent at a time when demand was such that he could easily have raised them instead. Mass production was the consequence, not the cause, of his low prices.

Management and managers were dismissed by Ford as largely unnecessary—but his lack of faith in management, along with a total reliance on the Model T, later proved the undoing of the company.

CONTRIBUTION
1. Pricing and Costs
Ford stated his policy as being,

> to reduce the price, extend the operations, and improve the article. The reduction of price comes first. We have never considered any costs as fixed. Therefore we first reduce the price to the point where we believe more sales will result. Then we go ahead and try to make the prices. We do not bother about the costs. The new price forces the costs down. The more usual way is to take the costs and then determine the price, and although that method may be scientific in the narrow sense, it is not scientific in the broad sense. What use is it to know the cost, if it tells you that you cannot manufacture at a price at which the article can be sold?

Ford's commitment to lowering prices cannot be doubted. Between 1908 and 1916 he reduced prices by 58 percent at a time when demand was such that he could easily have raised them.

2. Marketing
In a sense Ford was both the most brilliant and the most senseless marketer in U.S. history. He was senseless because he refused to give the customer anything but a black car. He was brilliant because he fashioned a production system designed to fit market needs. We usually celebrate him for the wrong reason, his production genius. His real genius was marketing.

3. Standardization
Ford realized that the mass car market existed; it just remained for him to provide the products the market wanted. Model Ts were black, straightforward, and affordable. At the center of Ford's thinking was the goal of standardization—something continually emphasized by the automakers of today.

4. Problems of a Single Product

The problem was that when other manufacturers added extras, Ford kept it simple and dramatically lost ground.

Such was Ford's commitment to the unadulterated version, he is reputed to have kicked a slightly modified Model T to pieces. But the company's reliance on the Model T nearly drove it to self-destruction. The man with a genius for marketing lost touch with the aspirations of customers.

> I have no use for a motor car which has more spark plugs than a cow has teats.

5. Mass Production

Ford is celebrated for his transformation of the production line into a means of previously unimagined mass production. He calculated that the production of a Model T required 7,882 different operations. Production was based around strict functional divides or demarcations. Ford believed in people getting on with their jobs and not raising their heads above functional parapets. He didn't want engineers talking to salespeople or people making decisions without his say-so.

6. Authoritarian Control

Management and managers were dismissed by Ford as largely unnecessary, and he made a systematic, deliberate, and conscious attempt to run the billion-dollar business without managers. Ford's lack of faith in management proved the undoing of the huge corporate empire he assembled. Without his autocratic belligerence to drive the company forward, it quickly ground to a halt.

7. Innovation in Business

In some respects Ford remains a good role model. He was an improviser and innovator who borrowed ideas and then adapted and synthesized them. He developed flow lines that involved people; now, we have flow lines without people, but no one questions their relevance or importance.

Though he is seen as having dehumanized work, Ford provided a level of wealth for workers and products for consumers that weren't previously available. He introduced the $5 a day wage for his workers, which at that time was around twice the average for the industry.

He had an international perspective that was ahead of his time. His plant at Highland Park, Detroit, produced his cars, but the world, not just the United States, bought them.

Ford was acutely aware that time was an important competitive weapon. "Time waste differs from material waste in that there can be no salvage," he wrote.

CONTEXT

My Life and Work is a robust account of Ford's life and business philosophy, although it is notable for the dominance of the former and the lack of the latter. Ford's business achievements and contribution to the development of industrialization are likely to be remembered long after his theories on politics, history, motivation, or humanity.

FOR MORE INFORMATION

Ford, Henry. *My Life and Work*. Rev. ed. North Stratford, NH: Ayer Company Publishers, 2000.

My Years with General Motors
ALFRED P. SLOAN JR.

WHY READ IT?
Alfred P. Sloan Jr. is one of the very few figures who undoubtedly changed the world of management. He was also one of the first managers to write an important theoretical book. *My Years with General Motors* is an account of his remarkable career and the creation of a new organizational form that spawned a host of imitators.

GETTING STARTED
Alfred P. Sloan Jr., a leading figure at General Motors from 1917, became its chief executive in 1946 and honorary chairman from 1956 until his death in 1966.

When he joined the company, the automobile market was dominated by Ford, and GM's market share was a mere 12 percent. GM was then an unwieldy combination of companies with eight models that competed against each other as well as against Ford. Sloan cut the eight models down to five and targeted each at a particular segment of the market. The five ranges were updated regularly and came in more than one color—unlike Ford's Model T. Sloan also reshaped the organization so that it was better suited to deliver his aspirations.

He created eight divisions—five auto and three component divisions. In today's jargon, these were strategic business units. Each had responsibility for its own commercial operations and its own engineering, production, and sales departments. The divisions were supervised by a central staff responsible for overall policy and finance.

Despite GM's recent parlous state (it filed for bankruptcy protection in June 2009), the main interest of *My Years with General Motors* for modern management thinkers lies in how Sloan managed to coordinate the semiautonomous divisions with the center and balance flexibility with control.

CONTRIBUTION
1. Balancing Flexibility with Control
The policy that Sloan labeled "federal decentralization" marked the invention of the decentralized, divisionalized organization. The multidivisional form enabled Sloan to utilize the company's size without making it cumbersome. Executives had more time to concentrate on strategic issues, and operational decisions were made by people in the front line rather than at distant headquarters.

By 1925, with its new organization and commitment to annual changes in its models, GM had overtaken Ford. Sloan's segmentation of the company changed the structure of the auto industry and also provided a model for how companies could do the same in other industries.

> I had learned that increased productivity would support higher wages.

2. Commitment to Employees
The book reveals that Sloan was committed to what at the time would have been regarded as progressive human resource management. In 1947 he established GM's employee-research section to look at employee attitudes, and he invested a large amount of his own time in selecting the right people for the job.

3. Problems in Decentralization

The decentralized structure revolved around a reporting and committee infrastructure that eventually became unwieldy. As time went by, more and more committees were established. Stringent targets and narrow measures of success stultified initiative. The organization proved quite incapable of creating and developing new businesses internally. This inability to manage organic expansion into new areas was caused by many factors:

- Operating responsibilities and measurement systems focused on profit and market share in existing markets.
- Business unit managers were not expected to look for new opportunities.
- The boxes in the organizational chart defined their product or geographic scope.
- Small, new ventures could not absorb the large central overheads and return the profits needed to justify the financial and human investments.

As Sloan himself put it: "In practically all our activities we seem to suffer from the inertia resulting from our great size. There are so many people involved and it requires such a tremendous effort to put something new into effect that a new idea is likely to be considered insignificant in comparison with the effort that it takes to put it across."

CONTEXT

Sloan established GM as a benchmark of corporate might, a symbol of U.S. strength and success. "What's good for GM is good for America," ran the popular mythology. Peter Drucker and Alfred Chandler celebrated his approach, but the deficiencies of the model were apparent to Sloan himself and were manifested in the decline of GM.

By the end of the 1960s the delicate balance that he had brilliantly maintained between centralization and decentralization was lost. Finance emerged as the dominant function, and GM became paralyzed by what had once made it great.

Gary Hamel commented:

> Can you be big and nimble? The question is as timely today as it was when Sloan took over General Motors. Despite divisionalization and decentralization, Sloan's organizational inventions, GM still fell victim to its size. . . . [T]he corporate superstructure that emerged to manage GM's independent divisions was more successful in creating bureaucracy than in exploiting cross-divisional synergies. The challenge of achieving divisional autonomy and flexibility on one hand, while reaping the benefits of scale and coordination on the other, is one that has eluded not only GM, but many other large companies as well.

One thing that should not be forgotten is that Sloan believed in managers and management in a way that his great rival Henry Ford did not. Nevertheless, as *The Economist* said: "Alfred Sloan did for the upper layers of management what Henry Ford did for the shop floor: he turned it into a reliable, efficient, machine-like process."

Of the book as a whole, Peter Drucker remarked: "It is perhaps the most impersonal book of memoirs ever written. And this was clearly intentional. Sloan's book knows only one dimension: that of managing a business so that it can produce effectively, provide jobs, create markets and sales, and generate profits."

FOR MORE INFORMATION

Sloan, Alfred P., Jr. *My Years with General Motors*. Rev. ed. New York: Doubleday, 1990.

Natural Capitalism
PAUL HAWKEN, AMORY B. LOVINS, AND L. HUNTER LOVINS

WHY READ IT?
The book offers an environmental perspective on economic activities. It includes practical advice on ways to transform business so that the earth's resources are protected.

GETTING STARTED
Natural Capitalism recognizes the critical relationship between the traditional creation of financial capital and the maintenance of natural resources. The book suggests an approach for reconciling ecological and economic priorities, one that not only protects the earth's environment but also improves profits and competitiveness. Environmental and economic priorities are normally considered contradictory, so that any state of balance requires tradeoffs. However, the authors believe that the best solutions may be based on design integration at all levels of economic activity, an approach they call "natural capitalism."

CONTRIBUTION
1. The Concept of Natural Capital
"Natural capital," according to the authors, comprises the world's resources, living systems, and ecosystem services. These, they feel, are being depleted at a dangerous rate. They explain how increased resource productivity would enable business and consumers to obtain the same amount of utility from a product or process while using less material or energy. These natural efficiencies go way beyond industry's current marginal performance gains. They believe that, if natural capitalism became widely accepted, resource productivity could grow at least fourfold, allowing people to live twice as well, yet use half as much.

2. The Stages of Natural Capitalism
The authors divide natural capitalism into four key strategies:

- radical resource productivity
- biologically inspired production models
- a solutions-based business model
- reinvesting in natural capital

These strategies, they say, offer benefits and opportunities in markets, finance, materials, distribution, and employment.

3. Radical Resource Productivity
According to the authors, radical resource productivity is the cornerstone of natural capitalism. It means obtaining the same amount of utility or work from a product, while using fewer materials and less energy. In simple terms, this means doing more with less. The authors believe that fundamental changes in production design and technology offer the opportunity to develop ways to make natural resources such as energy, minerals, water, and forests stretch 5, 10, even 100 times further than they do today.

In manufacturing, transportation, forestry, construction, energy, and other industrial sectors, the authors' evidence suggests that radical improvements in resource productivity are both practical and cost-effective. Designers, they believe, are already developing ways to make natural resources work much harder. These efficiencies transcend the marginal gains in performance that industry constantly seeks as part of its evolution. According to the authors, these revolutionary leaps in design and technology will alter industry itself.

4. Biologically Inspired Production Models

Taking examples from the natural world, the authors show how living organisms can produce complex "products" from recycled materials using minimal amounts of sustainable resources. Some of these products, such as the spider's silk or the cellulose produced by trees, have qualities that outperform their human-made equivalents. The authors argue that industry should learn from these natural techniques, a process they call "bio-mimicry." This approach seeks not only to reduce waste but to eliminate the very concept of waste.

5. A Solutions-based Business Model

The business model of traditional manufacturing rests on the sale of goods: A consumer uses the product for a limited period and disposes of it at the end of its useful life. This process, the authors argue, is extremely wasteful. They offer an alternative model, whereby a physical product owned by a consumer is replaced by a flow of services.

A simple example might be a washing machine that is owned, maintained, and upgraded by the manufacturer. When its useful life is finished, the manufacturer is responsible for recycling the product. Another example would be providing access to the entire catalogs of music companies by subscription rather than purchasing individual CDs. This shift of responsibility, they claim, would reduce consumption, but improve consumer choice.

> Companies and designers are developing ways to make natural resources—energy, metals, waters, and forests—work five, ten, even one hundred times harder than they do today.

6. Reinvesting in Natural Capital

According to the authors, sustaining, restoring, and expanding natural stocks of capital would work toward reversing worldwide planetary destruction, and governments are already recognizing the importance of using resource productivity to achieve this. The authors use terms such as "Factor Four," which means that resource productivity can and should grow fourfold; in other words, the amount of wealth extracted from one unit of natural resources can quadruple.

CONTEXT

Natural Capitalism is one of the increasing number of books that argue for a more ecologically sound approach to business. Unlike many more confrontational books that attack industry and offer no solution, *Natural Capitalism* shows how industry can adapt by learning from the natural world. Whereas most commentators believe that environmental and economic priorities are contradictory, this book attempts to reconcile them. Above all, it indicates opportunities that could lead to nothing less than a transformation of commerce and all societal institutions.

FOR MORE INFORMATION

Hawken, Paul, Amory B. Lovins, and L. Hunter Lovins. *Natural Capitalism: The Next Industrial Revolution*. Boston: Back Bay Books, 2000.

The Nature of Managerial Work
HENRY MINTZBERG

WHY READ IT?
Mintzberg is regarded by many as a leading contemporary management thinker, and this book was the first to explore what managers actually do at work. It goes behind the myths and the self-perceptions to describe the day-to-day work of a manager.

GETTING STARTED
What managers actually do, how they do it, and why are fundamental questions. Managers believe they deal with big strategic issues, but in reality they move from task to task dogged by diversions. Managerial work in general is marked by variety, brevity, and fragmentation.

Managers have three key roles, and the prominence of each role varies in different managerial jobs.

CONTRIBUTION
1. What Managers Do—The Myth
There are a number of generally accepted myths. Managers believe
- that they sit in solitude contemplating the great strategic issues of the day;
- that they make time to reach the best possible decisions; and
- that their meetings are high-powered, concentrating on the meta-narrative rather than the nitty-gritty.

The reality went largely unexplored until Henry Mintzberg's book.

2. What Managers Do—The Reality
Mintzberg went in search of the reality. He simply observed what a number of managers actually did. The resulting book blew away the managerial mystique.

Managers did not spend time contemplating the long term. They were slaves to the moment, moving from task to task, with every move dogged by another diversion, another call. The median time spent by a manager on any one issue was a mere nine minutes.

3. The Characteristics of the Manager at Work
Mintzberg observed that the typical manager
- performs a great quantity of work at an unrelenting pace;
- undertakes activities marked by variety, brevity, and fragmentation;
- has a preference for issues that are current, specific, and nonroutine;
- prefers verbal rather than written means of communication;
- acts within a web of internal and external contacts; and
- is subject to heavy constraints but can exert some control over the work.

4. Managers' Key Roles
From these observations, Mintzberg identified the manager's work roles as
- interpersonal,
- informational, and
- decisional.

Interpersonal Roles

- Figurehead: representing the organization/unit to outsiders
- Leader: motivating subordinates, unifying effort
- Liaiser: maintaining lateral contacts

> The manager undertakes activities marked by variety, brevity, and fragmentation.

Informational Roles

- Monitor: overseeing information flows
- Disseminator: providing information to subordinates
- Spokesman: transmitting information to outsiders

Decisional Roles

- Entrepreneur: initiating and designing change
- Disturbance handler: handling nonroutine events
- Resource allocator: deciding who gets what and who will do what
- Negotiator: negotiating

All managerial work encompasses these roles, but the prominence of each role varies in different managerial jobs.

CONTEXT

Henry Mintzberg is perhaps the world's premier management thinker, according to Tom Peters. His reputation has been made not by popularizing new techniques, but by rethinking the business fundamentals of strategy and structure, management, and planning.

His work on strategy—in particular his ideas of emergent strategy and grassroots strategy making—has been highly influential for years.

Best-selling author and management guru Gary Hamel commented: "Five reasons I like Henry Mintzberg: he is a world class iconoclast. He loves the messy world of real companies. He is a master storyteller. He is conceptual and pragmatic. He doesn't believe in easy answers."

The Nature of Managerial Work has produced few worthwhile imitators, but Mintzberg's rigor and originality have given his ideas staying power.

FOR MORE INFORMATION

Mintzberg, Henry. *The Nature of Managerial Work*. New York: Harper & Row, 1973.

The New Corporate Cultures
TERRENCE DEAL AND ALLAN KENNEDY

WHY READ IT?

Deal and Kennedy wrote the first significant book on corporate culture, *Corporate Cultures: Rites and Rituals of Corporate Life*, in 1982. Their later book, *The New Corporate Cultures*, reexamines its role in the light of accelerating changes in the business environment. They set out to demonstrate how organizations with a strong culture have survived and succeeded, despite the impact of globalization, information technology, mergers, and downsizing, and how an understanding of corporate cultures, coupled with strong leadership, can prove an effective model for business.

GETTING STARTED

The authors argue that corporate culture is a unifying factor that enables people to cooperate to achieve a common goal. However, a number of factors have militated against the development and maintenance of an effective culture: the demand for short-term results, the impact of downsizing and mergers, the introduction of outsourcing, and the effect of computers on business relationships. Organizations wishing to regain lost ground must now rebuild their cultures from the bottom up through strong leadership and high performance.

> The key to effective leadership in corporations is reading and responding to cultural clues.

CONTRIBUTION
1. Culture Breeds Financial Success

The authors demonstrate the value of corporate culture by analyzing financial performance. The companies they identified as top performers in 1982 outperformed average stock market growth by nearly 50 percent.

2. The Impact of Short-term Needs

They also explain, however, how the rise of stockholder value played a key role in reducing the importance of corporate culture. The emphasis on short-term results, coupled with a growth in institutional ownership, meant that long-term actions proved unattractive to many organizations. Cutting costs to achieve short-term results led to a wave of downsizing and reengineering. This, in turn, ended the concept of lifetime employment and destroyed trust within organizations.

3. Outsourcing, Downsizing, Mergers, and IT

Downsizing, say the authors, damages a corporate culture by destroying trust and breaking the link between leaders and employees. Outsourcing, they claim, has a similarly damaging effect, because when organizations focus on their core activities and outsource everything else, employees may be transferred to other organizations, losing benefits and severing their links with the original employer.

The rapid increase in mergers has likewise tested corporate cultures. Mergers create a climate of uncertainty for employees, because there are always winners and losers.

Information technology also has, in the authors' view, had a significant adverse effect. Although personal computers empower the people who use them, they can also isolate people from each other and break the informal links that are an important part of corporate culture.

4. The Effect of Globalization

Globalization, according to Deal and Kennedy, has accelerated the outsourcing and down-sizing trends by enabling companies to source from around the world. Management is also affected by globalization, as multinational managers struggle to operate in different cultures.

5. The Need for Cultural Leadership

The authors believe that cultural leadership is key to overcoming the problems that have emerged. Managers must find out what employees really believe about the company and translate that into a statement that represents the company's position. Finding the common ground and turning it into a set of shared beliefs helps to shape the overall corporate vision.

6. Challenge People

It is important, the authors suggest, to measure the progress of cultural revitalization in financial terms. Celebrating victories can bring people together. However, performance standards should not necessarily be based on financial targets. Setting people other challenges can help to create a strong culture. Companies must rebuild trust by emphasizing the importance of employees to the business. Transparency is an important part of that process. To ensure a high standard of performance, the authors recommend hiring and rewarding the right people. However, they point out that the organizational structure must be right to get the most from people. A rigid divisional structure tends to isolate people, so transferring them can help to redress the balance.

7. Building Teamwork

The authors recommend the introduction of cultural revitalization teams with access to senior management. The team should try to identify subcultures, small informal groups who work together and can form the basis of strong teams. Encouraging formal and informal meetings also helps to rebuild the connections inside a company. The authors explain how factors such as job security, job satisfaction, and a socially rewarding environment create a more attractive culture.

CONTEXT

When Deal and Kennedy introduced the term *corporate cultures* in 1982, it received a mixed reaction. Supporters believed it provided a valuable insight into the inner workings of an organization. Critics felt it was a superficial application of the discipline of anthropology to management.

The term is now an accepted part of business language and forms a key element of corporate strategy. Edgar Schein, writing in *Organization, Culture, and Leadership*, expresses his belief that the only important thing leaders do is create and manage corporate culture.

FOR MORE INFORMATION

Deal, Terrence, and Allan Kennedy. *The New Corporate Cultures*. Reading, MA: Perseus Books, 2000.

FURTHER READING

Deal, Terrence, and Allan Kennedy. *Corporate Cultures: Rites and Rituals of Corporate Life*. Reading, MA: Perseus Books, 2000.

New Patterns of Management
RENSIS LIKERT

WHY READ IT?
The author was a pioneer of attitude surveys and introduced an attitude scale that is now widely used in business research. The book explains how he used his research tools to identify patterns of participative management and organization that would bring success in an increasingly competitive environment.

GETTING STARTED
Rensis Likert was a pioneer of attitude surveys and poll design, as well as social research as a whole. According to Likert, there are four types of management style:
- exploitative and authoritarian
- benevolent autocracy
- consultative
- participative

Participative management is the best option, as increased participation and individualism is essential to meet increased competition. Participative groups can improve management and performance. The greater the loyalty of a group, the greater the motivation to achieve its goals.

An organization's style can be linked directly to its performance. The route to understanding managerial performance is improved measurement.

CONTRIBUTION
1. Measuring Attitudes
In Likert's doctoral thesis, written in 1932 while he was at Columbia University and entitled "A Technique for the Measurement of Attitudes," he introduced a straightforward five-point scale by which attitudes could be measured. The now well-known scale ranges from "strongly agree" to "strongly disagree" and is known as the Likert Scale.

2. The Contribution of Participative Groups
Likert's business research focused on the ways in which participative groups could improve management and performance. It also examined the human systems that exist in organizations. He concluded that the greater the loyalty of a group, the greater is the motivation among members to achieve the goals of the group, and the greater the probability that the group will achieve its goals.

3. Management Styles
Likert identified four types of management style, each of which tends to mold people in its own image. Authoritarian organizations tend to develop dependent people and few leaders. Participative management was seen by Likert as the best option, both in a business and a personal sense. In his view, participative organizations tend to develop emotionally and socially mature people capable of effective interaction, initiative, and leadership.

4. Organizational Style and Performance

"Managers with the best records of performance in American business and government are in the process of pointing the way to an appreciably more effective system of management than now exists," Likert writes in the book's opening. With the assistance of social science research, it is now possible to state a generalized theory of organization based on the management practices of these highest producers.

5. The Importance of Participation

Increased participation in the workplace and individualism are necessary consequences of increased competition and quickly accelerating technological improvement. Likert asserts that there is a much greater need for cooperation and participation in managing the enterprise than when technologies were simple and the chief possessed all the technical knowledge needed.

> Authoritarian organizations tend to develop dependent people and few leaders.

6. The Importance of Measurement

Management can make a difference, and the route to understanding managerial performance is improved measurement. In the author's opinion, an organization should be outstanding in its performance
- if it has competent personnel;
- if it has leadership that develops highly effective groups and uses the overlapping group form of structure; and
- if it achieves effective communication and influence, decentralized and coordinated decision making, and high performance goals coupled with high motivation.

CONTEXT

Likert's research highlights the importance of participative styles of management. This book bids farewell to the world of blind obedience and corporate man or woman. Likert picks up the mood of individualism, which was to sweep the world later in the 1960s. The book provides a blueprint for the ideal organization that has largely stood the test of time.

FOR MORE INFORMATION

Likert, Rensis. *New Patterns of Management*. New York: McGraw-Hill, 1961.

No Logo
NAOMI KLEIN

WHY READ IT?
No Logo is not a business handbook; it is an analysis of the impact of unchecked globalization. The book posits that nation-states have been rendered powerless, while corporations have gained de facto power. Klein's controversial political opinions earned her the sobriquet "Marx for the new millennium." Drawing on four years' research, *No Logo* details the origins of a global economic system and explores anticorporate "resistance." After the collapse of the WTO trade talks in Seattle in 1999 following massive street protests and the now seemingly routine demonstrations that dog any international trade meeting, Klein's message would make many a chief executive sit up and take notice.

GETTING STARTED
No Logo sets out to show how three forces have given rise to waves of anticorporate activism: the subverting of indigenous cultures through global branding; the loss of choice as brands overrule demand through predatory franchising, mergers, aggressive advertising, and corporate censorship; and the changes in global labor markets toward cheap labor, temporary work, and "portfolio" careers. Corporate social responsibility is rejected because it "favours only those being responsible." Klein's focus is on the reaction to this, and she does not support the suggestion that the world is "getting smaller." Instead, she questions how "small" the world actually is by dispelling the romantic myth of the tribal nomad in a jungle playing video games via a broadband satellite connection, and by drawing attention to the "digital divide." Klein argues that public activism is the only democratic alternative to unchecked globalization.

CONTRIBUTION
1. The Birth of the Brand
According to Klein, the development of economies of scale has required production to shift to locations that can offer suppliers the cheapest prices. Fashion and familiarity are essential to generating sales, as symbolized by Philip Morris's acquisition of Kraft for $12.6 billion— six times the company's real equity. The high price derived from Kraft's brand; its name brought tangible sales. Distinguishing between advertising—merely informing customers of something—and branding, Klein argues that communicating a powerful, emotionally resonant "image" distorts markets through changing tastes. The number of channels communicating "brands" are increasing: even schools grant exclusive advertising rights in canteens, corridors, and toilets. Klein suggests that brands put image before products. For example, IBM does not sell computers, it sells "solutions." Richard Branson argues that brands revolve solely around reputation, a fragile strategy. If Branson's Virgin trains are late, though, Klein argues, people will lose trust in his airline, record shops, and financial products.

2. Space, Choice, and Jobs
In Klein's view, big brands force out small businesses by using mergers, predatory pricing, and economies of scale to ensure that they cannot survive. Branding ensures there is only a market for specific "images," which creates monopolies. Only multinationals can employ such anticompetitive measures; gaining ever-greater levels of market share, they take over a

disproportionate amount of physical space. Starbucks coffee shops operate by "clustering," saturating areas with branches to force local cafes out of the market. Klein suggests that this removes consumer choice and destroys the local culture. A few corporations—a plutocracy—have unprecedented control.

According to the author, this has altered the labor market. After a century of improvements in working standards, corporations in both the developed and developing world are abusing their position. Klein suggests that scenes common during the Industrial Revolution recur in the developing world today. Child labor, excessive working hours, low pay, and hazardous conditions put a downward pressure on wages globally. "Outsourcing" produces lower wages and higher unemployment in rich countries. Globalization makes this inevitable in Klein's view: maximizing profit means producing where labor is cheaper. The author uses the example of Cavite, the Filipino free-trade zone, where workers face rules against talking and smiling and must endure forced overtime. Klein argues that branding prevents consumers from questioning multinational corporations and their unethical actions and removes the incentive to behave responsibly. Now, concern about unethical practices is pressuring corporations into being socially responsible. One urban teenager said, "Nike, we made you. We can break you." This, Klein suggests, is the new democracy.

> Nike, we made you. We can break you.

3. No Logo

No Logo shows how resistance to brands has developed as consumers feel rising resentment at brands' colonization of their lives, some even suggesting that the backlash is comparable to the civil rights campaigns of earlier generations. There are boycotts against "unethical" companies, and activists are "as global and capable of co-ordinated action as the multinational corporations they seek to subvert." Some successful corporations pride themselves on being "responsible"; Shell, for example, commits resources to developing "clean" fuels. Klein argues that consumers are becoming cynical, though. Nike has advertised that "high heels are a conspiracy against women," which is often interpreted as a self-serving attempt to both be antisexist and justify exorbitant prices. The "brand backlash" has begun.

CONTEXT

Critics view the anticorporate movement as having no common ideology except angry anarchism. When "indigenous" cultures choose development, they are denounced as being "exploited" by "imperialists." In fact, many East Asian Tiger economies, such as Taiwan and Japan, have become as rich as the societies they trade with. However, if consumers are antagonized by those aiming to serve their needs, something is wrong. If corporations put "image" before delivering value, consumers will lose trust in them. Reflecting the fact that the anticorporate movement is in its infancy, *No Logo* ignores the benefits of the system it condemns—including the greater accountability brands have to local businesses or technology transfer to low-cost locations—while providing few practical solutions. What it does do, however, is draw its readers' attention to the need for greater—and genuine—corporate social responsibility.

FOR MORE INFORMATION

Klein, Naomi. *No Logo*. New York: Picador USA, 2000.

Now, Discover Your Strengths
MARCUS BUCKINGHAM AND DONALD CLIFTON

WHY READ IT?
Most firms, according to the authors, go about things the wrong way when training their staff. They try to make up for their employees' weaknesses and concentrate on filling in gaps. The right thing to do, the authors advise, is to identify the special talents that employees possess and work on them to build up their strengths.

GETTING STARTED
On the basis of a wide-ranging survey, Buckingham and Clifton claim to have identified over 30 main "themes" of human talent. The particular gifts of each and every human individual can be described in terms of these themes, they say. Their book presents these themes in their various manifestations, explains how a strength profile works, and shows how the results can be translated into the everyday business of management.

CONTRIBUTION
1. The Anatomy of a Strength
Three tools are required to make use of one's own and other people's strengths:
- an ability to distinguish innate talents from things that can be learned;
- a system to enable one to recognize the predominant talents in oneself and others; and
- a common language to describe talents.

If we want to build up strengths, say the authors, we need know-how as well as knowledge. Know-how gives structure to knowledge derived from experience, inasmuch as it enables accumulated knowledge to be formalized as a series of steps, which, if followed, will produce results. Know-how enables us to avoid proceeding by trial and error and to incorporate the best insights in our performance. Buckingham and Clifton define talent as any persistent pattern of thought, feeling, or behavior that can be made use of productively. Talents, they say, are unique, dependable, and long-lasting.

2. Recognizing the Origins of Strengths
The authors claim that anybody can determine where his or her greatest strength potential lies by using their "StrengthFinder Profile" which includes, among others, achiever, activator, adaptability, analytical, belief, command, communication, competition, connectedness, context, deliberative, discipline, empathy, fairness, focus, futuristic, harmony, ideation, input, learner, relator, restorative, self-assurance, significance, and strategic.

3. Making Use of Strengths
The main purpose of the StrengthFinder is to achieve the best possible performance over time. The authors claim, for example, that it is possible to use this system to uncover one's own strongest talent themes, come to grips with them, and combine them into strengths. By concentrating on our strengths, we also find ways to manage our weaknesses.

There are five separate strategies for weakness management, discussed by the authors:
- getting a little better in the area of weakness,
- developing a support system,
- deploying a strong talent to overcome the weakness,

- finding a complementary partner, and
- accepting the weakness.

With the help of the talent themes listed in the book, employees can be successfully managed and their needs satisfied in ways such as these:

- Employees with analytical gifts should be presented with precise and well-founded figures and facts, and the logic of any decisions affecting them should be explained.
- Adaptable employees should be deployed for short-term tasks that demand immediate action.
- "Arrangers" should be given as much responsibility as possible, taking into account their knowledge and abilities.
- Employees with authority should be given as much scope as possible to make their own decisions, but prevented from building up their own little empires.
- Cautious employees should be kept away from any tasks that demand quick decisions and instead be made members of teams.
- Disciplined employees should be given the opportunity to bring order to a planless or chaotic situation.
- Enthusiastic employees should be given scope to bring drive and energy to their jobs or their teams.

> You will be most successful when you craft your role to play to your signature talents most of the time.

4. Building the Strength-based Business

The book describes four steps to constructing an organization built on people's strengths:

1. Management should spend a lot of time and money finding and appointing the right employees. It is a matter of discovering the "right" talent for every job.
2. The talents of each individual are unique. Consequently the company should concentrate on foregrounding results, instead of trying to press everybody into the same stylistic mold.
3. The main potential for growth in every person lies in the area of his or her greatest strengths. Training, therefore, should be focused on people's strong points and on ways of building these further.
4. Since people are best able to move on in the areas in which they are naturally gifted, management should do its best to find ways of furthering employees' careers without necessarily forcing them up the company ladder or promoting them out of areas where their strengths are most effective.

These four steps, say Buckingham and Clifton, represent a systematic process whereby the values bound up in a company's "human capital" can be maximized.

CONTEXT

The book is based on two long-term studies by the Gallup Institute, in which more than a million employees were surveyed and interviews were conducted with more than 80,000 managers. The authors defined their talent themes on the basis of this material. Their "talents" make individuals act in particular ways that management can make use of. Ultimately, then, the book is a plea for a very individual style of management.

FOR MORE INFORMATION

Buckingham, Marcus, and Donald Clifton. *Now, Discover Your Strengths*. New York: Free Press, 2000.

On Becoming a Leader
WARREN BENNIS

WHY READ IT?

Warren Bennis is widely respected as one of the foremost thinkers on leadership, and this book is regarded as a classic. It explains how people become leaders, how they lead, and how organizations respond to leadership. It is not based on academic theory, but rather offers practical advice based on interviews with a mix of leaders from many different fields.

GETTING STARTED

Bennis believes that there is no exact science of leadership. Leaders vary in background, education, and experience. However, he identifies certain characteristics as essential for success. According to Bennis, leaders should know what they want and should be able to communicate what they want to others to gain their support. Leaders should also understand their own strengths and weaknesses and use them to achieve their goals. Bennis explains the phenomenon of leadership by defining its distinctive qualities, especially those that set a leader apart from a boss or manager; highlighting the experiences that were vital to the development of leaders; identifying the turning points; and examining the role of failure.

CONTRIBUTION
1. The Importance of Leadership
Bennis explains that leaders are important for three reasons:
- They are responsible for the effectiveness of organizations.
- They provide a focal point.
- They provide a recognizable constant in the midst of rapid change.

2. Leading and Managing
According to Bennis, the ingredients of leadership are wide-ranging, and they include guiding vision, passion, integrity, self-knowledge, trust, and daring. Leaders, he argues, may be highly competent, but can fail to win the hearts and minds of the people they are leading.

Bennis believes that there is a significant difference between a leader and a boss, especially a boss in a results-driven management role. The drive for short-term results can run counter to the effectiveness of a visionary leader.

There are also many important differences between managers and leaders, he argues. The former have short-term rather than long-term perspectives, focus on systems rather than people, accept the status quo rather than challenging it, and exercise control instead of inspiring trust.

3. Leaders and Learning
Leaders, according to Bennis, are their own best teachers. They accept responsibility and gain from their own experience and that of others.

He distinguishes between maintenance learning and shock learning, both of which are familiar to managers, and what he calls innovative learning, which involves listening to others. This type of learning, he explains, means that people are free to express themselves, rather than just explain themselves. True intellect, he believes, is being able to see how things can be different.

4. The Value of Failure

Bennis suggests that leaders also learn from adversity. Making mistakes should not be punished. Leaders must operate on instinct, a process based on the use of the left- and right-hand sides of the brain. Managers, in contrast, rely on tried and tested processes.

According to Bennis, leaders should try everything, even in the face of failure. Few people venture into uncharted waters because of the risk of failure.

5. Achieving Goals

Leaders should be able to shift perspective so that they can see what is most important.

Bennis argues that leadership, unlike any other skill, cannot be broken down into a series of repeatable maneuvers. The creative process involved in reaching a goal is infinitely complex. As he explains, leaders have to be able to move through chaos and synthesize all the elements needed for success.

6. Gaining Support

Bennis argues that leaders must get people on their side to effect change. Empathy is therefore an important characteristic of leadership. This, he explains, is in contrast to theories of leadership by force.

Leadership, he believes, requires persuasion, not giving orders. This requires an understanding of the needs of other people and the ability to communicate a vision.

CONTEXT

Leadership did not attract serious academic interest until the 1985 publication of *Leaders: Strategies for Taking Change*, written in conjunction with Burt Nanus. It is now one of the most popular topics in management literature and training, and Warren Bennis has made an important contribution.

Bennis's work is based on extensive research with leaders in every field. One project involved interviews with 90 of America's leaders, including astronaut Neil Armstrong, the coach of the LA Rams, orchestral conductors, and businesspeople such as Ray Kroc of McDonald's.

Bennis argues that leadership is not a rare skill. Leaders are made rather than born; they are usually ordinary, or apparently ordinary, people rather than obviously charismatic figures. Leadership, moreover, is not solely the preserve of those at the top of the organization—it is relevant at all levels.

> Leaders today sometimes appear to be an endangered species, caught in the whirl of events and circumstances beyond rational control.

FOR MORE INFORMATION

Bennis, Warren. *On Becoming a Leader*. 2nd ed. Cambridge, MA: Perseus, 2003.

FURTHER READING

Bennis, Warren, and Burt Nanus. *Leaders: Strategies for Taking Charge*. 2nd ed. New York: Collins, 2003.

On the Economy of Machinery and Manufactures
CHARLES BABBAGE

WHY READ IT?

Charles Babbage was one of the great minds of the first Industrial Revolution. He is credited with pioneering the computer and wrote extensively about the importance of data and manufacturing. This book offers fascinating insights into the early development of manufacturing techniques.

GETTING STARTED

In an age of economic theory, Babbage argued for a highly scientific approach. His emphasis on fact finding influenced not only the practical elements of factory management in the early industrial era, but the formation of interpretive theory. Mechanical principles govern manufacturing, and merchants and manufacturers are the best people to supply the data on which all the reasoning of political economists is founded. People should not fear bad deductions from good facts.

Good factory organization is important, and factories require an entire system of operation. The most important principle of manufacture is the division of labor.

It is vital to calculate the life expectancy of capital equipment. In five years capital equipment ought to have paid for itself, and in ten it should be superseded by a better version.

CONTRIBUTION
1. Mechanical Principles Govern Manufacturing

Babbage's fundamental approach was highly scientific. He held that mechanical principles regulate the application of machinery to arts and manufacture.

First, he said, it's essential to gather the evidence. Babbage did so through touring factories exhaustively in the United Kingdom and Europe. The book provides helpful hints and a checklist of questions on how to find the best information when touring a factory.

2. Make Use of Facts

Political economists have been reproached with too small a use of facts and too large an employment of theory. "If facts are wanting, the closet-philosopher is unfortunately too little acquainted with the admirable arrangements of the factory," Babbage wrote. "The merchant and manufacturer are the best people to supply readily, and with so little sacrifice of time, the data on which all the reasoning of political economists are founded."

3. Collecting Data Is Essential

People should not fear that erroneous deductions may be made from recorded facts. The errors that arise from the absence of facts are far more numerous and more durable than those that result from unsound reasoning based on true data.

Babbage encouraged managers to follow his example and gather their own data. Collecting data is essential for manufacturers who want to know how many additional customers they will acquire by a given reduction in the price of the articles they make.

4. Good Factory Organization Is Important

The arrangements that should regulate the interior economy of a factory are founded on deeply rooted principles. Babbage recognized that the factory requires an entire system of operation. It needs to be organized in a vastly different way from the conventional means of production.

Babbage's book provides insights in two central areas; economies of scale and the division of labor.

5. Calculating the Right Division of Labor

Perhaps the most important principle on which the economy of manufacture depends is the division of labor among the people who perform the work.

"The number of operations performed in a given time may frequently be counted when the workman is quite unconscious that any person is observing him," Babbage said. "For example, the sound made by the motion of a loom may enable the observer to count the number of strokes per minute, even though he is outside the building in which it is contained."

6. Life Expectancy of Capital Equipment

Machinery for producing any commodity in great demand seldom actually wears out. New improvements, by which the same operations can be executed either more quickly or better, generally supersede it long before that time arrives. To make such an improved machine profitable, it is usually reckoned that in five years it ought to have paid for itself, and in ten it should be replaced by a better machine.

> Political economists have been reproached with too small a use of facts, and too large an employment of theory.

CONTEXT

The book was a best seller in its time. Babbage was one of the first to recognize the importance of factories, economically and socially. In that sense, the book is like the first one on the potential of the Internet.

Babbage was a pioneer of modern management. His approach bears more than a passing resemblance to that later adopted by the U.S. champion of scientific management, Frederick Taylor. He beckoned in the industrial era and, in doing so, laid the intellectual groundwork for Marx, Engels, and John Stuart Mill. Contrasts can be made with Adam Smith, whose economic viewpoint remained stuck in the agricultural era.

Joseph Schumpeter described this book as "a remarkable performance of a remarkable man."

FOR MORE INFORMATION

Babbage, Charles. *On the Economy of Machinery and Manufactures*. New York: Dodo Press, 2006.

On War
KARL VON CLAUSEWITZ

WHY READ IT?
Von Clausewitz believed that comparisons between military action and commerce are valid and useful. His book explains this comparison in detail and provides examples based on key concepts such as strategy, use of resources, and response to competitors. Other management thinkers agree that military thinkers like von Clausewitz can provide valuable insight for business.

GETTING STARTED
Military and commercial comparisons are valid for a number of reasons. Commerce, like war, is a conflict of interests and activities. Plans must be flexible and take account of competitors—and the best way to achieve flexibility is to operate along a line that offers alternative objectives. Theory is only an aid to decision making, and it is important to achieve results through minimal effort. It is important to remember that strategy and tactics are different and that objectives should be concentrated on one at a time.

CONTRIBUTION
1. Military and Commercial Comparisons Are Valid
Karl von Clausewitz firmly believed that comparisons between the military and commercial worlds were both valid and useful.

"Rather than comparing it [war] to art we could more accurately compare it to commerce, which is also a conflict of interests and activities," he wrote. "It is still closer to politics, which in turn may be considered as a kind of commerce on a larger scale."

2. Plans Must Be Flexible
To be practical, any plan must take account of the enemy's power to frustrate it. The best chance of overcoming obstruction is to have a plan that can easily be varied to fit the circumstances. To maintain such adaptability while still keeping the initiative, the best way is to operate along a line that offers alternative objectives.

3. Theory Is Only an Aid to Decision Making
Knowing is different from doing, and therefore theory must never be used as the norm for a standard, but merely as an aid to judgment.

Pragmatism is combined with a desire to achieve results through minimal effort.

A prince or general can best demonstrate his genius by managing a campaign exactly to suit his objectives and his resources, doing neither too much nor too little.

4. Strategy and Tactics Are Different
Von Clausewitz differentiates between strategy, the overall plan, and mere tactics, the planning of a discrete part of the overall plan (the battle, for example). Grand strategy represents the overall political objectives. Arguments over the difference between strategy and tactics have raged inconclusively for many years.

5. Concentrate on One Objective at a Time

Success comes through concentrating on one battle at a time. This is the distant precursor of the managerial theory of management by objectives.

By looking at each engagement as part of a series, at least insofar as events are predictable, the commander is always on the high road to his goal.

CONTEXT

Soldiers have a surprisingly lengthy heritage as managerial exemplars, both in terms of practice and theory. Hadrian, for example, was a champion of "people power" long before the advent of human resource departments; his military reputation was forged on his willingness to share the same conditions as his troops. He was also a globe trotter—he didn't seek to control his empire from Rome but traveled throughout it. In modern parlance, he accepted the diversity of his empire. Hadrian was also reputed to have had an eye for financial management. He built up reserves to fund building projects and social welfare programs. At the same time, he didn't raise taxes.

> Rather than comparing it [war] to art we could more accurately compare it to commerce, which is also a conflict of interests and activities.

The Duke of Wellington can lay claim to "managing by wandering around" during the Napoleonic Wars. Historian John Keegan said, "Wellington's methods required a particularly intense managerial style—taking trouble with the battle."

Wellington said, "The general must make himself the eyes of his own army and must constantly change position to deal with crises as they occur along the front of his sheltered line; must remain at the point of crisis until it is resolved and must still keep alert to anticipate the development of crises elsewhere."

More recently, management thinkers have sought inspiration from leading military thinker Basil Liddell Hart, in particular from his 1967 book, *Strategy*. Management gurus including Richard Pascale have examined military approaches to such issues as leadership, training, motivation, and strategy.

FOR MORE INFORMATION

von Clausewitz, Karl. *On War*. Princeton, NJ: Princeton University Press, 1989.

Onward Industry
JAMES MOONEY AND ALAN REILEY

WHY READ IT?
The book provides insights into early thinking about the nature of organizations and their impact on the performance of industry. The authors argue that organization is a universal phenomenon and benefits the overall standard of living.

GETTING STARTED
Organization is a universal phenomenon that has existed throughout history. The organization of businesses is crucial to prosperity and living standards.

Production without distribution is worthless; the emphasis must be on finding and exploiting markets. Industry should encourage participation in business so that purchasing capacity can be created and extended. Organizational size is less important than knowing what to do with the organization.

CONTRIBUTION
1. Organization Is a Universal Phenomenon
People love to organize, and organization is as old as human society itself. Consider the scalar organization of the Catholic Church, governmental organization, and the evolution of various forms of organization from Roman times, to medieval times, to the company of the early 20th century.

2. Organization Is Crucial to Standards of Living
The organization of businesses is crucial to overall standards of living. There is a direct link between industrial prosperity, built on modern management techniques, and the affluence of society as a whole.

"The highest development of the techniques both of production and distribution will be futile to supply the material wants of those who, because of poverty, are unable to acquire through purchase," the authors write. The final task of industry, therefore, is to organize participation in these activities, even in the poorest communities and countries, through which purchasing capacity can be created and extended.

3. Production without Distribution Is Worthless
Before the 1930s, production was the overarching driving force. Later the emphasis shifted to finding new markets and enhancing and expanding distribution to make inroads into these markets.

4. The Value of Size
Size isn't everything. Modern business leadership has generally been characterized by the capacity to create large organizations, but also by failure in knowing exactly how to make effective use of them.

5. Key Organizational Principles
Mooney and Reiley's theory of organizations identified three important organizational principles:

- the coordinative principle, leading to effective coordination
- the scalar process, resulting in functional definition
- the functional effect, leading to interpretative functionalism

> Organization is as old as human society itself.

CONTEXT

The book provides an organization model that is firmly of its time. It applies the reasoned science of Frederick W. Taylor to the broader organizational canvas. The argument that production without distribution is worthless marks something of a watershed. Before the 1930s, production was the overarching driving force. After World War II the emphasis shifted to finding new markets and enhancing and expanding distribution to make inroads into those markets.

FOR MORE INFORMATION

Mooney, James, and Alan Reiley. *Onward Industry*. Rev. ed. Bristol, UK: Thoemmes Continuum, 2004.

The Organization Man
WILLIAM WHYTE

WHY READ IT?
From the viewpoint of the age of uncertainty, downsizing, reengineering, and "discontinuous change," the 1950s and 1960s can easily seem like a golden age. The careers enjoyed by corporate executives were built on solid foundations, workers had jobs for life, suburbia was heaven, and everything seemed set to go on and on and on. William Whyte showed the downside to this corporate utopia. Read his brilliant, witty, and often poignant analysis to put both the postwar past and the present in perspective.

GETTING STARTED
William Whyte joined the staff of *Fortune* magazine in 1946 after graduating from Princeton and serving in the U.S. Marines during World War II. *The Organization Man* is based on articles he wrote for the magazine. He subsequently left *Fortune* and, in his later years, wrote mainly on the subject of urban sprawl, urban planning, and human behavior in urban spaces.

In the 1950s the United States still publicly and privately subscribed to the idea that rugged individualism was the hallmark of the American character and the cornerstone of American success. According to Whyte, this was a delusion. Average citizens in fact subscribed to a collectivist social ethic that was turning them into organization people—and they needed to realize the fact and do something about it.

CONTRIBUTION
1. The Social Ethic
Whyte believed that the condition he was analyzing did not affect the United States alone; he referred to "a bureaucratization that has affected every country."

The bureaucratic or collectivist ethic rested on three major principles:
- a belief in the group as the source of creativity;
- a belief in "belongingness" as the ultimate need of every individual; and
- a belief in the application of science to achieve "belongingness."

Above all he believed that, "the fundamental principle of the new model executive is . . . that the goals of the individual and the goals of the organization will work out to be one and the same."

2. The Importance of Loyalty
Gray-suited and obedient, corporate man was unstintingly loyal to his employer. He spent his life with a single company and rose slowly, but quietly, up the hierarchy. Loyalty and solid performance brought job security. This was mutually beneficial. The executive gained a respectable income and a high degree of security. The company gained loyal, dependable, hardworking executives.

> The fault is not in organization, in short, it is in our worship of it.

But while loyalty is a positive quality, it can easily become blind. What if the corporate strategy is wrong, or the company is engaged in unlawful or immoral acts? The corporation becomes a self-contained and self-perpetuating world supported by a complex array of checks, systems, and hierarchies. The company is right.

In a remark reminiscent of George Orwell's *1984*, Whyte suggested that the organization man "must not only accept control, he must accept it as if he liked it."

3. Low-risk Environment

Customers, who exist outside the organization, are often regarded as peripheral. It sometimes appears that in the 1950s, 1960s, and 1970s, no executive ever lost his or her job by delivering poor quality or indifferent service. In some organizations, executives only lost their jobs for defrauding their employer or insulting their boss. Jobs for life was the refrain and, to a large extent for executives, the reality.

Clearly, such an environment was hardly conducive to the fostering of dynamic risk-takers. It rewarded the steady foot soldier, the safe pair of hands, the organization man living with his organization wife.

CONTEXT

Reviewing the book in the *New York Times*, C. Wright Mills wrote: "Whyte understands that the work-and-thrift ethic of success has grievously declined, except in the rhetoric of top executives; that the entrepreneurial scramble to success has been largely replaced by the organizational crawl."

Chester Barnard noted in *The Functions of the Executive*: "The most important single contribution required of an executive, certainly the most universal qualification, is loyalty [allowing] domination by the organization personality."

Twenty years after the publication of Whyte's book, things had not changed very much. When she came to examine corporate life for the first time in her 1977 book, *Men and Women of the Corporation*, Rosabeth Moss Kanter found that the central characteristic expected of a manager was dependability.

Fortune founder Henry Luce commented:

> It was *Fortune's* William H. Whyte, Jr. who made the "organization man" a household word, and the organization wife too. His was a fine achievement in sociological reporting. In it he related the phenomenon of the business organization to questions of human personality and values. The kind of people who are eager to hear the worst about U.S. society assumed that Mr. Whyte was predicting the destruction of individualism by the organization.

Whyte was uneasy about corporate life, which seemed to stifle creativity and individualism. He was also uneasy about the subtle pressures in the office and at home that called for smooth performance rather than daring creativity. However, he did not urge organization men to leave their secure environment. Rather, he urged them to fight against the organization when necessary, and he was optimistic that the battle could be successful.

FOR MORE INFORMATION

Whyte, William. *The Organization Man*. Rev. ed. Philadelphia: University of Pennsylvania Press, 2002.

Organizational Culture and Leadership
EDGAR H. SCHEIN

WHY READ IT?

Organizational Culture and Leadership clarified the entire area of corporate culture in a way no previous book had. It brought culture into the management debate and paved the way for a plethora of further studies. Even today, its perspectives on culture as a constantly changing force in corporate life remain as disconcerting as they are valuable.

GETTING STARTED

Schein is sometimes seen as the inventor of the term *corporate culture;* he is, at the very least, one of its originators. After a long and distinguished academic career, he is currently the Sloan Fellows' Professor of Management Emeritus at the MIT Sloan School of Management.

In this book he not only provides a sophisticated definition of culture, but he turns the abstract concept into a tool to assist managers in understanding the dynamics of organizations. In addition, he tackles the vital question of how an existing culture can be changed—one of the toughest challenges for leadership.

CONTRIBUTION
1. The Basis of Corporate Culture

According to the author, culture is a pattern of basic assumptions invented, discovered, or developed by a given group as it learns to cope with its problems of external adaptation and internal integration. These assumptions have worked well enough to be considered valid and, therefore, to be taught to new members as the correct way to perceive, think, and feel in relation to those problems.

The assumptions can be categorized into five dimensions.

- Humanity's relationship to nature: Whereas some companies regard themselves as masters of their own destiny, others are submissive, willing to accept the domination of their external environment.
- The nature of reality and truth: Organizations and managers adopt a wide variety of methods to reach what becomes accepted as the organizational truth.
- The nature of human nature: Organizations differ in their views on human nature. Some follow McGregor's Theory X and work on the principle that people will not do the job if they can avoid it. Others regard people in a more positive light and attempt to enable them to fulfill their potential for the benefit of both sides.
- The nature of human activity: The West has traditionally emphasized tasks and their completion rather than the more philosophical side of work. Achievement is all. Schein suggests an alternative approach, "being-in-becoming," emphasizing self-fulfillment and development.
- The nature of human relationships: Organizations make a variety of assumptions about how people interact with each other. Some facilitate social interaction, whereas others regard it as an unnecessary distraction.

These categories are not mutually exclusive, but are in a constant state of development and flux. Culture never stands still for long.

2. Shaping Organizational Values

Key to the creation and development of corporate culture are the values embraced by the organization. A single person can shape these values and, as a result, an entire corporate culture. The heroic creators of corporate cultures include such people as Henry Ford and IBM's Thomas Watson Sr.

3. Development of Corporate Culture

There are three stages in the development of a corporate culture:

- Birth and early growth: The culture may be dominated by the business founder. It is regarded as a source of the company's identity, a bonding agent protecting it against outside forces.

> Through debate, dictatorship, or through simple acceptance, if something achieves the objective, it is right.

- Organizational midlife: The original culture is likely to be diluted and undermined as new cultures emerge and there is a loss of the original sense of identity. At this stage, there is an opportunity for the fundamental culture to be realigned and changed.

- Organizational maturity: Culture is regarded sentimentally. People are hopelessly addicted to how things used to be done and unwilling to contemplate change. Here the organization is at its weakest, as the culture has been transformed from a source of competitive advantage and distinctiveness to a hindrance in the marketplace. Only through aggressive measures will it survive.

4. Changing Corporate Culture

Each stage of the culture's growth requires a different method of change. If culture is to work in support of a company's strategy, there has to be a level of consensus covering five areas:

- the core mission or primary task
- goals
- the means to accomplish the goals
- the means to measure progress
- remedial or repair strategies

Achieving cultural change is a formidable challenge, one that well-established executives in strong cultures often find beyond them. The exceptional executives who achieve cultural change from within a culture they are closely identified with (such as GE's Jack Welch) are rarities and are known as cultural hybrids.

CONTEXT

Schein's findings gave rise to a host of other studies of the subject. His basic assumptions are rephrased and reinterpreted elsewhere in a variety of ways. Perhaps Chris Argyris comes closest when discussing "theories-in-use."

Gary Hamel says of Schein: "It is impossible to change a large organization without first understanding that organization's culture. Ed Schein gave us an ability to look deeply into what makes an organization what it is, thus providing the foundation of any successful effort at transformation or change. *Organizational Culture and Leadership* remains essential reading for all aspiring change agents."

FOR MORE INFORMATION

Schein, Edgar H. *Organizational Culture and Leadership*. 3rd ed. San Francisco, CA: Jossey-Bass, 2004.

Organizational Learning
CHRIS ARGYRIS AND DONALD SCHÖN

WHY READ IT?
This book shows why organizational learning is the ultimate competitive advantage. It also explains two of the central paradoxes of business life: how individual initiative and creativity can work in an organizational environment, where rules will always exist, and how team-working and individual working can coexist fruitfully.

GETTING STARTED
Learning is a key business activity. Many organizational models only achieve *single-loop learning*, which—though it permits a company to carry on its present policies and achieve its current objectives—is limited to detection and correction of organizational error.

Double-loop learning, on the other hand, enables organizations to detect and correct errors in ways that involve the modification of underlying norms, policies, and objectives. With double-loop learning, managers can act on information and learn from others. Most organizations do quite well in single-loop learning, but have great difficulties with double-loop learning.

Deutero-learning is the process of inquiring into the learning system by which an organization detects and corrects its errors. It underpins the concept of the learning organization.

Increasingly, the art of management is managing knowledge—and effective leadership means creating the conditions that enable people to produce valid knowledge. Success in the marketplace increasingly depends on learning, yet most people don't know how to learn.

CONTRIBUTION
The authors investigate two basic organizational models.

1. The Weakness of Single-loop Learning
Model 1 is based on the premise that we seek to manipulate and form the world in accordance with our individual aspirations and wishes. In Model 1, managers concentrate on establishing individual goals. They keep to themselves and don't voice concerns or disagreements. The onus is on creating a conspiracy of silence in which everyone dutifully keeps his or her head down. Defense is the primary activity in a Model 1 organization, though occasionally the best means of defense is attack. Model 1 managers are prepared to inflict change on others, but resist any attempt to change their own thinking and working practices.

Model 1 organizations are characterized by single-loop learning—the detection and correction of organizational error that permits the organization to carry on its present policies and achieve its current objectives.

2. The Importance of Double-loop Learning
Model 2 organizations emphasize double-loop learning, wherein organizational error is detected and corrected in ways that involve the modification of underlying norms, policies, and objectives.

In Model 2 organizations, managers act on information. They debate issues and respond to change, as well as being prepared to change themselves. They learn from others. A virtuous circle emerges of learning and understanding.

3. The Challenge of Deutero-learning

Deutero-learning offers even greater challenges. This is the process of inquiring into the learning system by which an organization detects and corrects its errors. The examination of learning systems is central to the contemporary concept of the learning organization.

4. The Importance of Managing Knowledge

Learning is powerfully practical, and increasingly the art of management is managing knowledge. Organizations should not manage people per se, but rather the knowledge that they carry.

> Increasingly, the art of management is managing knowledge.

Leadership means creating the conditions that enable people to produce valid knowledge, and to do so in ways that encourage personal responsibility. Knowledge must relate to action, rather than being knowledge for the purpose of understanding and exploring.

5. The Learning Imperative

There is a natural temptation for organizations and individuals to limit themselves to single-loop learning rather than its more demanding alternatives. However, the need to better understand learning in all its dimensions is now imperative. Any company that aspires to success in the tougher business environment of the 1990s and beyond must embrace learning—yet most people don't know how to learn. Those members of an organization who are assumed by many to be the best at learning are, in fact, not very good at it.

CONTEXT

Organizational Learning grew out of the authors' 1974 book, *Theory in Practice*.

Chris Argyris was part of the human relations school of the late 1950s and involved in the work of the National Training Laboratories. He was drawn to the riddles of human nature—in particular, why people fail to live up to their own professed ideals, and why so much human behavior is self-frustrating, particularly within the context of organizations.

Argyris's ideas became fashionable following the upsurge of interest in the concept of the learning organization. *Organizational Learning* first appeared in 1978, but it took the 1990 best seller from Peter Senge of MIT (Massachusetts Institute of Technology), *The Fifth Discipline*, to propel the learning organization from an academic concept to mainstream acceptance.

Charles Hampden-Turner of the University of Cambridge's Judge Institute of Management says, "There is an urgent need for alternative visions of science and Schön's work, along with that of Argyris, provides some of the best ideas and answers. Few have gone so far in reconciling the vigor of relevance and in building a bridge between the isolated academic fortresses of the sciences and the humanities."

Gary Hamel concurs: "If your organization has not yet mastered double-loop learning, it is already a dinosaur. No one can doubt that organizational learning is the ultimate competitive advantage. We owe much to Argyris and Schön for helping us learn about learning."

Anyone wishing to trace the roots of the learning organization would invariably read *Organizational Learning*.

FOR MORE INFORMATION

Argyris, Chris, and Donald Schön. *Organizational Learning*. 2nd ed. New York: Addison-Wesley, 1995.

Out of the Crisis
W. EDWARDS DEMING

WHY READ IT?
This book is regarded as a classic of the literature on quality management. It reflects Deming's experience in introducing quality to Japan, and its goal was to transform the style of U.S. management. Deming is regarded as the leading figure on quality, and this book sets out the methods that taught industry the power of quality.

GETTING STARTED
Deming argues that profit comes from repeat customers—and they respond to good quality. Statistical quality control produces spectacular results, so senior managers must take charge of quality, and quality training should begin at the top of the organization.

Quality is a way of living, Deming says; it is not the preserve of the few but the responsibility of all. Deming argues that factory workers already understand the importance of quality but have been stymied by managers focused on increasing productivity regardless of quality. Japanese culture is uniquely receptive to the quality message.

CONTRIBUTION
1. The Importance of Quality
Profit comes from repeat customers, who boast about a product and service and bring friends with them.

Quality is more than statistical control, though this is important. Statistical quality control produces spectacular results by using tools to improve processes in ways that minimize defects and eliminate rejects, rework, and recalls. Deming's work bridges the gap between science-based application and humanistic philosophy.

2. The Quality Gospel
The book's quality gospel revolves around a number of basic precepts:
- If consistent quality is to be achieved, senior managers must take charge of it.
- Implementation requires a cascade, with training beginning at the top before moving down through the hierarchy.
- The use of statistical methods of quality control is necessary so that, finally, business plans can be expanded to include clear quality goals.
- Quality is a way of living, the meaning of industrial life, and, in particular, the meaning of management.

3. Deming's Fourteen Points
1. Create constancy of purpose for improvement of product and service.
2. Adopt the new philosophy.
3. Cease dependence on inspection to achieve quality.
4. End the practice of awarding business on the basis of price tag alone. Instead, minimize total cost by working with a single supplier.
5. Improve constantly and forever every process for planning, production, and service.
6. Institute training on the job.
7. Adopt and institute leadership.

8. Drive out fear.
9. Break down barriers between staff areas.
10. Eliminate slogans, exhortations, and targets for the workforce.
11. Eliminate numerical quotas for the workforce and numerical goals for management.
12. Remove barriers that rob people of pride of workmanship. Eliminate the annual rating or merit system.
13. Institute a vigorous program of education and self-improvement for everyone.
14. Put everybody in the company to work to accomplish the transformation.

4. The Importance of Empowerment

The simplicity of the fourteen points disguises the immensity of the challenge, particularly that facing management. Quality is not the preserve of the few but the responsibility of all.

People all over the world think that it is the factory worker who causes problems. He or she is not the problem: "Ever since there has been anything such as industry, the factory worker has known that quality is what will protect his job. He knows that poor quality in the hands of the customer will lose the market and cost him his job. He knows it and lives with that fear every day. Yet he cannot do a good job. He is not allowed to do it because the management wants figures, more products, and never mind the quality."

> Quality is not the preserve of the few but the responsibility of all.

5. The Problem of Management

Management is 90 percent of the problem, a problem caused in part by the Western enthusiasm for annual performance appraisals. Japanese managers receive feedback every day of their working lives.

The Japanese culture was uniquely receptive to Deming's message for a number of reasons. Its emphasis on group rather than individual achievement enables the Japanese to share ideas and responsibility. It also promotes collective ownership in a way that the West often finds difficult to contemplate, let alone understand.

CONTEXT

W. Edwards Deming has a unique place among management theorists. He had an impact on industrial history that others only dream of.

Deming visited Japan after World War II on the invitation of General MacArthur and played a key role in the rebuilding of Japanese industry. During the 1950s Deming and the other U.S. standard bearer of quality, Joseph Juran, conducted seminars and courses throughout Japan. Deming and Japanese management were eventually discovered by the West in the 1980s. British author Robert Heller says, "Deming didn't invent quality but his sermons had a uniquely powerful effect because of this first pulpit and congregation: Japan and Japanese managers."

Management guru Gary Hamel adds: "Of all the management gurus . . . there is only one who should be regarded as a hero by every consumer in the world—Dr. Deming."

FOR MORE INFORMATION

Deming, W. Edwards. *Out of the Crisis*. Rev. ed. Cambridge, MA: MIT Center for Advanced Engineering Study, 2000.

Parkinson's Law
C. NORTHCOTE PARKINSON

WHY READ IT?
Parkinson's Law, like *The Dilbert Principle*, takes a cynical look at business. The book treats the growth of bureaucracy and red tape in a humorous way, but the findings reflect real-life situations, particularly in government organizations.

GETTING STARTED
According to the author, companies grow without thinking of how much they are producing and without making any more money. The time taken to complete a task depends on the person doing the job and his or her unique situation. Work also expands to fill the time available for its completion, and officials make work for each other.

CONTRIBUTION
1. How Organizations Grow
Parkinson's Law is simply that work expands to fill the time available for its completion. As a result, companies grow without thinking of how much they are actually producing. Even if growth in numbers doesn't make them more money, companies grow, and people become busier and busier.

The author contends that an official wants to multiply subordinates, not rivals, and that officials make work for each other.

2. Work Expands to Fill the Time
The notion of a particular task having an optimum time for completion is wrong. There are no rules—it depends entirely on the person doing the job and his or her unique situation. An elderly lady of leisure may spend an entire day writing and dispatching a postcard to her niece. The total effort that would occupy a busy person for three minutes might, in this fashion, leave another person prostrate after a day of doubt, anxiety, and toil.

3. Administration Expands
Faced with the decreasing energy of age and a feeling of being overworked, administrators have three options:
- resign
- halve the work with a colleague
- ask for two more subordinates

There is probably no instance in civil service history of choosing any but the third alternative.

For example, the number of admiralty officials in the British Navy increased by 78 percent between 1914 and 1928, while the number of ships fell by 67 percent and the number of officers and men by 31 percent. The expansion of administrators tends to take on a life of its own. The author's conclusion is that officials would have multiplied at the same rate had there been no actual seamen at all.

CONTEXT

Parkinson's Law is an amusing interlude in management literature. It is a kind of *Catch-22* of the business world, by turns irreverent and humorous, but with a darker underside of acute, critical observation.

The book was written in the late 1950s, when the human relations school in the United States was beginning to flower and thinkers were actively questioning the bureaucracy that had grown up alongside mass production.

Max Weber's model of a paper-producing bureaucratic machine appeared to have been brought to fruition as the arteries of major organizations became increasingly clogged with layer upon layer of managerial administrators.

Gary Hamel had this to say of this book, "Yes, I know that bureaucracy is dead. We're not managers any more, we're leaders. We're not slaves to our work, we've been liberated. And all those layers of paper-shuffling administrators between the C.E.O. and the order-takers—they're all gone, right? Well then, why does a re-reading of *Parkinson's Law*, written in 1958, at the apex of corporate bureaucracy, still ring true? *Parkinson's Law* was to the fifties what *The Dilbert Principle* is to the 1990s."

> Work expands to fill the time available for its completion.

FOR MORE INFORMATION

Parkinson, C. Northcote. *Parkinson's Law*. Rev. ed. Cutchogue, NY: Buccaneer Books, 1993.

The Peter Principle
LAURENCE PETER

WHY READ IT?
This book is one of the most enduring publications to take a cynical view of management. It is a humorous book that sets the tone for later works like *The Dilbert Principle*.

GETTING STARTED
According to the author, in a hierarchy every employee tends to rise to his or her level of incompetence. There are no exceptions to the Peter Principle. In time, every post tends to be occupied by an employee who is incompetent to perform his or her duties. There are two kinds of failures: those who thought and never did, and those who did and never thought. There are two sorts of losers—the good loser, and the one who can't act.

CONTRIBUTION
1. Finding a Level of Incompetence
According to the author, a position of incompetence is the apotheosis of a corporate career—or, indeed, of any career in any profession in which there is a hierarchy. The author contends that for each individual, the final promotion is from a level of competence to a level of incompetence. So, given enough time—and assuming the existence of enough ranks in the hierarchy—each employee rises to, and remains at, his or her level of incompetence.

2. Dealing with Failure
The author's view is that if at first you don't succeed, you may be at your level of incompetence. If you don't know where you are going, you will probably end up somewhere else.

Human inadequacy is universal, as is the human capacity to build vacuous power structures. In our supposedly leaner and fitter times, there are still hierarchies aplenty. The difference is, perhaps, that we have simply become more adept at disguising them.

Fortune knocks once, but misfortune has much more patience.

3. Computerized Incompetence
Computerized incompetence can be either the incompetent application of computer techniques or the inherent incompetence of a computer, says Peter.

CONTEXT
Cynicism about the way businesses and managers operate is nothing new. For example, *The Dilbert Principle* is simply an accurate and amusing portrayal of corporate cynicism, 2000s-style.

From *Murphy's Law* to *Parkinson's Law*, from Pudd'nhead Wilson to Stanley Bing, a steady infusion of comic skepticism has been injected into the corporate canon, and *The Peter Principle* is perhaps the most enduring, cynical classic.

The book carries many echoes of that other humorous classic of the 1960s, Joseph Heller's *Catch-22*. It remains a poignant antidote to the blind optimism and sugary outlook of most business books. It is a reminder that corporate reality is not usually about grand designs and great decisions. It is more mundane and frustrating; too mundane and too frustrating ever to be taken too seriously.

Dilbert creator Scott Adams commented, "Now, apparently, the incompetent workers are promoted directly to management without ever passing through the temporary competence stage. When I entered the workforce in 1979, *The Peter Principle* described management pretty well. Now I think we'd all like to return to those Golden Years when you had a boss who was once good at something."

The book remains relevant today. When Peter refers to codophilia (defined as speaking in letters and numbers instead of words), he could be describing today's business consultants.

Bill Gates echoes Peter: "The art of management is to promote people without making them managers."

> If at first you don't succeed, you may be at your level of incompetence.

FOR MORE INFORMATION
Peter, Laurence. *The Peter Principle*. Rev. ed. Cutchogue, NY: Buccaneer Books, 1993.

Planning for Quality
JOSEPH M. JURAN

WHY READ IT?

Juran, like W. Edwards Deming, was one of the key figures in the quality revolution. In this book he stresses that the human aspect of quality management is as important as statistical control. The book underscores the contribution that quality teams and empowerment make to the quality process.

GETTING STARTED

Unlike the West, the Japanese have always made quality a priority at the top of the organization. The key elements in a quality philosophy are

- quality planning;
- quality management; and
- quality implementation.

Juran contends that quality is nothing new, but it has become ignored in the West, where it is treated as an operational issue. There is more to quality than specifications and rigorous testing: it cannot be delegated and has to be the goal of each employee, individually and in teams. Quality can be seen as an invariable sequence of steps. Planning consists of developing processes to meet customers' needs; the human side is just as important.

CONTRIBUTION
1. National Attitudes to Quality Matter

Talking to Japanese audiences in the 1950s, Joseph Juran's message was enthusiastically absorbed by groups of senior managers—the Japanese have made quality a priority at the top of the organization. In the West, Juran's audiences were made up of engineers and quality inspectors. Quality was delegated downward—an operational rather than a managerial issue.

After World War II, U.S. businesses were taken by surprise by Japanese business success because

- they assumed their Asian adversaries were copycats rather than innovators, and
- chief executives were too obsessed with financial indicators to notice or heed any danger signals.

2. The Quality Trilogy

Juran's quality philosophy is built around a "quality trilogy" based on "Company-Wide Quality Management" (CWQM), which aims to create a means of disseminating quality to all. Juran insisted that quality cannot be delegated, and he was an early exponent of what has become known as empowerment. Quality has to be the goal of each employee, individually and in teams, through self-supervision.

3. The Historical Context of Quality

Manufacturing products to design specifications and then inspecting them for defects to protect the buyer is something the Egyptians mastered 5,000 years ago when building the pyramids. The ancient Chinese established a separate department of the central government to establish quality standards and maintain them.

Juran's message, therefore, is that quality is nothing new. But if it is so elemental and elementary, why had it been ignored in the West?

4. The Human Side of Quality
Juran regarded the human side of quality as critical. He developed all-embracing theories of what quality should entail.

5. The Quality Planning Process
Quality planning includes the following activities:
- identifying the customers and their needs,
- developing a product that specifically responds to those needs,
- developing a process able to produce that product.

Quality planning can be produced through an invariable sequence of steps:
- Identify the customers.
- Determine their needs.
- Translate those needs into our language.
- Develop a product that can respond to those needs.
- Optimize the product features to meet our needs as well as customers' needs.
- Develop a process that can produce the product.
- Optimize the process.
- Prove that the process can produce the product under operating conditions.
- Transfer the process to those who will be operating it.

> Quality planning consists of developing the products and processes required to meet the customers' needs.

CONTEXT
Juran is critical of Deming (*Out of the Crisis*) for being overreliant on statistics. His approach is less mechanistic than Deming's and places greater emphasis on human relations. Juran was an early exponent of what has become known as empowerment and believed that quality should be the goal of each employee.

Gary Hamel commented: "The impact of Juran, and of Deming as well, went far beyond quality. By drawing the attention of Western managers to the successes of Japan, they forced Western managers to challenge some of their most basic beliefs about the capabilities of their employees and the expectations of their customers."

FOR MORE INFORMATION
Juran, Joseph M. *Planning for Quality*. New York: Free Press, 1988.

The Practice of Management
PETER F. DRUCKER

WHY READ IT?

Peter Drucker was regarded as the major management and business thinker of the 20th century. *The Practice of Management* is a book of huge range, encyclopedic in its scope and historical perspectives. It laid the groundwork for many of today's accepted management practices and is an excellent primer in management thinking.

GETTING STARTED

Drucker asserts that management will remain a basic and dominant institution, with managers being at the epicenter of economic activity. A business's purpose is to create a customer, and the two essential functions of business are marketing and innovation. Organization is a means to achieving business performance and results.

There are five basics of the managerial role. Management has a moral responsibility and must be driven by objectives.

CONTRIBUTION
1. The Importance of Management

Rarely has a new basic institution emerged as fast as has management since 1900, and never before has a new institution proved indispensable so quickly.

2. A Marketing Attitude Is Critical

According to Drucker, markets are created by businesspeople. The want they satisfy may have been felt previously by the customer, but it was theoretical. Only when the action of businesspeople provides a means to satisfy that want is there a customer, a market.

Since the role of business is to create customers, its only two essential functions are marketing and innovation. Marketing is not an isolated function; it is the whole business seen from the customer's point of view.

3. The Nature of Organizations

Though indispensable, organization is not an end in itself, but a means to achieving performance and results. The wrong structure will seriously impair performance and may even destroy the business.

The first question in discussing structure must be, what is our business, and what should it be? Organizational structure must be designed in such a way that it's possible to achieve business objectives for 5, 10, and 15 years hence.

4. The Managerial Role

The five basics of the managerial role are to
- set objectives,
- organize,
- motivate and communicate,
- measure, and
- develop people.

The function that distinguishes the manager above all others is educational. The unique contribution he or she must make is to give others vision and ability to perform.

5. The Importance of Moral Responsibility

It is vision and moral responsibility that, in the final analysis, define the manager, says Drucker. This morality is reflected in five areas.

- There must be high performance requirements: no condoning of poor or mediocre performance, and rewards must be based on performance.
- Each management job must be rewarding in itself, rather than just a step on the ladder.
- There must be a rational and just promotion system.
- Management needs clear rules about who has the power to make life-and-death decisions affecting a manager, and there should be some way to appeal to a higher court.
- In its appointments, management must realize that integrity is the one quality that a manager has to bring to the job and cannot be expected to acquire later on.

> Management will remain a basic and dominant institution perhaps as long as Western civilization itself survives.

6. Management by Objectives

A manager's job should be based on tasks, the performance of which will help attain the company's objectives. The manager should be directed and controlled by the objectives of performance, rather than by his or her boss. Drucker argues that the manager must know and understand what the business goals demand of him or her in terms of performance, and his or her superior must judge the manager accordingly.

7. Tasks for Future Managers

Drucker identified six new tasks for the manager of the future. Given that these were laid down over 40 years ago, their prescience is astounding. Tomorrow's managers must

1. manage by objectives;
2. take more risks for longer;
3. be able to make strategic decisions;
4. be able to build an integrated team, each member of which is capable of managing his or her own performance in relation to the common objectives;
5. be able to communicate information; and
6. be able to see the business, and the industry, as a whole and to integrate his or her function with it.

CONTEXT

The Practice of Management laid the groundwork for many of the developments in management thinking during the 1960s and is notable for its ideas about the tools and techniques of management. The book is also important because it argues that management has a central role in modern society.

Drucker coined phrases such as "privatization" and "knowledge worker" and championed concepts such as management by objectives. Many of his innovations have become accepted facts of managerial life. *The Economist* commented, "In a field packed with egomaniacs and snake-oil merchants, he remains a genuinely original thinker."

FOR MORE INFORMATION

Drucker, Peter F. *The Practice of Management*. Rev. ed. New York: Collins, 1993.

The Prince
NICCOLÒ MACHIAVELLI

WHY READ IT?
Although written almost 500 years ago, Machiavelli's advice to leaders remains relevant to managers today and covers many popular topics such as motivation, dealing with change, and leadership qualities.

GETTING STARTED
Change management, leadership style, motivation, and international management were just as relevant in the 16th century as they are today. Executives continue to see themselves as natural rulers of an organization, and to the leader, presentation is as important as ability.

Introducing change is extremely difficult. According to Machiavelli, it's essential to keep motivation high—success is not the result of luck or genius, but happy shrewdness. Leaders who rise rapidly often fall just as quickly, and people ruling foreign countries should be on the spot to prevent trouble. When necessary, leaders have to practice evil.

CONTRIBUTION
1. Executives Have Not Changed
Machiavelli covered topics as apparently contemporary as change management, leadership style, motivation, and international management. Like the leaders Machiavelli sought to defend, some executives tend to see themselves as natural rulers, in whose hands organizations can be safely entrusted.

Theories abound about their motivation: Is it a defensive reaction against failure, or a need for predictability through complete control? The effect of the power-driven Machiavellian manager is usually plain to see.

2. Presenting the Right Image
According to Machiavelli, "It is unnecessary for a prince to have all the good qualities [I have] enumerated, but it is very necessary to appear to have them. It is useful to be a great pretender and dissembler."

3. Managing Change and Motivation
Machiavelli wrote that, "There is nothing more difficult to take in hand, more perilous to conduct, or more uncertain in its success, than to take the lead in the introduction of a new order of things. A leader ought above all things to keep his men well organized and drilled, to follow incessantly the chase."

4. Managing Internationally
Machiavelli pointed out that, "When states are acquired in a country with a different language, customs, or laws, there are difficulties; good fortune and great energy are needed to hold them. It would be a great help if he who acquired them should go and live there. If one is on the spot, disorders are seen as they spring up, and one can quickly remedy them; but if one is not at hand, they are heard of only when they are great, and then one can no longer remedy them."

5. The Qualities of Leadership

In the author's opinion, success is not the result of luck or genius, but happy shrewdness. He felt that a prince "ought to have no other aim or thought, nor select anything else for his study, than war and its rules and discipline; for this is the sole art that belongs to him who rules."

"In addition, those who solely by good fortune become princes from being private citizens have little trouble in rising, but much in keeping atop," wrote the author. "They have no difficulties on the way up, because they fly, but they have many when they reach the summit."

It is all very well being good, the author stated, but the leader "should know how to enter into evil when necessity commands."

> It is unnecessary for a prince to have all the good qualities I have enumerated, but it is very necessary to appear to have them.

CONTEXT

The Prince is the 16th-century equivalent of Dale Carnegie's *How to Win Friends and Influence People*. Many of its insights are as appropriate to today's managers and organizations as they were half a millennium ago. Antony Jay's 1970 book, *Management and Machiavelli*, explored the similarities.

This book offers something for everyone. It covers topics as apparently contemporary as change management, leadership style, motivation, and international management.

Gary Hamel has said of this book:

> We occasionally need reminding that leadership and strategy are not modern inventions. It's just that in previous centuries they are more often the concerns of princes than industrialists. Yet power is a constant in human affairs, and a central theme of Machiavelli's *The Prince*. It is currently out of fashion to talk about power. We are constantly reminded that in the knowledge economy, capital wears shoes and goes home every night. No place here for the blunt instrument of power politics? But would Sumner Redstone, Bill Gates, or Rupert Murdoch agree? What is interesting is that after nearly 500 years, Machiavelli is still in print. What modern volume on leadership will be gracing bookstores in the year 2500? Does Machiavelli's longevity tell us anything about what are the deep, enduring truths of management?

FOR MORE INFORMATION

Machiavelli, Niccolò. *The Prince*. New York: Penguin, 2003.

Principles of Political Economy
JOHN STUART MILL

WHY READ IT?
Can liberalization and ethics be combined? Is there a just way of distributing wealth? These are still very relevant issues in the age of globalization and neoliberalism. They also exercised the mind of John Stuart Mill (1806–1873) in the middle of the 19th century. He gave lucid and humane expression to the view that the objective of economic policy must be to ensure an appropriate material livelihood for everyone. Rejecting the premises of "homo economicus," the rational maximizer of profit and consumption, and the unrestricted belief in the progress of his age, he evolved a concept of the "good" society that is ultimately a vision of unilaterally cooperative socialism.

GETTING STARTED
Mill dealt with the principles of production and distribution, embedding economic issues in a broader sociopolitical context. Free competition is necessary, Mill believed, in order to liberate useful social energies. However, the state is not thereby relieved of all its responsibilities, though the scope of its interventions should be strictly limited. Mill drew together the conclusions of a whole period of scientific research and connected economic principles with their practical applications.

CONTRIBUTION
1. Production and Distribution
The national economy, Mill argued, has to be redefined. Production and distribution must be separated. Whereas the laws of production may be natural laws, the only laws to be investigated in the case of distribution are human-made.

2. Progress
Belief in progress should not, he believed, be unqualified. A "stationary" state, in which economic production stagnates, is not a crisis signal or catastrophe for industrialized countries, but an opportunity to develop a more just, leisured, and cultivated society. It is not an unhappy and discouraging prospect, but a chance to create a harmonious social order. Mill confessed that he was "not charmed with the ideal of life held out by those who think that the normal state of human beings is that of struggling to get on; that the trampling, crushing, elbowing, and treading on each other's heels, which form the existing type of social life are the most desirable lot of human kind or anything but the disagreeable symptoms of one of the phases of industrial progress."

Progressive economic development, Mill thought, is characterized by the continuing and unlimited growth of human control over nature and the constant increase in the security of persons and property.

3. Production and Prosperity
In Mill's view, increase in production remains significant only for underdeveloped countries. Distribution is much more important for developed countries. The objective there is not merely an increase in the result of aggregate production, but prosperity for all.

Where producers join together to form cooperatives, Mill suggested, the overall productivity of industry increases. A strong impetus is given to productive energy, inasmuch as the workers are placed in relation to their work as a single body. But the material benefit is nothing in comparison to the moral transformation of society that would accompany this. Cooperatives reduce the profits of capitalists.

> Human improvement has no tendency to correct the intensely selfish feelings engendered by power.

4. Private Property

The principle of private property, according to Mill, is important for three reasons. First, individuals have a right vis-à-vis society, a claim to the rewards of their labor or their frugality. Second, the criterion of economic efficiency is operative in that people are motivated to perform to the best of their abilities when they can appropriate the results of their efforts to their own use. Third, private property develops as a function of individuality itself.

5. State Interference

In Mill's opinion, state interventions in the economy are to be rejected. For one thing, individuals know what benefits them and what harms them; for this reason, state interventions are always inferior to private initiatives. For another, state interventions increase the power of the state and tend to lead to despotic and centralized rule.

6. The Good Society

In Mill's words, a happy society is characterized by the following elements:
- "a well-paid and affluent body of laborers"
- "no enormous fortunes, except what were earned and accumulated during a single lifetime"
- "a larger body of people than at present not only exempt from coarser toils, but with sufficient leisure . . . to cultivate freely the graces of life, and afford examples of them to the classes less favourably circumstanced for their growth"

Modern states, he said, will need to learn the lesson that the welfare of a nation must rest on the justice and the judicious self-determination of its individual citizens. Progress in the future depends on the degree to which they are educated to be able to think for themselves.

CONTEXT

The English economist, philosopher, and logician John Stuart Mill was one of the chief exponents of empirically oriented thought and utilitarianism. He made his name as an advocate of radical reform in political and social life and of equality for women. He wished to unite the political economy of capital with the demands of the working class. His thoroughgoing investigation of the methodological questions relating to national economies made him the epistemologist of the liberal school. His inquiries at the interface of pure economics, social philosophy, and ethics gave liberalism a new social cast and are still relevant today. Mill's reflections have once again attracted attention in the course of the debate on "the limits of growth."

FOR MORE INFORMATION

Mill, John Stuart. *Principles of Political Economy with Some of Their Applications to Social Philosophy*. New York: Oxford University Press, 1999.

Principles of Political Economy and Taxation
DAVID RICARDO

WHY READ IT?
David Ricardo is one of the most important theorists in the history of political economy. *The Principles of Political Economy and Taxation* is one of the cornerstones of the classical approach to the subject. His ideas, especially the theory of comparative cost advantage, formed the basis for the discussion of free trade and protective tariffs throughout the 19th century. His work forms a bridge between that of Adam Smith, who was Ricardo's immediate inspiration, and that of Karl Marx. He is also often said to be the inspirer of the Chicago "monetarist" school, which had a profound influence on the economics and the politics of the late 20th century. The book is still acknowledged as a masterpiece today for its isolation and abstraction of basic principles, its synthesis, and its logic.

GETTING STARTED
In this book, first published in 1817, Ricardo came to grips with the concept of exchange value and expounded the theory of comparative cost advantage.

His central argument runs as follows: The exchange of goods between two countries is worthwhile for both, even if one country can produce all the goods more cheaply than the other. He used two trading nations, Britain and Portugal, and two types of goods, cloth and wine, as examples. In addition, he set out criteria for the objective valuation of goods. According to his doctrine, the value of any good is determined solely by how much labor is necessary for its production. He also dealt with prosperity and poverty in the social classes and the connections among the factors of production, labor, land, and capital, and developed general principles of taxation.

CONTRIBUTION
1. On Value
Ricardo stated that the value of a good depends on the relative quantity of labor required for its production. By this he meant not merely the labor expended in actually creating it, but also that expended on the machines, tools, and buildings that support the immediate work of production.

2. On Foreign Trade
Expansion of foreign trade will not, according to Ricardo, immediately increase the sum of value in a country. As the value of all foreign goods is measured by the quantity of the products of the country's soil and labor expended in exchange for them, it will not possess greater value if, through the discovery of new markets, it receives double the quantity of foreign goods for a specific quantity of its own.

3. On Taxes
Taxes, said Ricardo, are a part of the product of the land and labor of a country that is put at the disposal of the government. They are always paid out of the country's capital or revenue.

Taxes on luxury goods only affect those who use luxuries. Taxes on necessities, however, are a burden on consumers not only in proportion to the quantity they consume, but often in far greater measure. This is because, argued Ricardo, anything that increases wages reduces the profit from capital; any taxes on goods consumed by workers tend to bring down rates of profit.

Income taxes likewise increase wages and reduce the rate of profit on capital. Consequently, in Ricardo's view, only those who employ workers contribute to income tax, not money capitalists, nor landowners, nor any other social class.

He also argued, however, that a tax on essential consumer goods does not entail any particular disadvantage, insofar as it raises wages and lowers profits. Profits are indeed reduced, but only to the extent of the worker's contribution to the tax, which in any event must be borne either by the worker's employer or the consumers of the products of his or her labor.

4. On Currencies and Banks

The exchangeability of paper money for metal is not essential to ensure its value, Ricardo said. It is only necessary that its quantity be regulated in accordance with the value of the metal that has been declared as the standard. If gold of a specific weight and fineness is the standard, then the amount of paper money in circulation can be increased whenever gold declines in value or, which is the same thing in its effect, whenever the price of goods rises.

5. On the Influence of Supply and Demand on Prices

Production costs, Ricardo argued, determine the prices of goods, not the relationship between supply and demand. This relationship may influence the market price of a good for a time, until it is delivered in greater or lesser quantities depending on whether demand has risen or fallen. But this will only be a temporary effect.

CONTEXT

In his thoughts on foreign trade, Ricardo went against the spirit of his age. Whereas his homeland, Great Britain, protected its own economy with customs barriers, his theorem of comparative cost advantages argued in favor of free trade. His views on foreign trade continue to be a guiding light in the liberalization of world trade even today, and his portrait adorns the Web site of the World Trade Organization (WTO).

Ricardo's arguments on the value of goods and his ideas on the division of income among workers, capitalists, and landowners influenced many later economists. In particular, his theory of added value was taken up by Karl Marx and became a weapon in the arsenal of socialism.

Before he began writing, Ricardo was one of the best-known speculators of his time. As a young man, he was a dealer in government securities and made a fortune through the stock exchange. In Ricardo's system of distribution, however, landowners come off best in the long run. He himself acted in accordance with his own principles: He sold his securities and bought an estate.

FOR MORE INFORMATION

Ricardo, David. *The Principles of Political Economy and Taxation*. Amherst, NY: Prometheus Books, 1996.

The Principles of Scientific Management
FREDERICK WINSLOW TAYLOR

WHY READ IT?

At the time *The Principles of Scientific Management* was published, "business management as a discrete and identifiable activity had attracted little attention," as Lyndall Urwick, the British champion of scientific management, said. The book put management on the map, and its influence on working methods and managerial attitudes for most of the 20th century, especially in mass-production industries, was enormous. Taylor's principles have been alternately reviled, rejected, and rediscovered. They remain undeniably significant even today.

> The determination of the best method of performing all of our daily acts will, in the future, be the work of experts.

GETTING STARTED

Frederick Winslow Taylor was a U.S. engineer and inventor, whose fame rests chiefly on this book. He shares with Henry Ford the dubious distinction of founding an "-ism." Taylorism is the practice of the principles of scientific management, which emerged from Taylor's work at the Midvale Steel Works. It involves rigorous measurement of work processes, total objectivity in the assessment of which methods work best, and the consequent mechanization of work and elimination of the human element. The objective standards arrived at, however, are as binding on managers, who have to enforce them, as on the workers, who have to meet them. Like the assembly line, scientific management imposes its discipline on everyone. To most members of the humanistic school of management, it is the enemy par excellence.

CONTRIBUTION
1. Measuring Work

Taylor's science consisted of the minute examination of individual tasks. Having identified every single movement and action involved in doing something, he could determine the optimum time required to complete a task. Armed with this information, the manager could determine whether a person was doing the job well.

2. Putting Science before Opinion

The most obvious consequence of scientific management is a dehumanizing reliance on measurement. The experts, who first analyze and then accurately time the various ways of doing each piece of work, will finally know from exact knowledge, and not from anyone's opinion, which method will accomplish the results with the least effort and in the least time.

According to Taylor, the exact facts will have in this way been developed, and they will constitute a series of laws, which are destined to control the vast multitude of our daily personal acts that at present are the subjects of individual opinion.

3. A System with No Initiative

The Taylorist system envisages no room for individual initiative or imagination. People are labor, mechanically accomplishing a particular task and doing what they are told.

According to Robert McNamara, under Taylor's system, "Those who were so important in the early stages of American manufacturing, the foremen and plant managers, were disenfranchised. Instead of being creators and innovators, as in an earlier era, now they depended on meeting production quotas. They could not stop the line and fix problems as they occurred; they lost any stake in innovation or change" (quoted in Debora Shapley, *Promise and Power*). On the other hand, Taylor's program for objectively determining best practices for every imaginable job could be said to have freed frontline workers from the capricious discipline of unscientific, turn-of-the-century foremen.

CONTEXT

Though Taylor's concepts are now usually regarded in a negative light, the originality of his insights and their importance are not in doubt. He himself announced that he was ushering in a revolution, "a complete mental revolution on the part of the working man engaged in any particular establishment or industry, a complete mental revolution on the part of these men as to their duties toward their work, toward their fellow men, and toward their employees."

Peter Drucker observed in *The Practice of Management*: "Few people had ever looked at human work systematically until Frederick W. Taylor started to do so around 1885. Work was taken for granted and it is an axiom that one never sees what one takes for granted. *Scientific Management* was thus one of the great liberating, pioneering insights."

Lyndall Urwick added: "At the time Taylor began his work, business management . . . was usually regarded as incidental to, and flowing from knowledge of . . . a particular branch of manufacturing, the technical know-how of making sausages or steel or shirts. The idea that a man needed any training or formal instruction to become a competent manager had not occurred to anyone."

The legacy of Taylor's work is most obvious in companies that tend to emphasize quantity over quality. His ideas were enthusiastically taken up by Henry Ford in the development of mass-production techniques.

Drucker also identified two fundamental flaws in scientific management: "The first of these blind spots is the belief that, because we must analyze work into its simplest constituent motions, we must also organize it as a series of individual motions, each if possible performed by an individual worker; the second that it divorces planning from doing."

Gary Hamel sums up the position on Taylor thus:

> The development of modern management theory is the story of two quests: to make management more scientific, and to make it more humane. It is wrong to look at the latter quest as somehow much more enlightened than the former. Indeed, they are the yin and yang of business. The unprecedented capacity of twentieth century industry to create wealth rests squarely on the work of Frederick Winslow Taylor. While some may disavow Taylor, his rational, deterministic impulses live on. Indeed, reengineering is simply late twentieth century Taylorism. Though the focus of reengineering is on the process, rather than the individual task, the motivation is the same: to simplify, to remove unnecessary effort, and to do more with less.

FOR MORE INFORMATION

Taylor, Frederick Winslow. *The Principles of Scientific Management*. Rev. ed. New York: 1st World Library, 2006.

Purple Cow: Transform Your Business by Being Remarkable
SETH GODIN

WHY READ IT?

To excel, organizations need to distinguish themselves from the competition. In this book, marketing guru Seth Godin likens the art of being recognized and of leading a market to a cow in a field in the countryside that will only be noticed by a passing driver if it is colored purple. His book is a manual for creating the remarkable and standing out from the crowd. With customers increasingly satisfied—even spoiled—organizations have to find ways of not just meeting their needs, but *exceeding them*, and of finding entirely new ways to deliver value.

GETTING STARTED

The book's title comes from a story Godin tells about when his family left the city to drive through the countryside and were (initially) excited at the sight of grazing cows. After driving for a few hours, however, looking at cows got boring; the only thing that would have been worth their attention, Godin says, would have been a *purple* cow. This feeling can be translated to a commercial setting. While the inventors of aspirin or the frozen pizza built their fortunes by selling a *new* product, today customers' needs are by and large met and already provided for in an increasingly competitive, saturated market. To succeed, one must market a "Purple Cow"—an iPod or a Frappucino™. While the original marketing mix included such "Ps" as Price, Product, Position, Publicity, Promotion, Packaging, and Permission, according to Godin, the most important "P" in the future may prove to be the "Purple Cow."

CONTRIBUTION
1. Death of a Salesman

Godin's first contribution is to challenge conventional marketing and public relations wisdom that ascribes success to "share of voice" in standard media streams, such as newspaper and television advertising. He points out that even Coca-Cola's fantastically expensive adverts do little to sell more cans of soft drinks and argues that the end of what he calls the "TV-Industrial Complex," with the saturation of global communication, places more emphasis on being people's first choice, rather than simply a close second.

2. Know Your Business and Be Passionate about It

By understanding exactly what your business or product is, you can target your marketing more exactly and prioritize tasks. Godin uses most of *Purple Cow* to explore practical examples of remarkable products and services. What they all had in common—from the maker of the internal combustion engine to a publicist for the plastic surgery industry—was a strategic focus on using their unique selling points to meet a previously unexplored market. A market for luxury iced coffees did not exist when Starbucks first marketed its Frappucino™, but by doing something different, it created a profitable product. Knowing what makes your business and customers tick will allow you more opportunity for success than ever before.

3. Brainstorm and Reinvent

Many marketers and salespeople understand the importance of being passionate about their product, but what about *developing* a product that compels people to make decisions with the same passion? Godin cites salt as an example. For years, it was a commodity manufactured in vast quantities with greater economies of scale but diminishing returns. Manufacturers are increasingly realizing the benefits of selling handmade, luxury brands—for instance, those targeted at gourmet restaurants—that add value in new ways and for which they can charge a premium. By developing radical, maverick products, or by reinventing old products so that they meet new needs in creative ways, marketing is at its most effective.

CONTEXT

The importance of being passionate about your product and of creating remarkable marketing strategies has been discussed by management guru Tom Peters (*The Pursuit of Wow*), and the way ideas travel through populations has been studied by Malcolm Gladwell in *The Tipping Point*. Godin, self-proclaimed "agent of change," argues that most marketers treat these concepts as fads and fall back on tried and tested but boring channel marketing strategies and advertising, hoping that word of mouth will do the rest. With consumers spoiled by choices in a global marketplace, learning how to create a "Purple Cow" is essential. In a trouble-beset global economy, the only way to create a truly winning product is to be revolutionary. With increasingly flat, globalized communication, customers reject otherwise decent products, seeking only the most extraordinary and unique.

FOR MORE INFORMATION

Godin, Seth. *Purple Cow: Transform Your Business by Being Remarkable.* London: Penguin, 2005.

Quest for Prosperity
KONOSUKE MATSUSHITA

WHY READ IT?
This book describes how Konosuke Matsushita built a global business—Panasonic—from nothing. It contains lessons on customer service, business ethics, and marketing that would benefit any business.

GETTING STARTED
According to the author, customer service is critical to success—customers want goods that will benefit them. Furthermore, after-sales service is more important than assistance before sales.

Business with a conscience cements loyalty. We are using precious resources that could be better used elsewhere unless we make a good profit. Production efficiency and quality products are key. The mission of a manufacturer should be to overcome poverty, to relieve society as a whole from misery, and to bring it wealth.

CONTRIBUTION
1. Building a Winning Business
The Matsushita story is one of the most impressive industrial achievements of the 20th century. The company's first break was an order to make insulator plates. The order was delivered on time and was high quality. Matsushita began to make money. He then developed an innovative bicycle light. Initially, retailers were unimpressed. Then Matsushita had his salesmen leave a light switched on in each shop. This simple product demonstration impressed the retailers, and the business took off.

2. The Importance of Customer Service
The company understood customer service before anyone in the West had even thought about it:
- Don't sell customers goods that they are attracted to. Sell them goods that will benefit them.
- After-sales service is more important than assistance before sales. It is through such service that one acquires permanent customers.

3. Efficiency and Quality
Matsushita emphasized the importance of efficient production and good quality products.

Managing stock levels is also essential; if you run out of stock (careless, according to Matsushita), apologize to the customers, ask for their address, and tell them that you will deliver the goods immediately.

4. Risk-taking Pays
Matsushita took risks and backed his beliefs at every stage. The classic example of this is the development of the videocassette. Matsushita developed VHS video and licensed the technology. Sony developed Betamax, which was immeasurably better, but failed to license the technology. Consequently, the world standard is VHS, and Betamax was consigned to history.

5. Business with a Conscience

Matsushita advocated business with a conscience, reflected in his paternalistic employment practices. During a recession early in its life, the company did not lay anyone off. This cemented loyalty.

According to Matsushita, it is not enough to work conscientiously. No matter what kind of job you are doing, you should think of yourself as being completely in charge of, and responsible for, your own work.

> We are going to win and the industrial West is going to lose out; there's not much you can do about it because the reasons for your failure are within yourselves.

6. The Role of the Leader

Big things and little things are the leader's job. Middle-level arrangements can be delegated. Matsushita also explained the role of the leader in more cryptic fashion: "The tail trails the head. If the head moves fast, the tail will keep up the same pace. If the head is sluggish, the tail will droop."

7. The Broader Objectives of Business

Matsushita mapped out the broader spiritual goals he believed a business should have. Profit was not enough. The mission of a manufacturer should be to overcome poverty, to relieve society as a whole from misery, and to bring it wealth.

He outlined his basic management objective in the following way: "Recognizing our responsibilities as industrialists, we will devote ourselves to the progress and development of society and the well-being of people through our business activities, thereby enhancing the quality of life throughout the world."

He viewed failure to make a profit as a sort of crime against society: "We take society's capital, we take their people, we take their materials, yet without a good profit, we are using precious resources that could be better used elsewhere."

According to the author, business is demanding, serious, and crucial: "Business, we know, is now so complex and difficult, the survival of companies so hazardous in an environment increasingly unpredictable, competitive, and fraught with danger, that their continued existence depends on the day-to-day mobilization of every ounce of intelligence."

CONTEXT

Matsushita created a $42 billion revenue business from nothing. He also created Panasonic, one of the world's most successful brands, and amassed a personal fortune of $3 billion. The book explains the key principles that made his business a global success.

FOR MORE INFORMATION

Matsushita, Konosuke. *Quest for Prosperity*. Kyoto: PHP Institute, 1988.

Real Time
REGIS MCKENNA

WHY READ IT?

Regis McKenna is regarded as one of the most important marketers in the technology business. This book provides valuable insights into the changing nature of new economy customers. It will be useful to anyone developing a marketing or customer relationship strategy.

GETTING STARTED

Customers want better quality, cheaper prices, and immediate response. This is changing traditional business models. According to the author, companies must become real-time businesses to survive and succeed, and understand how time, technology, and customer service are interrelated.

Technology compresses time, but business practices must also change. "Real-time managers" must focus on delivery, results, and customized service.

Creating a real-time company is difficult, but essential. Real-time systems will change working relationships inside and outside an organization. The systems will generate new product ideas, ways of gaining customer loyalty, and methods of team collaboration.

Information technology will become a valued corporate asset. It will support rapid and continuous business refinements.

CONTRIBUTION
1. Customer Demands Increasing

Customers are ever more demanding. They want better quality, they want cheaper prices, and above all, they want it now.

Traditional bookshop owners who need time to order in books see increasing volumes of business going to Internet sites like Amazon. Bank balances are now available online, more or less instantly, with no need for a visit to the branch.

2. Meeting the Challenge

Providing an immediate, customer-satisfying response to any request is a tough challenge for any business. Companies that wish to remain in the marketplace have only one choice—they must become real-time businesses in a world of instant gratification and infinite opportunity.

3. Achieving the Transformation

Companies must understand how time, technology, and customer service are interrelated. Great technology will help to compress time.

Companies must also challenge conventional wisdom about how they operate. Traditional facets of company life, such as hierarchy and long-term planning methodologies, have to go. They must be replaced by "real-time managers" who focus on delivery and results, and who recognize that customized service is the new corporate mantra.

4. Creating the Real-time Company

The task of implementing a real-time corporation is difficult and complex, but it is an essential investment in a competitive future. The implementation of real-time systems will have the effect of changing the working relationships within an organization, as well as those with partners and customers.

The application of technology will change corporate culture. As these systems are adopted, they will provide a number of benefits:

- new ideas for services and products
- new ways of gaining customer loyalty
- new methods of team collaboration

Then information technology will become a valued corporate asset.

5. Being Prepared for Anything

Companies will learn about the technologies of real time in the only way they can, by adopting them and putting them to practical use. They will deploy them, not to predict the future, but to live virtually on top of changing patterns and trends affecting every sphere of their business environment. This will enable them to make rapid and continuous refinements in their way of doing business.

New consumers are never satisfied customers.

CONTEXT

When *Real Time* was first published, it received excellent reviews in the United States, and a number of well-respected CEOs sang its praises. Although the messages of the book seem far less radical now, McKenna's analysis remains valid, as does his emphasis on customized service and time-based competition.

FOR MORE INFORMATION

McKenna, Regis. *Real Time: Preparing for the Age of the Never Satisfied Customer*. Boston: Harvard Business School Press, 1997. Web site: The McKenna Group, www.mckenna group.com

Reengineering the Corporation
JAMES CHAMPY AND MICHAEL HAMMER

WHY READ IT?
Reengineering the Corporation is seen as the key book in the reengineering revolution. It encourages organizations to take a fresh look at inefficient and outdated processes and to focus on dramatic improvements in cost, quality, service, and speed. Although the message has been misinterpreted, reengineering remains a powerful tool for change.

GETTING STARTED
In the authors' view, reengineering must focus on the fundamental rethinking and radical redesign of key business processes. Dramatic improvements in cost, quality, service, and speed are the objectives.

Reengineering should go far beyond altering and refining processes; the goal is "to reverse the Industrial Revolution."

Reengineering puts a premium on the skills and potential of the people at the center of the organization and should also tackle three key areas of management—managerial roles, styles, and systems.

CONTRIBUTION
1. Focus on Improving Core Processes
In the context of a fiercely competitive environment and the ability of IT to transform business processes, the book encourages organizations to take a fresh look at inefficient and outdated processes. Reengineering, according to the authors, is the fundamental rethinking and radical redesign of business processes.

2. Create a Lean Organization
The authors argue that organizations need to identify their key processes and make them as lean and profitable as possible. In some cases, peripheral processes and people need to be discarded.

Unfortunately, many organizations have taken this advice literally and downsized without reengineering. CSC, the consulting firm founded by Champy and Hammer, surveyed more than 600 companies involved in reengineering projects in 1994. In the United States, an average 336 jobs were lost on each project. In Europe, the figure was 760 jobs per project.

3. Achieve a Complete Corporate Revolution
Simple business process reengineering is not enough, say the authors. True reengineering is a recipe for a corporate revolution and should go far beyond altering and refining processes. The past is history; the future is there to be coerced into the optimum shape.

The authors believe that reengineering is concerned with rejecting conventional wisdom and received assumptions about the past. However, this can mean ignoring the experiences and lessons of the past. Companies are discouraged from trying to understand why they have been successful and building on that.

4. Transform the Future

The authors suggest that organizations should start with a blank piece of paper. They should map out their processes to identify how their businesses should operate, and then attempt to translate the paper into concrete reality.

> I tell them what I really do is I'm reversing the Industrial Revolution.

In practice, this has proved difficult to achieve. The authors now believe that companies tend not to cast the reengineering net widely enough; they find processes that can be reengineered quickly and stop at that point. They lack a vision for the future and the revolutionary approach to take reengineering forward.

5. Reengineer Management as Well

Part of the problem, the authors believe, is that managers fail to impose change on themselves—they concentrate on tearing down processes, but they leave their own jobs and management styles intact. However, the old ways of management could eventually undermine the very structure of their rebuilt enterprise. The reengineering process should therefore tackle the three key areas of management—managerial roles, styles, and systems.

6. Reengineering Should Be Built on Trust, Respect, and People

The authors believe that reengineering actually puts a premium on the people at the center of the organization. Once peripheral activities have been cut away, the new environment puts a premium on skills of the people who are left. Experience suggests that this has not happened so far; downsizing creates a difficult environment in which trust is frequently absent.

CONTEXT

Reengineering is seen by some as an old concept with a new label. Frederick W. Taylor's *Scientific Management* advocated similar change, but at an individual rather than an organizational level. Gary Hamel pointed out that reengineering followed a line from scientific management, industrial engineering, and business process improvement.

The mechanistic theme has been a key issue for critics, who have made the point that reengineering owes more to visions of the corporation as a machine, rather than a human system. Peter Cohan, a former colleague said the authors ignored the importance of people, describing them as objects who handle processes.

Christopher Lorenz of the *Financial Times* believed that the authors failed to state whether organizations should undertake behavioral and cultural changes in parallel with reengineering.

It has also been easy to take the book's messages too literally. Reengineering has been seen as a synonym for redundancy, and the book has been blamed for a wave of downsizing.

FOR MORE INFORMATION

Champy, James, and Michael Hammer. *Reengineering the Corporation*. Rev. ed. New York: Collins, 2004.

Relationship Marketing
REGIS MCKENNA

WHY READ IT?
Relationship marketing has become one of the most important determinants of corporate success. Retaining customers and maximizing lifetime customer value are critical to long-term revenue and profitability. Regis McKenna's book sets out the principles of building successful relationships, using technology to understand and communicate with customers.

GETTING STARTED

> Marketing is everything.

Business has moved away from mass marketing to customization and personalization. Technology is the enabler in this change, allowing companies to deal with the growing power of the customer.

CONTRIBUTION
1. Integrating the Customer
Technology and the choices it offers are transforming the marketplace. All companies, he claims, are technology companies, using technology to customize and offer unlimited choice. The knowledge and understanding available through technology are changing the nature of marketing. The objective now is to integrate the customer into the company.

2. Dominating Markets
A strong brand is the reflection of a successful relationship. Market dominance is vital to attracting customers, business partners, and the best employees. The starting point is to define a narrow market and dominate it, before expanding the relationships.

3. Dialog with Customers
Companies need to have dialogue with customers using trials, user groups, and other feedback mechanisms. He calls this "experience-based marketing."

4. Merger of Products and Services
The author points out that, in industries like computing, around 75 percent of the business consists of services such as consulting, systems integration, and customer support. These are all essential to customers and form part of a solution that builds relationships.

5. Faster Time to Market
Companies must reduce time to market as much as possible—delay leads to lost opportunities. The marketplace is changing rapidly, so it is important to stay close to customers.

6. Market Creation Replaces Market Sharing
Companies must differentiate their products to dominate a market, which may mean starting with small sectors and acting like entrepreneurs. Market creation also means educating customers and listening to them. However, quantitative information can distract companies from entering small sectors. Qualitative judgment may be more important.

7. Relationships

Relationships are more important with complex, high-risk products. Customers need reassurance, education, support, and services to build and maintain their confidence in a company.

8. Dynamic Positioning

The author explains how dynamic positioning differs from traditional positioning. In dynamic positioning,

- product positioning determines how a product fits into a competitive market;
- market positioning requires a company to understand the infrastructure, influences, and distribution channels in its market; and
- corporate positioning determines whether a company is perceived as a credible supplier.

9. Product Positioning

Product positioning must be based on an understanding of the market environment, according to McKenna. It must also focus on the intangible factors that are important to customers. Trust is the logical outcome when customers have a strong relationship and continue to buy.

10. Product Success

McKenna cites ten characteristics of a successful product:

- It appeals to a new market.
- It takes advantage of the best technologies.
- It depends on the market infrastructure for newly developed technologies.
- Its timing is right.
- It is adapted to market requirements.
- It is developed by small entrepreneurial teams.
- Its customers are involved in its development.
- It is adopted by early users.
- It generates a new language.
- It is used in demonstrations, workshops, and user groups.

11. Developing Relationships

According to McKenna, successful companies develop relationships with the whole market, not just customers. This is the market infrastructure, and it includes analysts, developers, retailers, journalists, suppliers, and other organizations who are mutually dependent. The leaders set the standard for their market, and everyone else works with them.

12. Selling to the Right Customers

McKenna places buyers in four categories:

- innovators
- early adopters
- the majority
- laggards

CONTEXT

This book was one of the first to highlight the importance of relationships with customers, suppliers, distributors, and other players in the marketplace. Since the book's publication, the practice of relationship marketing has been further refined by the development of personalization techniques and one-to-one marketing via the Internet.

FOR MORE INFORMATION

McKenna, Regis. *Relationship Marketing: Successful Strategies for the Age of the Customer.* Cambridge, MA: Perseus Books, 1993.

Riding the Waves of Culture
FONS TROMPENAARS AND CHARLES HAMPDEN-TURNER

WHY READ IT?
Riding the Waves of Culture is an examination of the cultural imponderables faced by managers in the global village. Based on exhaustive research, it systematically "dimensionalizes" cultural differences, identifying seven areas, such as attitude to rules and awareness of time, in which different nations have fundamentally different conceptions. Anyone whose work involves dealing with people from other cultures would benefit from reading it.

GETTING STARTED
Fons Trompenaars studied at a top U.S. business school, where he started thinking about cultural differences. "I started wondering if any of the American management techniques I was brainwashed with in eight years of the best business education money could buy would apply in the Netherlands, where I came from, or indeed in the rest of the world."

Charles Hampden-Turner is an international authority on cross-cultural communication who taught for many years in the United States and, like his coauthor, worked for Shell.

The book is based on meticulous quantitative research (over 15 years, 15,000 people from 50 countries were surveyed) and more than 900 seminars presented in 18 countries. Its main contentions are that basic to understanding other cultures is the awareness of cultural difference; that cultural difference can be systematically analyzed; that flexibility, a certain amount of humility, and a sense of humor are needed in dealing with cultures other than our own; and that the reconciliation of difference is the supreme managerial art.

CONTRIBUTION
1. Culture
Culture is a series of rules and methods that a society has evolved to deal with the recurring problems it faces. They have become so basic that we no longer think about how we approach or resolve them.

First, people should be aware that they belong to a culture and have a specific way of doing things, and second, they should be prepared for a different response from the one they are accustomed to receiving when they do business with someone whose culture differs from theirs.

2. Seven Dimensions of Culture
In analyzing cultural differences, the authors identify seven dimensions in which different or contrasting attitudes are particularly crucial:
- universalism vs. particularism
- individualism vs. collectivism
- neutral vs. emotional
- specific vs. diffuse
- achievement vs. ascription
- attitude toward time
- attitude toward the environment

Universalism and Particularism   There are two fundamentally distinct ways of dealing with situations that the book labels "universalism" and "particularism." Universalists (including Americans, Canadians, Australians, and the Swiss) advocate one best way, "what is good and right can be defined and always applies." They focus on rules and procedure. Particularists (e.g., South Koreans, Chinese, and Malaysians) feel that circumstances dictate how ideas and practices should be applied. They focus on the peculiar nature of any given situation and on particular relationships.

Universalists doing business with particularists should be prepared for meandering or irrelevancies that do not seem to be going anywhere. Particularists doing business with universalists should be prepared for rational and professional arguments and presentations, and little else.

> Culture is the way in which people resolve dilemmas emerging from universal problems.

Individualism and Collectivism   The book also contrasts the collectivist mind-set with the individualist one. The United States again comes at one extreme of the spectrum, emphasizing the individual before the group. Countries such as Egypt and France are at the other end.

Individualists working with collectivists must tolerate time taken to consult and negotiators who only agree tentatively and may withdraw after consulting with superiors.

3. The Role of the International Manager

Given the wide range of basic differences in how cultures perceive the world, it is evident that the international manager is moving in a world riddled with potential pitfalls. There are also profound differences between those who show their feelings (such as the Italians) and those who hide them (such as the Japanese), and those who accord status on the basis of achievement and those who ascribe it on the basis of family and age.

The international manager needs to go beyond awareness of cultural differences. He or she needs to respect these differences and take advantage of diversity through reconciling cross-cultural dilemmas. In the end, the only positive route forward is through reconciliation. Those societies that can reconcile better are better at creating wealth.

CONTEXT

Tom Peters called *Riding the Waves of Culture* a masterpiece. "What's not okay is cultural arrogance. If you come to another's turf with sensitivity and open ears . . . you're halfway home."

Gary Hamel takes the authors to task for their criticisms of U.S. cultural inflexibility: "So Americans will never understand foreign cultures? Funny how American companies are out-competing their European competitors in Asia and Latin America. . . . Where I agree with Trompenaars is that the future belongs to the cosmopolitans."

The cultural aspects of managing internationally are likely to gain in importance as the full force of globalization affects industries and individuals. In this respect the value of the book's contribution is undeniable. It has been argued, however, that its stress on cultural relativism and adaptability might become outmoded if capital markets were to enforce "global rules of the game" independent of different cultures.

FOR MORE INFORMATION

Trompenaars, Fons, and Charles Hampden-Turner. *Riding the Waves of Culture*. 2nd ed. New York: McGraw-Hill, 1997.

The Rise and Fall of Strategic Planning
HENRY MINTZBERG

WHY READ IT?
Mintzberg shows how overemphasizing analysis and hard facts limits strategic planning. Planning should be something visionary and creative. This book has become an influential classic.

GETTING STARTED
Planning is concerned with analysis; strategy making is concerned with synthesis. According to the author, strategic planners tend to be detached from action and the reality of the organization.

Planners typically gather hard data on their industry, markets, and competitors. Soft data—such as networks of contacts, talking with customers, suppliers, and employees—have been ignored. Strategy formulation has been dominated by logic and analysis. This narrows options. Intuition and creativity need to become part of the process.

CONTRIBUTION
1. Strategy and Planning
Planning codifies, elaborates, and operationalizes existing company strategy. In contrast, strategy is either an emergent pattern or a deliberate perspective and cannot be planned. Whereas planning is concerned with analysis, strategy making is concerned with synthesis.

2. The Nature of Planners

> **Strategy cannot be planned.**

Mintzberg asserts that planners do have value, but only as strategy finders, analysts, and catalysts. At their most effective, they unearth strategies in unexpected pockets of the organization, whose potential can then be explored.

3. Problems with Planning Practices
The author identifies the three main pitfalls of planning practices as
- the assumption that discontinuities can be predicted,
- the fact that planners are detached from the reality of the organization, and
- the assumption that strategy making can be formalized.

The Assumption That Discontinuities Can Be Predicted   Forecasting techniques often assume that the future will resemble the past. This gives artificial reassurance and creates strategies that disintegrate rapidly as they are overtaken by events.

Planners' Detachment from the Reality of the Organization   If the system does the thinking, strategy must be detached from operations, and thinkers from doers. This disassociation of thinking from acting lies at the root of the problem.

The Assumption That Strategy Making Can Be Formalized   The emphasis on logic and analysis creates a narrow range of options. Alternatives that do not fit into the predetermined structure are ignored.

The right side of the brain, with its emphasis on intuition and creativity, needs to become part of the process. Planning defines and preserves categories. Creativity creates categories or rearranges established ones. Thus strategic planning can neither provide creativity, nor deal with it when it emerges. Mold-breaking strategies grow initially like weeds—they are not cultivated and can take root anywhere.

4. Hard Data and Soft Data

Hard data are often anything but. There is the fallacy of measuring what's measurable. There is a tendency to favor cost-leadership strategies (emphasizing operating efficiencies, which are generally measurable) over product-leadership strategies (emphasizing innovative design or high quality, which tends to be less measurable).

To gain useful understanding of an organization's competitive situation, soft data need to be dynamically integrated into the planning process. They may be difficult to analyze, but they are indispensable for synthesis—the key to strategy making.

5. The Nature of Strategy Making

Mintzberg defines strategy making thus:

- It is derived from synthesis.
- It is informal and visionary, rather than programmed and formalized.
- It relies on divergent thinking, intuition, and using the subconscious. This leads to outbursts of right-brain creativity as new discoveries are made.
- It is irregular, unexpected, ad hoc, and instinctive. It upsets stable patterns.
- Managers are adaptive information manipulators.
- It is done in times of instability characterized by discontinuous change.
- It results from an approach that takes in broad perspectives and is, therefore, visionary, and involves a variety of actors capable of experimenting and then integrating the results.

CONTEXT

This book reflects a general dissatisfaction with strategic planning. Research by the U.S. Planning Forum found that only 25 percent of companies considered that their planning was effective.

The book attracted much attention and debate. It also brought a spirited response from the defenders of strategy. Andrew Campbell, coauthor of *Corporate-Level Strategy*, wrote: "Strategic planning is not futile. Research has shown that some companies—both conglomerates and more focused groups—have strategic planning processes that add real value." Campbell further argues that the corporate center must develop a value-creating, corporate-level strategy and build the management processes needed to implement it.

Management guru Gary Hamel commented: "Henry views strategic planning as a ritual, devoid of creativity and meaning. He is undoubtedly right when he argues that planning doesn't produce strategy. But rather than use the last chapter of the book to create a new charter for planners, Henry might have put his mind to the question of where strategies actually do come from!"

FOR MORE INFORMATION

Mintzberg, Henry. *The Rise and Fall of Strategic Planning*. New York: Free Press, 1994.

Small Is Beautiful
E. F. SCHUMACHER

WHY READ IT?
Schumacher's book has become one of the most influential works ever on environmental issues and business. It looks at traditional Western economics in a radical way, arguing that big is not always best. His work has struck a chord with politicians, environmentalists, and a growing number of business leaders.

GETTING STARTED
Schumacher argues that the relentless pursuit of profit and progress has resulted in economic inefficiency, environmental pollution, and inhumane working conditions. Instead, he proposes greater use of "intermediate technology," based on smaller work units, communal ownership, and the use of local labor and resources.

CONTRIBUTION
1. The Problem of Production
Schumacher believes that business has not solved the problem of production. Businesses are using up the store of natural capital, and he cites the spiraling demands on fossil fuels and other finite natural resources. The proposal to replace fossil fuels with human-made energy sources such as nuclear fuels creates its own problems.

The author's view is that the concept of peace through universal prosperity is also unachievable. He argues that if prosperity grew in line with population growth, the impact on fuel consumption and subsequent atmospheric pollution would be extremely damaging.

2. Changing the Emphasis of Economics
The solution, he claims, lies in a reorientation of science and technology. The emphasis should not be on concentrating production in larger and larger units; it should be on making technology accessible and suitable for small-scale application. He also believes that technology should leave room for human creativity, rather than replacing it.

Traditional economic theories are driven by market forces. Schumacher believes that they ignore humanity's dependence on the natural world. Economics, he says, is also overdependent on quantitative measures such as gross domestic product and consequently overlooks qualitative measures such as the impact of the economy on the environment.

According to Schumacher, economics looks upon human labor as a necessary "input" to wealth. Business takes every opportunity to reduce the cost, making work meaningless. An alternative point of view says that work should enable people to utilize their faculties and join in a common cause. This is in contrast to the theory that consumption is the only real end.

3. Toward a Smaller Scale
Schumacher points out that scale is another important element of economic thinking. The traditional theory is that economic organizations, such as businesses, should be as large as possible. He counters that they only need to be big enough to meet real needs.

Schumacher also argues for the more effective use of land. It is not simply a factor of production. He cites the flight from the land as evidence of this misunderstanding.

4. The Efficiency Gap

The author is critical of modern industrial efficiency. The United States, for example, has around 5 percent of the world's population, yet requires almost 40 percent of the world's primary resources to sustain its economy.

Apart from the demand on resources, Schumacher argues that this situation also creates problems between producer and consumer countries. An economy that is so dependent on other resources must in the long term suffer.

5. A Human Face for Technology

Schumacher believes that technology needs a human face. It should free people from the burdens of work. He describes how the Intermediate Technology Development Group aims to broaden the use of technology, supporting production by the masses, instead of mass production. This approach, he feels, would be an effective way to support regional economic development around the world.

Despite his emphasis on small-scale regional development, Schumacher accepts that large organizations will remain an important part of the economy. He believes that setting up smaller units within a larger organization could help to overcome any inherent problems of size.

CONTEXT

Schumacher, like Hawken, Lovins, and Lovins in *Natural Capitalism*, highlights the conflict between business growth and the destruction of natural resources. He proposes a system of environmentally friendly business that takes account of limited resources and offers everyone a stake in success.

He draws on a wide variety of influences and sources to develop his themes, including Buddhist economics, Adam Smith, Gandhi, and economists such as Galbraith.

Although Schumacher's work could be regarded as utopian, he proposes practical working solutions, some of which have already been put into practice successfully.

> One of the most fateful errors of our age is the belief that the problem of production has been solved.

FOR MORE INFORMATION

Schumacher, E. F. *Small Is Beautiful: A Study of Economics as If People Mattered.* New York: HarperCollins, 1999.

FURTHER READING

Hawken, Paul, Amory B. Lovins, and L. Hunter Lovins. *Natural Capitalism: The Next Industrial Revolution.* Boston: Back Bay Books 2000.

Strategy and Structure
ALFRED CHANDLER

WHY READ IT?
Chandler's book is regarded by many commentators as a masterpiece. It demonstrates the critical link between a company's strategy and its structure and played an influential role in the profitable decentralization of many leading corporations. The book's findings remain relevant to new forms of organization such as the federated organization, the multicompany coalition, and the virtual company.

GETTING STARTED
According to the author, structure should be driven by strategy—and if it isn't, inefficiency results. The structure of many corporations is driven by market forces: Recognition that production had to be market-driven led large organizations to change to a looser divisional structure.

Increases in scale also led to business owners having to recruit a new breed of professional manager, as professional management coordinates the flow of product to customers more efficiently than market forces can ever do.

The author asserts that a planned economy is important to long-term organizational success.

CONTRIBUTION
1. Structure Should Be Driven by Strategy
Strategy is the determination of the long-term goals and objectives of an enterprise, and the adoption of courses of action and the allocation of resources necessary for reaching these goals. A company's structure is dictated by its chosen strategy—and unless structure follows strategy, inefficiency results. A company should establish a strategy and then seek to create the structure appropriate to achieving it.

2. Structure Driven by Market Forces
Organizational structures in companies such as Du Pont, Sears Roebuck, General Motors, and Standard Oil were driven by the changing demands and pressures of the marketplace. The market-driven proliferation of product lines in Du Pont and General Motors led to a shift from a functional, monolithic organizational form to a more loosely coupled divisional structure.

3. The Rise of the Multidivisional Organization
The multidivisional organization removed the executives responsible for the destiny of the entire enterprise from the more routine operational responsibilities. It gave them the time, information, and even psychological commitment needed for long-term planning and appraisal.

4. The Professionalization of Management
The managerial revolution was fueled by a variety of factors: the rapid rise of oil-based energy; the development of the steel, chemical, and engineering industries; and a dramatic rise in the scale of production and the size of companies.

Increases in scale led to business owners having to recruit a new breed of professional manager. The roles of the salaried manager and technician are vital, as the visible hand of management coordinates the flow of product to customers more efficiently than Adam Smith's "invisible hand" of the market.

5. The Importance of a Planned Economy
Organizations and their managements require a planned economy rather than a capitalist free-for-all dominated by the unpredictable whims of market forces.

> Unless structure follows strategy, inefficiency results.

CONTEXT
The book is based on Chandler's research into major U.S. corporations between 1850 and 1920. Its subtitle is *Chapters in the History of the American Industrial Enterprise*, but its impact went far beyond that of a brilliantly researched historical text. Alfred Chandler's *Strategy and Structure* is a theoretical masterpiece that has had profound influence on both practitioners and thinkers.

Chandler was highly influential in the trend among large organizations for decentralization in the 1960s and 1970s. While in 1950 around 20 percent of Fortune 500 corporations were decentralized, this had increased to 80 percent by 1970. In the 1980s, Chandler's thinking was influential in the transformation of AT&T from what was in effect a production-based bureaucracy to a marketing organization.

Until recent times, Chandler's conclusion that structure follows strategy has largely been accepted as a fact of corporate life. Now the debate has been rekindled.

Tom Peters said, "I think he got it exactly wrong. For it is the structure of the organization that determines, over time, the choices that it makes about the markets it attacks."

In *Managing on the Edge*, Richard Pascale said, "The underlying assumption is that organizations act in a rational, sequential manner. Yet most executives will readily agree that it is often the other way around. The way a company is organized, whether functional focused or driven by independent divisions, often plays a major role in shaping its strategy. Indeed, this accounts for the tendency of organizations to do what they best know how to do—regardless of deteriorating success against the competitive realities."

Gary Hamel, author of *Leading the Revolution*, said:

> Those who dispute Chandler's thesis that structure follows strategy miss the point. Of course strategy and structure are inextricably intertwined. Chandler's point was that new challenges give rise to new structures. The challenges of size and complexity, coupled with advances in communications and techniques of management control, produced divisionalization and decentralization. These same forces, several generations on, are now driving us toward new structural solutions—the federated organization, the multi-company coalition, and the virtual company. Few historians are prescient. Chandler was.

FOR MORE INFORMATION
Chandler, Alfred. *Strategy and Structure*. Cambridge, MA: MIT Press, 1962.

The Theory of Economic Development
JOSEPH A. SCHUMPETER

WHY READ IT?
Rated as one of the greatest economists of the 20th century, Schumpeter was among the first to set out a clear concept of entrepreneurship and its function within an economy. The key factor is innovation. Entrepreneurs innovate. Innovations create dynamism. Schumpeter's work was for a long time overshadowed by that of Keynes, but increased interest in innovation since the 1980s has led to a renaissance of Schumpeterian economics and a renewal of interest in this book in particular.

GETTING STARTED
This book sets out to uncover the forces within an economy that produce endogenous change. Schumpeter explains the processes of economic development by means of microtheory; he bases his study on innovative entrepreneurs and uses them to make large-scale factors, such as capital accumulation, interest, and company profits, understandable as dynamic processes.

CONTRIBUTION
1. Static and Dynamic Phenomena
According to Schumpeter, static general concepts of the workings of national economies are inadequate to explain the periodic changes in their stationary equilibrium—that is, the fluctuations of the economic cycle—and economic progress. This is because such concepts ascribe change solely to external influences. The central element in any overall concept ought, in his view, to be economic development, which alters the existing balance from within.

It is necessary then to distinguish between static phenomena, in which no changes take place, and dynamic ones, which lead to changes until counteracting forces bring the economy into a new state of balance. This development is apparent in phases of boom and recession, which consequently represent necessary manifestations accompanying economic development.

2. The Stationary Economy
Schumpeter's starting point is a stationary economy, that is, a system in a state of balance that periodically repeats itself. These are some of its features:
- All economic plans are aimed at achieving an optimum and need only be updated from period to period.
- In all households and businesses, income corresponds exactly to outgoings.
- In each period only those goods are consumed that were produced in the foregoing period and then exchanged.
- The possibilities of production are fixed in advance. The production function is invariable, and there are no possibilities for improvement or further investment.
- Perfect competition reduces aggregate profit to zero and consequently removes any incentive to entrepreneurial action.

But the function of capitalism is not, says Schumpeter, to administer existing structures, but to change them:
- In the static concept, there is no endogenous mechanism that could lead out of the status quo. Consequently, changes can only be brought about exogenously, that is, by external factors: social, political, and cultural influences, such as population growth,

capital growth, or altered preferences and technical or organizational improvements (organic growth).

- In the dynamic concept, economic development originates in innovations. Here, too, progress in production methods and organizational improvements play a part, but as a result of entrepreneurial action.

3. Innovations

Innovations, according to Schumpeter, consist of the practical implementation of knowledge, ideas, or discoveries, and therefore rely not on inventiveness but on entrepreneurial abilities. Technically speaking, technological and organizational improvements could be described as new possibilities for factor combination. The innovation could therefore lie in the introduction of new products or production methods, in the opening up of new markets or supplies of resources, or in organizational changes.

These innovations are put into practice by dynamic entrepreneurs; they represent the microfoundation of the macrophenomenon of social development. Schumpeter posits two conditions as necessary for innovative entrepreneurs to appear as economic actors:

- Development takes place by means of individual actions and of incentives and appears as the aggregate of the consequences of individual actions. Only when profits can be realized through innovations will the latter happen.
- Companies must have the opportunity to react to these incentives by changing the way they act. In balanced conditions, all production capacity is fully exploited. Consequently banks must make capital available so that potentially profitable investment opportunities can be realized through a change in the input of resources.

4. The Outcomes of Innovation

Profits from innovation make it possible to meet interest payments. As a result, the rate of interest will be determined by the demand for capital, and this demand, in turn, by the extent of profitable investment opportunities. Interest rates are consequently an indicator of economic progress. Profit and interest can thus be explained as outcomes of economic dynamism.

CONTEXT

Joseph Schumpeter (1883–1950) was an Austrian professor of political economy who belonged to the Vienna School of national economics. He later emigrated to the United States and held a professorship at Harvard.

The roots of his theories lay in Marxism, but since Marx's doctrine of the value of labor was in disrepute, he chose the neoclassical theory of value as the foundation for his work. This makes it difficult to assign Schumpeter a place in economic history. He proclaimed the significance of the business organization, but at the same time believed in the victory of socialism, famously answering "No" when asked if capitalism would survive. He realized himself that his work was likely to be overshadowed by Keynes's, and for most of the latter part of the 20th century this indeed proved to be the case.

> Can capitalism survive? No, I do not think it can.

FOR MORE INFORMATION

Schumpeter, Joseph A. *The Theory of Economic Development.* Trans. Opies. New Brunswick, NJ: Transaction Publishers, 1983.

The Theory of Social and Economic Organization

MAX WEBER

> Large organizations require that the people involved put the cause of the organization before their own aspirations.

WHY READ IT?

It is quite easy to make Weber's book sound as if it was intended to be a source text for Franz Kafka's novels and Charlie Chaplin's film *Modern Times*, not to mention George Orwell's *1984*. Weber is often incorrectly assumed to have been an advocate of bureaucracy and a mechanistic society, rather than someone who described bureaucracy—with at least some degree of correctness—as the most efficient and rational means of organization. In fact, as R. J. Kilcullen puts it, "bureaucracy was for Weber what capitalism was for Marx, the admired enemy." No understanding of the way modern organizations work would be complete without a study of this book.

GETTING STARTED

Max Weber was a versatile thinker who was a professor of political economy at the universities of Freiburg and Heidelberg in Germany. He is best known today as one of the founding fathers of modern sociology.

The Theory of Social and Economic Organization grew out of his philosophical inquiries into the nature of authority and how it is transmitted. Weber identified three types of authority: the "charismatic," based on the individual qualities of a leader and reverence for them among his or her followers; the "traditional," based on custom and usage; and the "rational-legal," based on the rule of objective law. According to the author, bureaucracy is the most efficient way of implementing the rule of law.

CONTRIBUTION

1. How Bureaucracy Works

There are four main principles characteristic of a rational-legal bureaucracy:

- The organization is structured around official functions, which are bound by rules, each area having its own specified competence.
- Functions are structured into offices organized into a hierarchy that follows technical rules and norms, for which training is provided.
- The administration is separated from the ownership of the means of production.
- The rules, decisions, and actions of the administration are recorded in writing.

2. The Impersonality of Bureaucracy

According to Weber, the most important feature of bureaucracy—its main strength as well as its main weakness—is its impersonality. Impersonality is a strength in that it minimizes the potential abuse of power by leaders because

- offices are ranked in hierarchical order;
- operations are conducted in accordance with impersonal rules;
- officials are allocated specific duties and areas of responsibility; and
- appointments are made on the basis of qualifications and suitability for the post.

It is a weakness in that
- the characteristic information processing and filtering to the top makes bureaucracies cumbersome and slow;
- the machinery makes it difficult to handle individual cases, because rules and procedures require all individuals to be treated as if they were the same;
- bureaucratization leads to depersonalization, because the roles of officials are circumscribed by written definitions of their authority, and there is a set of rules and procedures to cater to every contingency.

3. Toward Ultimate Efficiency

For Weber, the purely bureaucratic type of administrative organization is, from a purely technical point of view, capable of attaining the highest degree of efficiency. It is, in this sense, the most rational known means of carrying out imperative control over human beings. It is superior to any other form of organization in precision, in stability, in the stringency of its discipline, and in its reliability.

CONTEXT

Bureaucratic organization as expounded by Max Weber became the model for the 20th-century organization and was encapsulated in Alfred Sloan's General Motors and Harold Geneen's ITT. Strictly implemented, and in combination with regimented mass production as practiced by Henry Ford, who echoed some of Weber's thoughts in his faith in strict demarcations and his fervently mechanistic approach to business, it could produce a nightmare scenario for the world of work in the 20th century.

Weber himself could see no realistic substitute for bureaucracy. He regarded its triumph with distaste, but as inevitable. Only in the latter part of the 20th century did new and more humane concepts of the organization emerge and start to win adherents. The roots of some of the latest theories are in biology and the new sciences of chaos and complexity, areas unknown to Weber. Today's organizations are talked of in terms of fractals and amoebae—they are imagined as elusive and ever-changing rather than efficient and static.

The regularity of the machine age has given way to the tumult, ambiguity, and complexity of the information age. Even so, Max Weber remains important. In his book *Gods of Management*, Charles Handy chose as one of the gods Apollo, who is characterized by a Weber-like faith in rules and systems. Aspects of the bureaucratic model remain alive and well in a great many organizations where hierarchies, demarcations, and exhaustive rules dominate.

The influential author Gary Hamel notes:

> Every organization wrestles with two conflicting needs: the need to optimize in the name of economic efficiency, and the need to experiment in the name of growth and renewal. Authoritarian bureaucracies, of the sort that rebuilt the Japanese economy after the war, serve well the goal of optimization. While there is experimentation here, it is tightly constrained. Anarchical networks, of the sort that predominate in Italy's fashion industry, allow for unfettered experimentation, but are always vulnerable to more disciplined competitors. Weber staked out one side of the argument; Tom Peters the other. As always, what is required is a synthesis.

FOR MORE INFORMATION

Weber, Max. *The Theory of Social and Economic Organization* (originally published 1924). New York: Free Press, 1997.

Theory Z
WILLIAM OUCHI

WHY READ IT?
The book is subtitled *How American Business Can Meet the Japanese Challenge*, and the issue is still as important as it was when *Theory Z* was published in 1981. Ouchi believes that one of the major differences between Japanese and Western companies is their respective approach to managing people. Western companies who adopt the Japanese approach and adapt it to the Western business environment will be able to transform their business.

GETTING STARTED
Ouchi believes that Japanese success is derived from a very strong company philosophy, a distinct corporate culture, long-range staff development, and decision making based on consensus. The result, he claims, is lower staff turnover, increased job commitment, and higher productivity—all important factors in determining competitiveness. He argues that Western companies should not simply adopt Japanese practices, but adapt them.

CONTRIBUTION
1. The Real Forces behind Productivity
Ouchi believes that productivity is not just working harder. Trust is an essential factor, enabling people to make a contribution that will be respected. Subtlety allows teams to balance their skills in line with their roles, rather than seniority. Intimacy is a feature of all aspects of Japanese life, and this enables people to cooperate effectively at work.

2. Lifetime Employment
Major Japanese companies hire people just once a year. Staff are guaranteed employment until their retirement at age 55, and any promotion takes place from within. The employment system is mirrored in the satellite system of suppliers and subcontractors that surround a major company and its bank. The trading relationships are permanent and stable.

3. Job Rotation
Ouchi points out that the Japanese employment system features nonspecialist career paths so that staff gain a broader experience of the ways of the whole company. This is a form of lifelong job rotation. The Western system, he claims, rewards specialists, and there is less chance of interaction between staff.

4. Working to Common Objectives
According to the author, the basic mechanism of control in Japan is the corporate philosophy and objectives. All other company policy is derived from that. The company values and beliefs are also derived from the overall philosophy.

5. Decision Making by Consensus
Ouchi explains that, in this method of decision making, everyone gets involved. This may not result in the best decision, but it means that everybody understands the reasons for the decision and shares a commitment and responsibility for its success.

6. Japanese and Western Companies Compared

According to Ouchi, the key differences are

- lifetime employment versus short-term employment,
- slow promotion versus rapid promotion,
- nonspecialist career path versus specialist career path,
- implicit control mechanisms versus explicit ones,
- collective decision making versus individual decision making, and
- collective responsibility versus individual responsibility.

> Productivity and trust go hand in hand.

7. Type Z Companies

Ouchi uses the term to describe Western companies that have adapted Japanese practices. They encourage employees to stay longer, but have a faster promotion ladder. They substitute "management by walking about" for the job rotation of Japanese companies. Type Z companies encourage collaboration, but still maintain individual responsibility for decision making.

8. Creating a Type Z Company

The author outlines the key stages for leaders who want to transform their company:

- Understand a Type Z company and your own role in it.
- Audit your company's philosophy to detect inconsistencies.
- Define a suitable company philosophy.
- Create structures and incentives to support the new philosophy.
- Develop staff interpersonal skills.
- Involve employees and unions in the transformation.
- Stabilize employment.
- Broaden career path development.
- Encourage participation.

CONTEXT

Comparing Japanese and Western business practice has a long tradition.

W. Edwards Deming, paradoxically, took Western ideas on quality to Japan after World War II. He made an important contribution to Japanese economic recovery and the country's subsequent reputation for quality. It was only when Western observers realized the potential impact of Japan on Western economies that they took notice of Deming's writings.

William Ouchi offers a valuable insight into the human factors that make Japanese business so successful. However, Nonaka and Takeuchi, in their 1994 book *The Knowledge-creating Company*, caution readers about overreliance on contributory factors such as lifetime employment. They focus on the management of innovation within Japanese companies as a key competitive weapon.

Richard Pascale's *The Art of Japanese Management*, argues that Japanese success is largely attributable to what he called "soft factors"—style, shared values, skills, and staff. Western companies concentrated on "hard factors" such as strategy, structure, and systems.

FOR MORE INFORMATION

Ouchi, William. *Theory Z*. Reading, MA: Addison-Wesley, 1981.

The Third Wave
ALVIN TOFFLER

WHY READ IT?
The obvious reason for reading a work of futurology more than 20 years after its publication is to see if the futurologist got it right. In many respects Toffler did. Toffler predicted the electronic office and its effects. Now that most people work in electronic offices and live with their effects, perhaps it seems redundant to read a book simply to be able to congratulate the author on his foresight. What is startling about *The Third Wave* is that it was written so recently, and yet the technological leaps made since its publication have been so immense. The intriguing thing is whether the author's broader analysis encompassed the developments that flowed from the developments he immediately foresaw. For many people Toffler's ideas are still intriguing.

GETTING STARTED
Alvin Toffler began his career as a journalist but shot to international fame as a futurologist with the publication of his first book, *Future Shock*, in 1970. *The Third Wave* appeared ten years later, and *Power Shift* ten years after that.

The "Third Wave" referred to in the title is the super-industrial society that emerged toward the end of the 20th century and is still taking shape. It succeeded the "Second Wave," the industrialized society produced by the Industrial Revolution, which itself succeeded the agricultural phase of human development, the "First Wave." Each new wave was ushered in by the development of revolutionary new technology. Electronics brought in the third.

Though the various waves followed one another in time, they did not affect the whole of the human race simultaneously—many people are still living under First Wave conditions. Toffler's main concern is with the transition from the Second to the Third Waves in advanced societies, but he also deals with possible areas of friction between people coexisting at different stages of development.

CONTRIBUTION
1. Toward Mass Customization
The Third Wave, according to Toffler, is characterized by mass customization rather than mass production.

The essence of Second Wave manufacture was the long run of millions of identical standardized products. By contrast, the essence of Third Wave manufacture is the short run of partially or completely customized products.

The Second Wave strictly separated consumer and producer. The Third Wave will see the two become almost indistinguishable, as the consumer becomes involved in the actual process of production, expressing choices and preferences.

2. The Growth of Flexible Working
Toffler predicted the demise of the nine to five working day.

Machine synchronization shackled the human to the machine's capabilities and imprisoned all of social life in a common frame. It did so in capitalist and socialist countries alike. Now, as machine synchronization grows more precise, humans, instead of being imprisoned, are progressively freed. They are freed into more flexible ways of working, whether it is flextime or working at home.

3. Changes in Working Relationships

A partial shift toward the electronic office will be enough to trigger an eruption of social, psychological, and economic consequences. The coming wave of change means more than just new machines. It promises to restructure all the human relationships and roles in the office.

Toffler predicted that the Third Wave will produce anxiety and conflict as well as reorganization, restructuring, and, for some, rebirth into new careers and opportunities. The new systems will challenge all the old executive turfs, the hierarchies, the sexual role divisions, and the departmental barriers of the past.

4. The Impact on the Corporation

Instead of clinging to a sharply specialized economic function, the corporation, prodded by criticism, legislation, and its own concerned executives, is becoming a multipurpose institution, according to Toffler.

> Old ways of thinking, old formulas, dogmas, and ideologies, no matter how cherished or how useful in the past, no longer fit the facts.

The organization is being driven to redefinition through five forces:

- Changes in the physical environment. Companies must take greater responsibility for the effects of their operations on the global environment.
- Changes in the lineup of social forces. The actions of companies now have greater impact on those of other organizations such as schools, universities, civil groups, and political lobbies.
- Changes in the role of information. As information becomes central to production, as information managers proliferate in industry, the corporation, by necessity, impacts the informational environment exactly as it impacts the physical and social environments.
- Changes in government organization. The profusion of government bodies means that the business and political worlds interact to a far greater degree than ever before.
- Changes in morality. The ethics and values of organizations are becoming more closely linked to those of society. Behavior once accepted as normal is suddenly reinterpreted as corrupt, immoral, or scandalous. The corporation is increasingly seen as a producer of moral effects.

The organization of the future will be concerned with ecological, moral, political, racial, sexual, and social problems, as well as traditional commercial ones.

CONTEXT

Other studies of the future of working life tend to plunge head-first into celebrations of the miracles of technology, with little attempt to understand the human implications. Toffler is aware of them.

Many of his ideas have since been developed further by others. Charles Handy, for instance, has done a lot of work on the rise of homeworking.

Gary Hamel, influential author of *Leading the Revolution*, commented: "The post-industrial society is here! And Alvin Toffler saw it coming in 1980. . . . One of the challenges for anyone reading Toffler, or any other seer, is that there is no proprietary data about the future. Your competitors read Toffler, Naisbitt, and Negroponte too! The real challenge is to build proprietary foresight out of public data."

FOR MORE INFORMATION

Toffler, Alvin. *The Third Wave*. New York: Bantam, 1980.

The Tipping Point
MALCOLM GLADWELL

WHY READ IT?
The Tipping Point explains Gladwell's "laws of epidemics." Beyond his entertaining anecdotes and illustrations lies an exploration of the forces driving the spread of products, ideas, and other phenomena. The "tipping point" is the dramatic moment when everything changes simultaneously because a threshold has been crossed, although the situation might have been building for some time. According to Gladwell, epidemics can be either "good" or "bad." The spread of HIV is catastrophic, but it thrives on the same mechanism that spreads positive things—like fashions or health warnings. Underpinning this mechanism lie three fundamental forces driving all epidemics.

GETTING STARTED
The spread of some products or ideas while others decline is rarely understood. Gladwell's insight into social dynamics posits concrete laws governing the trends of human behavior. He likens rapid growth, decline, and coincidence to epidemics. Ideas are "infectious," fashions represent "outbreaks," and new ideas and products are "viruses." For example, advertising is a way of infecting others. Developing his analogy, Gladwell shows how a factor "tips"—that is, when a critical mass catches the infection and passes it on. This is when a shoe becomes a "fashion craze," social smoking becomes "addiction," and crime becomes a "wave." *The Tipping Point* is a manual for understanding and directing change, a revolutionary's handbook, in fact.

CONTRIBUTION
1. The Law of the Few
Epidemics need only a small number of people to transmit their infection to many others. Transmission is not achieved by the majority, or even a large minority; it only takes a very few. This is apparent with the spread of disease: The few people who socialize and travel the most make the difference between a local outbreak and a global pandemic. Word of mouth is a critical form of communication when spreading ideas. Those who speak the most (and speak the best) create epidemics of ideas. Gladwell categorizes these decisive people into connectors, mavens, and salespeople.

Connectors bring people together, using their social skills to make connections. This affords them power over the spread of epidemics, as they communicate throughout different "networks" of people. They are masters of the "weak tie" (a friendly, superficial connection) and can spread ideas far. Since ordinary people form time-consuming relationships, they make fewer of them and affect fewer people.

Mavens (information specialists) are subtly different. They focus on the needs of others rather than their own, and they have the most to say. Examples of mavens are teachers.

Salespeople concentrate on the relationship, not the message, and are more persuasive because they have better sales skills, mastering nonverbal communication and "motor mimicry" (the imitation of another's emotions and behavior to gain trust). The product is not necessarily theirs. An individual might make smoking look "cool" to an impressionable teenager without owning the cigarette company. Without connectors, mavens, and salespeople, epidemics would not reach a "tipping point." Epidemics need surprisingly few such people.

2. The Stickiness Factor

Whereas the law of the few relates to communication, stickiness is about intrinsic qualities or appeal. With a product or idea, the extent to which it spreads and becomes well known depends as much on its attractiveness as it does on how it is promoted. Its "stickiness" determines whether it passes by or catches on. The author explains that to reach a tipping point, ideas have to be compelling. If the idea or product is unattractive, it will be rejected irrespective of how it is transmitted. The information age has created a stickiness problem: The "clutter" of messages we face leads to products and ideas being ignored. For those wishing to create epidemics (such as marketers), it has become increasingly important to pay attention to the message's presentation. If contagiousness is a function of the messenger, stickiness is a property of the message.

3. The Power of Context

We rarely appreciate how our personal lives are affected by circumstances. Changes in the context of a message can tip an epidemic. An example is the "broken windows theory." If people see a single broken window, they may believe there is an absence of control and authority. Consequently, they are more likely to commit other crimes. A broken window or wall covered in graffiti invites crime that is more serious, spawning a crime wave. Yet the origin of the epidemic might not be with the connectors, mavens, or salespeople, nor with the stickiness of the factor (assuming crime is not a necessary human act). It could result from an accident in the environment. Gladwell argues that our circumstances matter as much as character. This means that manipulating the environment can control tipping points.

> In a given process or system some people matter more than others.

CONTEXT

Gladwell's experience at the *Washington Post* and the *New Yorker* in business, science, and medicine left him with some excellent explanations for a diverse range of questions. *The Tipping Point* charts a common course among a range of different phenomena. Successful strategies require improvements in our thinking and a shift from an exclusive focus on cause and effect. Gladwell supports a "systems-thinking" approach. Behind all successful epidemics rests a belief that change is possible. Tipping points underline the power of intelligent action—always an empowering vision.

FOR MORE INFORMATION

Gladwell, Malcolm. *The Tipping Point*. Rev. ed. Boston, MA: Back Bay Books, 2002.

FURTHER READING

Shapiro, Andrea. *Creating Contagious Commitment: Applying the Tipping Point to Organizational Change*. Hillsborough, NC: Strategy Perspective, 2003.

Toyota Production System
TAIICHI OHNO

Toyota's emphasis therefore was on reducing costs rather than increasing the selling price.

WHY READ IT?

Since the 1940s, Western automakers have lurched from one crisis to another, seemingly always one step behind. The company they were often following was the Japanese giant Toyota, and the reasons for this are explained by Taiichi Ohno in his brief book *Toyota Production System: Beyond Large-scale Production*. The world's carmakers have suffered dramatically since the global financial crisis kicked in in 2008, but Ohno's findings transcend that industry and still have resonance today.

GETTING STARTED

The Toyota Production System was developed to help the company catch up with the United States, whose auto workers were producing nine times as much as their Japanese counterparts. The Toyota system differed from the Western approach, emphasizing a reduction in costs rather than an increase in selling price.

According to the author, the company should be seen as a continuous and uniform whole, including suppliers as well as customers. Asking the question "why?" five times at each stage helps identify and solve problems before moving on.

CONTRIBUTION
1. Catching Up with the West

The roots of the Toyota Production System lie in the years immediately after the Second World War. Toyoda Kiichiro, president of Toyoda Motor Company, demanded that the company catch up with the United States and gave it three years to do so. He anticipated that otherwise the Japanese auto industry would cease to exist. At that time in the auto industry, an average U.S. worker produced around nine times as much as a Japanese worker.

2. A Different Approach to Production

The Toyota Production System evolved by Ohno was strikingly different from approaches used in the West. There, selling price was regarded as the combination of actual costs plus profit. Toyota, believing that the consumer actually sets the price, concluded that profit resulted when costs were subtracted from the selling price. Its emphasis therefore was on reducing costs rather than increasing the selling price.

3. The Principles of the Toyota System

The system has three simple principles:

Just-in-Time Production There is no point in producing cars, or anything else, in the hope that someone, somewhere, will buy them; production has to be closely tied to the market's requirements.

Wider Responsibility for Quality Responsibility for quality rests with every individual in an organization. Any quality defects need to be rectified as soon as they are identified.

The Concept of Value Stream The company should not be seen as a series of unrelated products and processes, but rather as a continuous and uniform whole; a stream including suppliers as well as customers.

4. The Five Whys

Another central element in Ohno's system was that the process of asking "why?" five times about various parts of a problem would help get to the root of it and solve it.

CONTEXT

These concepts were brought to mass Western audiences thanks to work conducted at the Massachusetts Institute of Technology as part of its International Motor Vehicle Program. The MIT research took five years, covered 14 countries, and looked exclusively at the world-wide auto industry. The researchers concluded that U.S. automakers remained fixed in the mass-production techniques of the past. In contrast, Japanese management, workers, and suppliers all worked to the same goals, resulting in increased production, high quality, happy customers, and lower costs.

This research was the basis for the 1990 best seller by James Womack, Daniel Jones, and Daniel Roos, *The Machine That Changed the World.* From lean production, Womack and Jones went on to propose lean enterprise and lean management. As with most management fads, it was willfully misinterpreted and became linked with reengineering.

The reality is that lean production as introduced by Ohno and Toyota is a highly effective concept. It can provide the economies of scale of mass production, the sensitivity to market and customer needs usually associated with smaller companies, and job enrichment for employees.

The West continues to see lean production as a means of squeezing more production from fewer people. This is a fundamental misunderstanding. Reducing the number of em-ployees is the end rather than the means. Western companies have tended to reduce numbers and then declare themselves lean organizations. Womack argues that although lean produc-tion requires fewer people, the organization should then accelerate product development to tap new markets to keep the people in work.

Inevitably, lean production has its downside. The most obvious is that the car industry is its natural home. It can be more difficult to apply in other industries. The second obvious problem with lean production is that it fails to embrace innovation and product develop-ment. It is one thing to be able to make a product efficiently, but how does one originate exciting and marketable products in the first place?

Womack and Jones suggest that the critical starting point for lean thinking is value, but this is effectively one stage beyond the initial one of generating ideas. Even so, lean produc-tion has raised awareness, provided a new benchmark, and brought operational efficiency to a wider audience.

Harvard Business School's Michael Porter argues, "Organizations did well to employ the most up-to-date equipment, information technology, and management techniques to elim-inate waste, defects, and delays. They did well to operate as close as they could to the pro-ductivity frontier. But while improving operational effectiveness is necessary to achieving superior profitability, it is not sufficient."

FOR MORE INFORMATION

Ohno, Taiichi. *Toyota Production System.* Cambridge, MA: Productivity Press, 1988.

Up the Organization
ROBERT TOWNSEND

WHY READ IT?
Like any good satire, *Up the Organization* is not only irreverent and wickedly humorous, it is based on shrewd insight and sound common sense. Its questioning of the ghastly, stifling orthodoxies of corporate thinking, corporate behavior, and corporate society is, many commentators note regretfully, as relevant now as it was when the book was first published over 30 years ago.

GETTING STARTED
Townsend's first concern is for the people who are trapped in rigid organizational structures and unable to realize anything like their full potential. He has no time for the adornments of executive office or indeed anything that separates a management elite from the experiences of ordinary workers. Turning his attention to more general issues, he suggests that all major organizations are operating on the wrong assumptions.

CONTRIBUTION
1. The Organizational Trap
According to Townsend, in the average company, the boys in the mailroom, the president, the vice presidents, and the girls in the steno pool have three things in common: They are docile, they are bored, and they are dull.

He claims that they are trapped in the pigeonholes of organizational charts and have been made slaves to the rules of private and public hierarchies that run mindlessly on and on because nobody can change them.

2. The Problems of Business Schools
Townsend's advice to companies is not to hire Harvard Business School graduates. He believes that this so-called elite is lacking in some pretty fundamental requirements for success: humility; respect for people on the firing line; deep understanding of the nature of the business and the kind of people who can enjoy themselves making it prosper; respect from way down the line; and a demonstrated record of guts, industry, loyalty, judgment, fairness, and honesty under pressure.

3. The End of Executive Office Perks
All the special perquisites of executive office are anathema to Townsend. His list of no-nos includes
- reserved parking spaces;
- special-quality stationery for the boss and his elite;
- muzak;
- bells and buzzers;
- company shrinks;
- outside directorships and trusteeships for the chief executive; and
- the company plane.

4. The Wrong Kind of Leaders

According to Townsend, those with power, or who think they have power, are dangerous beings. He claims that there is nothing fundamentally wrong with the country except that the leaders of all our major organizations are operating on the wrong assumptions.

Townsend believes that the country is in this mess because for the last 200 years it has been using the Catholic Church and Caesar's legions as the patterns for creating organizations. He argues that until 40 or 50 years ago, that made sense. The average church-goer, soldier, and factory worker was uneducated and dependent on orders from above. And authority carried considerable weight because disobedience brought the death penalty or its equivalent.

> We're in this mess because for the last 200 years we've been using the Catholic Church and Caesar's legions as our patterns for creating organizations.

CONTEXT

Townsend's genius lies in debunking the modern organization for its excesses, stupidity, and absurdity. He collected his material in the course of his successful career as a director of American Express and president of Avis Rent-a-Car, then transformed himself into a witty commentator on the excesses of corporate life.

Up the Organization is subtitled *How to Stop the Corporation from Stifling People and Strangling Profits*. The influential author Robert Heller called the book the first pop best seller on business management. It is in the tradition of humorous best sellers debunking managerial mythology and the high-minded seriousness of the theorists. In the 1950s there was *Parkinson's Law*; at the end of the 1960s came Laurence Peter and Townsend; and more recently the *Dilbert* series has followed in their footsteps.

Townsend also belongs in the tradition of people-oriented business writing. His humor should not blind one to the underlying seriousness of his purpose.

Given that over 30 years have passed since its publication, the book still retains its freshness and originality, and its insights into the blind deficiencies of too many organizations remain sadly apt.

FOR MORE INFORMATION

Townsend, Robert. *Up the Organization*. New York: Fawcett Books, 1984.

Valuation
TOM COPELAND, JACK MURRIN, AND TOM KOLLER

WHY READ IT?
Prompted by more intensive competition, the restructuring of industries, and ever more sophisticated stockholders, managers are checking over their company portfolios more critically than ever before to find out precisely where value is being created or destroyed. At a time when stakeholder value is gaining ground and stock options play an ever more important role in the remuneration of leading employees, value-oriented portfolio structuring and resource allocation are becoming central factors in strategic thinking.

GETTING STARTED
The authors provide management with the necessary equipment to help them identify the sources and extent of value appreciation and depreciation within the company. In a series of theoretical analyses based on capital market research, they present the discounted cash flow (DCF) method and supplement their explanatory material with numerous case studies drawn from business practice.

CONTRIBUTION
1. Company Value and Company Strategy
Companies, say the authors, need competitive strategies, not only for the familiar goods and services markets, but also for the market in the disposal rights of companies. This is where the success of efforts to increase company value, which derives from cash flows, will be felt. Managers must pursue active value-management policies.

There are two stages in the development of a value-oriented policy:
- a restructuring that frees up the values locked into the company
- establishing priorities for enhancing value

Managers should regularly create and make use of opportunities to increase value, according to Copeland and his colleagues. In this way they can avoid having to react under pressure later.

2. Company Value on a Cash Flow Basis: A Guide for Practitioners
The procedure that combines best with the objective of long-term value enhancement, the authors suggest, is the discounted cash flow (DCF) method, which has the following advantages:
- The bases for valuation are free cash flows, as only these are available for servicing invested capital.
- Future expectations are systematically taken into account.
- Capital structure, financing costs, and risk are fully covered, so that the whole debit side of the company balance sheet is taken into consideration.
- An objective yardstick for comparing strategic options is created.
- Almost all the information needed to calculate the value of the company can be derived from existing and projected figures given in the company accounts.

In accordance with the DCF "component model," the value of a company's equity capital is equivalent to the value of various cash flows that lead ultimately to the cash flow to stockholders (dividends, stock repurchases, stock issues). This, say the authors, has four advantages:
1. Evaluating the components of the company helps to identify the individual sources of investment and finance that influence the value of the company.

2. It identifies operating drivers with the greatest prospects for enhancing value.
3. It can be applied at various levels and combined with investment accounting.
4. It is sufficiently differentiated to cope with complex situations and can be conducted using simple data-processing technology.

3. Using the DCF Component Model to Value a Company
The authors split this process into five stages:

- Analysis of historical performance. First the relevant components of free cash flows are determined. Then a comprehensive profile of past performance is drawn up. It provides important clues to forecasting future performance.
- Determining capital costs. The first step is to establish the capital structure of the company. From this the weighting factors for the weighted average cost of capital (WACC) formula can be derived. Next, external capital costs are determined. Finally, equity capital costs are assessed, a process best conducted using the capital asset pricing model (CAPM) or the arbitrage pricing model (APM).
- Prognosis of future performance. Here the assumptions and scenarios relevant to a prognosis of the company's economic situation and competitive position in its industry are worked out. Forecasts also need to be made for the decisive drivers of value: growth and return on capital.
- Estimating continuance value. First the most suitable DCF method to apply must be decided on. The choice is among the long-term detailed prognosis, the continuing-value formula taking account of growing cash flows, and the value factor formula. The time frame for a detailed prognosis is established. The parameters are then assessed; these are the operating result after tax, free cash flow, the return on new investment, the growth rate, and the WACC. Finally, the continuing value is discounted to the present.
- Calculation and interpretation of results. The final phase comprises the calculation and checking of the value of the company, together with the interpretation of the results in the light of the circumstances surrounding the decision.

This method of calculation, the authors say, is also suitable for valuing companies under more complex framework conditions. It allows the options price theory to be applied to both their assets and their liabilities.

CONTEXT
Insufficient attention to value has meant that the value of companies worldwide has been reduced without this becoming apparent in their published accounts. This development prompted the consultancy firm McKinsey to conduct extensive research that ultimately resulted in the DCF method. This book, whose three authors are partners at McKinsey, supplements accounting disciplines with a comprehensive plan for company evaluation. It was hailed on its appearance by finance experts worldwide as a must-read for managers, security analysts, and investors alike. The new edition shows how the system can be applied in the valuation of companies in the new economy.

FOR MORE INFORMATION
McKinsey & Co. Inc., Tom Copeland, Jack Murrin, and Tim Koller. *Valuation: Measuring and Managing the Value of Companies.* 3rd ed. Hoboken, NJ: Wiley, 2000.

The Visionary's Handbook
WATTS WACKER AND JIM TAYLOR

WHY READ IT?
This is a provocative book that challenges organizations to be unconventional. The authors show how organizations will face constant change and claim that the only way to survive is to turn conventional thinking on its head. A book to aid forward thinking, rather than day-to-day management.

GETTING STARTED
Constant change is a fact of business life. Constant change will become constant paradox—and the authors outline nine paradoxes of the new world:
1. The paradox of value: Intrinsic worth isn't.
2. The paradox of size: The bigger you are, the smaller you need to be.
3. The paradox of time: At the speed of light, nothing happens.
4. The paradox of competition: Your biggest competitor is your own view of your future.
5. The paradox of action: You've got to go for what you can't expect to get.
6. The paradox of leadership: To lead from the front, you have to stay inside the story.
7. The paradox of leisure: Relax, dammit; play is hard work.
8. The paradox of the visionary: Our reality is yours alone.
9. The paradox of reality: Your reality is ours alone.

CONTRIBUTION
1. From Constant Change to Constant Paradox
Constant change is now taken for granted on most corporate agendas, and business life in the hinterlands of the new economy is due for another shake-up.

Constant change will become constant paradox—a continuous collision of opposites that will affect us and the terms of our business and personal lives. There are nine paradoxes (listed above and discussed below).

2. The Paradox of Value: Intrinsic Worth Isn't
The value of any product becomes inseparable from a buyer's perception of worth. Instead of intrinsic value, we have relative value only. The products that a business makes bear diminished relations to the physical content of the offering.

3. The Paradox of Size: The Bigger You Are, the Smaller You Need to Be
Even if you're a large corporation, you need to think small to operate effectively in a world in which each individual is a microculture. To communicate effectively and directly to the interests of those microcultures, you have to atomize your organization and miniaturize its units.

4. The Paradox of Time: At the Speed of Light, Nothing Happens
To succeed in the short term, you need to think in the long term. Yet the greater your vision and the longer the time interval over which you predict results, the greater the risk that you will be unable to take the necessary steps in the short term to achieve the long-term goals. The tension between short- and long-term planning has never been more tormented.

5. The Paradox of Competition: Your Biggest Competitor Is Your Own View of Your Future

Competition comes from everywhere and nowhere at the same time. It needs to be viewed in both external and internal terms. Competition takes place in all three tenses.

6. The Paradox of Action: You've Got to Go for What You Can't Expect to Get

Nothing will turn out exactly as it's supposed to. You must act intuitively and be equally ready to take resolute, counterintuitive action.

7. The Paradox of Leadership: To Lead from the Front, You Have to Stay Inside the Story

In an inherently inconsistent world, consistency in our leaders is not the virtue it once was.

8. The Paradox of Leisure: Relax, Dammit; Play Is Hard Work

Play and work are blending and becoming indistinguishable.

9. The Paradox of the Visionary: Our Reality Is Yours Alone

The closer your vision gets to a provable truth, the more you are simply describing the present. The more certain you are of a future outcome, the more likely you will be wrong.

10. The Paradox of Reality: Your Reality Is Ours Alone

Every person has the potential to be connected to every other person. But every individual inhabits a world of his or her own and is a marketing segment of absolutely one. As our links become stronger, our individuation becomes starker.

CONTEXT

The authors focus on constant paradox, a continuous collision of opposites that will affect us and the terms of our business and personal lives every moment we are alive. They identify nine paradoxes in all.

> Your biggest competitor is your own view of your future.

To help readers come to grips with the implications of these paradoxes, Wacker and Taylor offer practical examples to illuminate their meaning, as well as numerous exercises and reflection points to enable readers to chart their personal course for the future. However, the book provides no prepackaged solutions. The authors claim this is one of the book's virtues.

The Visionary's Handbook captures the interlocking web of paradoxes that abound in business life and provides a map to help make the future work for every individual and every company in the challenging and uncertain times ahead.

FOR MORE INFORMATION

Wacker, Watts, and Jim Taylor. *The Visionary's Handbook*. New York: HarperBusiness, 2000.

The Visual Display of Quantitative Information
EDWARD R. TUFTE

WHY READ IT?

The book is widely regarded as one of the most authoritative guides to the graphical treatment of statistical information through charts, graphs, and other graphic devices. It draws on the work of experts in the field and includes hundreds of examples of good and bad design.

> Words, data, and graphics are different mechanisms with but a single purpose—the presentation of information.

GETTING STARTED

Statistical graphics are used to communicate complex information clearly through words, numbers, and pictures. The author reports that each year, somewhere between 900 billion and 2 trillion images of statistical graphics are produced, demonstrating the importance of the subject. Excellence, he believes, should lead the viewer to think about the content and explain complex ideas with clarity, precision, and efficiency.

CONTRIBUTION

Tufte illustrates how graphics should tell a story in a way that ordinary statistics could not do. He points out that good graphics must be based on sound data sources. However, graphics can sometimes be used to distort data. He distinguishes between perceived visual effects and attempts to deceive. Design variations, such as changing scale, can also distort information.

The author suggests two ways to avoid distortion:

- The representation of numbers should be directly proportional to the numbers themselves.
- Clear labeling should be used to remove ambiguity.

Tufte argues that it is a mistake to think that graphics should be used because data are intrinsically dull. This attitude, he claims, is responsible for overelaborate graphics produced by designers who may not understand the significance of the numbers. The use of graphics should not be treated as decoration.

The author sets out principles for good design:

- Above all else, show the data.
- Erase non-data information.
- Erase redundant data information.

He also suggests that presentation can be inspired by combining words, numbers, and pictures.

CONTEXT

The author is regarded as an authority on the presentation of statistical information. The book was based on a series of seminars on the use of statistical graphics. This, he believes, is an underdeveloped field. Most books on graphics concentrate on design technique, rather than on the information the graphics are communicating.

Tufte's collaboration with statistician John Tukey set out to bridge the gap. The collaboration, he believes, made the subject intellectually respectable. As well as giving the subject a more intellectual dimension, Tufte also uses the book to demonstrate the tradition of excellence in graphics since the 18th century.

FOR MORE INFORMATION
Tufte, Edward R. *The Visual Display of Quantitative Information.* 2nd ed. Cheshire, CT: Graphics Press, 2001.

The Wealth of Nations
ADAM SMITH

WHY READ IT?
Many books are claimed to be classics or seminal works: *The Wealth of Nations* is indisputably both. It is a broad-ranging exploration of commercial and economic first principles. In it Adam Smith laid the philosophical foundations for modern capitalism and the modern market economy. There are few economists over the last 200 years—and fewer politicians of a free-market persuasion—who have not been influenced by it. Smith has helped shape the economic policies of British prime ministers and chancellors of the exchequer, from the days of Lord North (1770–1782) to those of Margaret Thatcher—and even Tony Blair.

GETTING STARTED
Adam Smith was a Scottish philosopher. He was professor of logic and professor of moral philosophy at Glasgow University, but left his university posts to travel on the continent as tutor to a young nobleman. In France he was greatly influenced by a school of philosophical economists known as the "physiocrats." Returning to his native town of Kirkcaldy in Fife, he spent the next ten years preparing *An Inquiry into the Nature and Causes of the Wealth of Nations*, which was published—a significant coincidence perhaps—in the same year as the signing of the Declaration of Independence, 1776.

His central thesis is that capital can best be used for the creation of both individual and national wealth in conditions of minimal interference by government. The "invisible hand" of free-market competition ensures, in his view, both the vitality of commercial activity and the ultimate good of all a nation's citizens.

> The real and effectual discipline which is exercised over a workman is not that of his corporation, but that of his customers.

CONTRIBUTION
1. The Invisible Hand
According to Smith, conscious and well-meaning attempts to better the lot of a nation and its population are generally doomed to failure. The unintended cumulative effects of self-interested striving are far more effective. As he put it: "Every individual is continually exerting to find out the most advantageous employment for whatever he can command . . . [and] necessarily labors to render the annual revenue of the society as great as he can. He generally neither intends to promote the public interest nor knows how much he is promoting it. He intends only his own gain, and he is in this, as in many other cases, led by an invisible hand to promote an end which was no part of his intention."

2. Value and Labor
The value of a particular good or service is determined by the costs of production. If something is expensive to produce, then its value is similarly high. Smith wrote: "The real price of everything, what everything really costs to the man who wants to acquire it, is the toil and trouble of acquiring it. What everything is really worth to the man who has acquired it, and who wants to dispose of it or exchange it for something else, is the toil and trouble of which it can save himself, and which it can impose on other people."

He continued: "What is bought with money or with goods is purchased by labor, as much as what we acquire by the toil of our own body. They contain the value of a certain quantity of labor which we exchange for what is supposed at the time to contain the value of an equal quantity."

3. The Division of Labor

Smith's legacy to scientific management was the concept of the division of labor. "The division of labor occasions in every art a proportionable increase of the productive powers of labor. The separation of different trades and employments from one another seems to have taken place in consequence of this advantage," he wrote. "Men are much more likely to discover easier and readier methods of attaining any object when the whole attention of their minds is directed towards that single object than when it is dissipated among a great variety of things."

CONTEXT

For a book that is over 200 years old, there is a surprisingly modern-sounding ring to a great deal of what *The Wealth of Nations* has to say. This is mainly owing to the acuteness and lasting value of Smith's analysis—the book was the first comprehensive exploration of the foundations, workings, and machinations of a free-market economy—but also to the familiarity of many of its basic concepts. *The Wealth of Nations* continues to have a role as a right-wing manifesto, a gloriously logical exposition of the beauty of market forces. And the appeal is not only to the right wing in politics.

Smith's system of demarcation and functional separation provided the basis for the management theorists of the early 20th century, such as Frederick Winslow Taylor, and practitioners such as Henry Ford. They translated the economic rigor of his thinking to practices in the workplace, though in ways and on a scale that Smith could never have imagined.

History has, however, put its own limitations on Smith's theorizing.

- Physical labor is no longer so important.
- The 20th century saw the emergence of management as a profession. It was barely acknowledged by Smith.
- Smith wrote without knowledge of the power and scope of modern corporations, let alone the power of brand names and customer loyalty.
- He also wrote in harder times, when self-interest was not a choice but a necessity.

Nevertheless, as Gary Hamel commented: "Revisionists be damned. Citizens from Prague to Santiago to Guangzhou to Jakarta owe much of their new-found prosperity to the triumph of Adam Smith's economic ideals. [He] laid the philosophical foundations for the modern industrial economy. Enough said."

FOR MORE INFORMATION

Smith, Adam. *The Wealth of Nations*. New York: Bantam, 2003.

What They Don't Teach You at Harvard Business School

MARK H. MCCORMACK

WHY READ IT?

What They Don't Teach You at Harvard Business School is not an indictment of Harvard's business education program or of the merits of a business education elsewhere, but rather a testament to the importance of practical experience. Although an alumnus of Yale Law School, in this book McCormack argues that education is useful only when one understands its limitations; in his opinion, ignoring them leads to dangerous arrogance and a lack of understanding about the way the world works. MBAs and high IQs alone often indicate little about future success in business. The value of this book is to learn the lessons McCormack teaches, drawing on his experiences throughout a long and successful career. The "street smarts" that McCormack highlights were the critical factor in his business career and in understanding others' behavior.

GETTING STARTED

To get the most out of this book, you have to understand that what you know matters less than how you react to what you do not know. The book comprises many lessons, ranging from McCormack's opinion of the best way to dress in a business situation (conservatively) to how to impress and judge others.

McCormack founded the International Management Group (IMG) in the early 1960s with less than $500, few contacts, and a novel idea. It gave birth to a new industry, incorporating the lifestyle sector and, by the early 1980s, generated revenues of several hundred million dollars. IMG's business, in addition to television programming, is to market "sports personalities" as diverse and famous as Gary Player, Tiger Woods, Serena Williams, and Michael Schumacher. While IMG's fortunes are largely tied to its clients' success, it was the company's ability to construct a successful enterprise with a great brand, a deep reserve of talent, and a series of winning deals that bred its success.

McCormack shares his practical experience with entertaining anecdotes from his personal career. McCormack presents these as rules, showing how they contributed to the building of IMG, and organizes them into those concerning people, selling, and running a business.

CONTRIBUTION
1. People

The author offers advice on various aspects of dealing with people, but the general message is to be observant and diligent to create the right impression; build trust; and obtain winning advantages over rivals, competitors, and peers. These different skills are categorized into "reading people," "creating impressions," "taking the edge," and "getting ahead." Observing others effectively and influencing them—the "gamesmanship of business"—brings success. Perhaps the most interesting individual lesson McCormack teaches is the value of "working in the mailroom" or similar situations. This will not teach humility or how the company really works, but helps one to understand oneself—those who succeed are those who compete with themselves. However, one does not need to be genuinely the best to get ahead. As McCormack observes, "Carpenters that become contractors have a need to drive a nail straighter and truer than anyone else." However, "some executives, had they started in the mailroom, would still be sorting mail—and misrouting most of it." Knowing others is essential, but it is just as important to understand oneself and use this understanding as a practical advantage.

2. Sales and Negotiation

McCormack's advice on selling and negotiating includes tactics such as the importance of silence, to force the other person to talk or to make sure the right pitch is made at the right time. Moreover, he highlights that we are all "natural" salespeople. In school, we persuade peers to accept us and teachers to give us good grades. After this, we excel at selling ourselves to employers. However, when we actually go out to sell we often underperform for fear of rejection or underestimate the importance of salesmanship, neglecting "street wisdom" for that of the business school. The book describes the rules of selling, but the most important lesson is that failure in sales and negotiation usually comes from one's own psychological barriers, such as fear of failure; overcoming these is the secret to success.

3. Running a Business

Much of the literature about building a business is academic, covering different models for growth, acquisition, entrepreneurship, and countless other factors. However, McCormack uses his own experience in creating and building IMG to distill the realities of successful business management. His lesson is to avoid "reinventing the wheel": It is far better to use one's own common sense and apply proven rules to unique situations. Often, general rules—grow prudently, diversify risks and opportunities, manage talent, distinguish between short- and long-term opportunities, employ systems-based thinking while staying flexible, be efficient, and pay attention to detail—are ignored as managers apply more complicated strategies to gain competitive advantage. Most situations benefit from common sense, rather than complex solutions. For example, when IMG faced a lawsuit about their client Bjorn Borg, McCormack refused to seek legal advice, held a meeting with the plaintiffs to discuss their complaints, and eventually settled the matter to everyone's satisfaction.

> You don't have to be perfect, but you should learn from your imperfections.

CONTEXT

This book is not a substitute for real-world experience—it merely distills McCormack's personal experiences and values—but it *is* an autobiography that provokes and inspires. It should do so; Mark McCormack was at the top of his game until his death in 2003.

His most valuable lesson is that no one has to be perfect to be successful, as long as they play to their strengths. This is a key theme: that book-learned knowledge and scientific preparation is less important than being able to get things done in the real world. It may not be necessary to be perfect at something if there is an alternative or if you are at least good enough at that thing. However, worrying about being perfect is an excellent way to destroy confidence and to establish even greater barriers to success. In McCormack's words: "You don't have to be perfect, but you should learn from your imperfections."

FOR MORE INFORMATION

McCormack, Mark H. *What They Don't Teach You at Harvard Business School*. Reissue. New York: Bantam, 1986.

The Will to Manage
MARVIN BOWER

WHY READ IT?
Marvin Bower did more than anyone else to create the modern management consulting industry. The book provides valuable insight into the management practices that made McKinsey and Company such a long-lasting success.

GETTING STARTED
Marvin Bower's success was based on his principle that building trust with clients is critical to the consulting firm's success. The interests of the client should precede increasing the company's revenues.

He also believed that using values to help shape and guide an organization is extremely important. One of those values is that regard for the individual is based not on title, but on competence, stature, and leadership. Instead of experienced consultants, McKinsey recruited graduate students who could learn how to be good problem solvers and consultants. The company also developed "virtual" project teams, bringing in the best people in the organization wherever they were based in the world. Clear, simple employment policies and change through empowerment helped to maintain high professional standards.

CONTRIBUTION
1. A New Way of Looking at Consultancies
Bower did not change the name of his company, McKinsey, as he shrewdly decided that clients would demand his involvement in projects if his name was up in lights. His vision was to provide advice on managing to top executives and to do it with the professional standards of a leading law firm. Due to a belief that in all successful professional groups, regard for the individual is based not on title but on competence, stature, and leadership, McKinsey consultants were associates who had engagements, rather than mere jobs, and the firm was a practice rather than a business.

2. Building Trust with Clients
The entire ethos of McKinsey was to be very respectable, the kind of people CEOs naturally relate to. Bower's gospel was that the interests of the client should precede increasing the company's revenues; unless the client could trust McKinsey, the company could not work with them. If McKinsey looked after the client, the profits would look after themselves. High charges were not a means to greater profits, but a simple and effective means of ensuring that clients took McKinsey seriously.

Other central principles were that consultants should keep quiet about the affairs of clients, should tell the truth, and should be prepared to challenge the client's opinion. They should only agree to do work that is both necessary and that they can do well. Using values to help shape and guide an organization was extremely important.

3. New Patterns of Recruitment
Instead of hiring experienced executives with in-depth knowledge of a particular industry, Bower recruited graduate students who could learn how to be good problem solvers and

consultants. This changed the emphasis of consulting from passing on a narrow range of experience to using a wide range of analytical and problem-solving techniques.

4. Developing Virtual Project Teams

Another element of Bower's approach was the use of teams. He thought of McKinsey as a network of leaders. Teams were assembled for specific projects, and the best people in the organization were brought to bear on a particular problem, no matter where they were based in the world. McKinsey's culture fostered rigorous debate over the right answer, without that debate resulting in personal criticism.

5. Clear, Simple Employment Policies

The company's policy remains one of the most simple: Seniority in McKinsey correlates directly with achievement. If a consultant ceases to progress with the organization or is ultimately unable to demonstrate the skills and qualities required of a principal, he or she is asked to leave McKinsey.

> If you looked after the client, the profits would look after themselves.

6. Change through Empowerment

"There have been thousands of changes in methods, but not in command and control. Many companies say they want to change, but they need to empower people below. More cohesion is needed rather than hierarchy," Bower said in 1995.

CONTEXT

Under Bower's astute direction, McKinsey became the world's premier consulting firm. Recent years have also seen the structure and managerial style of the company receiving plaudits. McKinsey is special because it has developed a self-perpetuating aura that it is unquestionably the best. Marvin Bower was the creator of this organizational magic.

American Express chief Harvey Golub says that Bower led McKinsey according to a set of values, and it was the principle of using values to help shape and guide an organization that was probably the most important thing he took away from his contact with McKinsey.

FOR MORE INFORMATION

Bower, Marvin. *The Will to Manage*. New York: McGraw-Hill, 1966.

The Wisdom of Crowds
JAMES SUROWIECKI

WHY READ IT?

History tells us that change is always managed by a leader. In *The Wisdom of Crowds*, business journalist James Surowiecki argues that the crowd is often more rational and decisive than the individual. Understanding how people behave en masse is critical to analyzing any situation and an especially useful tool when it comes to comprehending markets. Studying a wide range of different "crowds"—including traffic, the scientific community, markets, and political democracies—Surowiecki develops a thesis that can be applied to diverse teams, companies, and problems. Understanding the wisdom of crowds promises to change the way we view our business decisions, structure our political systems, and organize our society. While Adam Smith's "hidden hand of the market"—the idea that individuals' self-interest creates economic efficiency—is widely embraced, looking at how the crowd behaves is vital to understanding how markets function and make decisions.

GETTING STARTED

Surowiecki uses anecdotes to demonstrate how large crowds make more rational decisions than individuals and smaller groups. For instance, he relates how the U.S. Navy located the wreckage of a lost submarine not by consulting with just a few experts, but rather by allowing a large group of people with diverse backgrounds to provide an estimate of its location and calculating the mean average of every estimate. When the submarine was eventually found, it was just 220 yards from where the group had said it would it be. The astonishing thing about this story is that the evidence that the group was relying on was virtually nonexistent. No one person knew why the submarine sank, how fast it was traveling, or how steeply it fell to the bottom, but the group as a whole came up with the right answers.

The author's definition of a "crowd" is very broad, ranging from game-show audiences, to large corporations, to herds of cars caught in traffic, to juries and management teams. He argues that collective intelligence can be applied to a wide variety of problems, but requires three conditions to be "smart": diversity, independence, and decentralization.

CONTRIBUTION
1. Diversity of Membership

Diversity among the members of the group is important because it helps to generate a wider set of possible solutions and makes it better at problem solving. It adds perspectives that would otherwise be absent and takes away (or weakens) some of the destructive characteristics of group decision making. Fostering diversity is actually more important in small groups and in formal organizations than in larger collectives, like markets or electorates, because the sheer size of the latter usually guarantees a minimum level of diversity. Too often, a few biased individuals exert undue influence, skewing the group's collective decision. Diversity makes it easier for a group to make a decision based exclusively on facts, rather than on emotional biases and allegiances; heterogeneous groups are less susceptible to "groupthink."

2. Independence of Opinion

Independence is a crucial ingredient in effective decisions but is notoriously fragile. By enabling each member of the group to make up his or her own mind, the rationality of a group decision is maintained. The fashion industry provides a good example: A product that sells more but does not offer good value can still succeed because people want to wear what others are already wearing, so that they'll gain approval. In this case, a lack of independent opinion leads the crowd to buy a product that is worse value than its competitors. Independence keeps the mistakes that people make from becoming correlated and systematic.

3. Decentralization

Surowiecki argues that to be rational, crowds must decentralize power and diffuse authority on a reasonably equal basis. Decentralization facilitates independence of opinion while allowing individuals to coordinate their activities and collaborate to solve their problems. However, decentralized systems need mechanisms for going beyond aggregating information to being able to make a coordinated judgment. In a democracy, voters base their voting decision on the available information, while the mechanism for pronouncing their judgment is the election itself. However, many crowds lack such a formal decision process, which can create anarchy. While maintaining a decentralized system, a crowd can best tackle a problem in situations in which the decision process would otherwise have a bias against individuals.

CONTEXT

As corporations' strategic decisions become increasingly complex, harnessing the wisdom of the crowd is increasingly vital. Too many organizations are hampered by rigid hierarchies that formalize individual leaders' power over their teams, leading to flawed and irrational decision making. Surowiecki's liberating analysis encourages democracy over despotism. A successful example of a company harnessing the wisdom of crowds is Hewlett-Packard's use of internal "decision markets," in which employees anonymously buy and sell shares to reflect their view of future sales of particular products.

In a commercial context, it is important to differentiate between the wisdom of small and large crowds. Small groups are unusual, as individuals have more impact on overall judgments—for example, each individual in a jury has more impact on others than each individual in the crude oil market. However, it seems that few organizations have figured out how to make internal groups work consistently well, preferring to discourage all dissent and in the process continue to make flawed decisions.

FOR MORE INFORMATION

Surowiecki, James. *The Wisdom of Crowds: Why the Many Are Smarter Than the Few*. New York: Doubleday, 2004.

Work This Way
BRUCE TULGAN

WHY READ IT?
Like Charles Handy in *The Age of Unreason* and Tom Peters in *The Brand You 50*, the author predicts the end of traditional career structures and jobs for life. The book provides a guide to the new career patterns and would be of interest to employers and employees who are planning their future careers.

GETTING STARTED
The traditional career is over. The working world is increasingly dominated by the knowledge economy, and organizations are showing increasing uncertainty about future direction. Individuals are experiencing uncertainties about future career and job prospects, as a job for life seems like a leftover concept from a very different era.

CONTRIBUTION
1. The New Pattern of Work
The traditional career is over. Most people believe it, but nobody really seems to know what is going to replace it. There are five essential ingredients for a reinvented career:
- Learn voraciously.
- Concentrate on relationships.
- Add value continuously.
- Be balanced.
- Take it one year at a time.

Learn Voraciously   The next generation of employees already has an insatiable appetite for information. According to Tulgan, we need to
- create our own opportunities to learn—the traditional education system by itself is no longer enough;
- take personal control of our postschool education by designing our own courses;
- maximize all corporate training opportunities and turn everyday life into a learning lab; and
- turn job-hopping into a personal training program.

Concentrate on Relationships   Relationships with individuals will be the most reliable institutions in the post-jobs era. We need to
- identify and seek out the real decision makers;
- turn every contact into a multiple contact;
- identify and win over gatekeepers;
- get on the right person's radar, then prove that we are more than a blip; and
- take personal responsibility for keeping relationships fizzing.

Add Value Continuously   The most successful workers today are chameleon-like, day-to-day value adders who are flexible and adapt well to changing circumstances.

Temporary workers are the fastest growing category of employees. Temping is not just for clerical workers anymore but also for doctors, lawyers, engineers, bankers, scientists, teachers, programmers, trapeze artists, and many other types of worker.

Be Balanced   Set clear priorities in our working and personal lives and then live by them, no matter what. It is essential to stay close to our deepest values and priorities, such as quality, integrity, fulfillment, and well-being.

> We should plan our lives and careers only one year at a time.

Take It One Year at a Time   In a changing environment, long-term goals are good, but long-term planning is useless. We should plan our lives and careers only one year at a time.

2. A Volatile Working Environment

The working world is increasingly dominated by the knowledge economy. Although we are still in the early stages of this knowledge revolution, we can already see evidence of its impact reflected in ever more volatile markets.

Organizations, large and small, are showing increasing uncertainty about future direction. Most individuals are experiencing huge uncertainties about future career and job prospects. Only 47 percent of people of working age in the U.K. are in full-time permanent roles these days—a drop of around 20 percent in as many years.

CONTEXT

Work This Way is a guide to the post-jobs era. It aims to provide a set of readily applicable strategies for prospering in an environment where many are intent on merely surviving.

Tulgan's previous book, *Managing Generation X*, looked at the career issues facing the generational successors to the postwar baby boomers—those born between 1963 and 1981. He found a group of people who value individualism and personal empowerment and who seem well equipped to handle life in the post-jobs era.

Work This Way marks an extension of his range to embrace the challenges facing anybody who expects to be working in the new millennium.

Charles Handy, writing in the October 1999 edition of *CBI News*, predicted that we are heading toward "a world of fleas and elephants, of large conglomerates and small individual entities" in which "elephants are a guarantee of continuity but fleas provide the innovation."

Organizations may need to acquire a new mind-set, an ability to think like a flea. Charles Leadbetter and Kate Oakley, in *The Independents*, give examples of "flea thinking."

FOR MORE INFORMATION

Tulgan, Bruce. *Work This Way: Inventing Your Career in the Workplace of the Future*. Mankato, MN: Capstone, 1998.

The World Is Flat
THOMAS FRIEDMAN

WHY READ IT?

Geographic barriers are collapsing, creating a freer, faster, "flatter" global economy. However, to succeed and compete in the new era of globalization, we must understand what is driving the integration of markets. In this book Friedman argues that free trade and the emergence of a single, global economy—often viewed as unequal and unfair—have spread opportunity, created new markets, and spawned unimaginable innovations.

GETTING STARTED

Due to "flatteners," the world is increasingly becoming a level playing field. While Columbus traveled West to show the world was round, the rise of Eastern economies—notably, though not limited to, India and China—has destroyed old Western-based prejudices and empowered individuals and corporations across the world to explore new opportunities.

CONTRIBUTION
1. The Ten Flatteners

1. Falling walls and rising windows. The fall of the Berlin Wall in 1989 was the symbol of the flattening of the political, commercial, and intellectual barriers between the East and West that had seemed fundamental during the Cold War. Freed markets bred opportunity, igniting a new phase of globalization.
2. Netscape. The invention of the Netscape browser brought the benefits of a modern graphic interface to help increasing numbers of people accessing the Internet.
3. Workflow software. Workflow software has created a global web of production. It has shifted from simply connecting people to the Internet to enabling them to collaborate and innovate.
4. Uploading. The Internet enables people to share information for free. Individuals can access unprecedented resources, and the disparity in opportunities between rich and poor has decreased.
5. Outsourcing. By enabling companies to concentrate on their core competencies while getting other essential jobs done cheaply overseas, productivity and innovation have increased, "flattening" the world.
6. Offshoring. With an increasing demand for capital and consumer goods, countries have had to integrate, harmonizing both political and economic policy. With reduced international risk, companies are increasingly willing to outsource their operations to third parties in offshore locations.
7. Supply chaining. With governments in consensus on the merits of free trade, companies can create more efficient, closely integrated supply chains that better serve markets.
8. Insourcing. By bringing the benefits of global supply chains and the returns to scale of a large operation to small and medium-size businesses that focus on niche markets and market "microtrends," even local economies can be part of the global, flat world. Fishermen in India can access reliable weather forecasts on the Internet to improve their catch, while UPS enables small businesses throughout the world to deliver merchandise on bespoke, branded vehicles.

9. In-forming. On an individual scale, the "information economy" empowers people to know and do more than was imaginable even a few years ago. With the erosion of the "digital divide," increasing numbers of people can search for information on Wikipedia and search for the solutions to their problems on Google.

10. The steroids. The global economy has flattened so rapidly because of the transformation in communication technology, which has enabled the other nine flatteners to work with far greater force than they may have done otherwise.

2. Playing on a Level Pitch

With emerging markets offering competitive labor costs and more aggressive companies, there is a fear that the developed world will lose out in the "flat" world. However, a free, global market will benefit all as innovation spawns new markets and new opportunities. Countries with a relative abundance of knowledge workers will engage in the more value-added sectors, while comparative advantage increases economic efficiency. There is, however, a danger that entire economies may be left behind in a flat world. To avoid this, Friedman argues, education and innovation will become ever more important.

CONTEXT

Friedman feels that globalization happened in three phases:

1. 1500–1800. With perceptions of the world shrinking from unimaginably large to just about conceivable, after Columbus's contact with the New World, new opportunities and new technologies accelerated global trade and integration.

2. 1800–2000. Interrupted only by two world wars, the world shrank from medium to small size. With the rise of multinational companies, global information networks, and supply chains, came the primacy of democracy and free, regulated markets.

3. 2000–Present. With the development of global communications networks providing instantaneous information and contact, the "global village" has become simultaneously competitive and rich with opportunity.

Although the world is now flatter than it has been, Friedman does acknowledge the problem created by persistent, absolute poverty. As the Bill and Melinda Gates Foundation—together with the champions of corporate social responsibility—argue, the world can only become truly flat when a humanitarian push comes from global business. Bill Gates told Friedman of his fear that the world will only be flat for its wealthiest three billion residents. Friedman cites Hewlett-Packard as an example of a firm that is not just socially responsible, but profitably engages in the poorest markets. However, while the push for creating a uniformly flat playing field may come from global business, countries lagging behind must themselves embrace reform. Friedman argues that "reform wholesale," opening a country to foreign trade and investment via "top-down" initiatives, is not sufficient, but must be followed by "reform retail"—offering the choice of how to develop infrastructure, regulatory institutions, education, and culture at all points in society.

FOR MORE INFORMATION

Friedman, Thomas. *The World Is Flat*. New York: Farrar, Straus, and Giroux, 2005.

AUTHOR INDEX